BUSINESS OVER BREAKFAST

Bree James & Andrew Griffiths

Chew.
Percolate.
Digest.

WHAT PEOPLE SAY

" A self-made man and a self-made woman team up to create a special brand of generosity. They share their menu of personally tested success hacks: hundreds of them. This is inspiration on toast with your morning coffee. Their excitement about small business is infectious. Try it. Business caffeine for the soul. **"**

> — **Rosemary Shapiro-Liu**, Author
> *The Mentor Within*
> www.triplewin.com.au

" My favourite thing about the collaboration between Andrew and Bree is the ease of application of their clever ideas and the wisdom they share. They understand what makes a business successful or not and everything they do is for the benefit of the end user . That's why I look to them for answers and support. **"**

> — **Andrea Tunjic**, Author
> *People Power*
> www.andreatunjic.com

" Big on knowledge. Big on passion. Another cracker, Andrew! **"**

> — **Robert Gerrish**, Co-Founder
> Flying Solo

" Bree and Andrew are very smart people, both forward thinkers who like to question the norm and with good reason. Their opinions are highly sought after, they are thought provoking and incredibly real. I'll continue to implement everything they say because this stuff works and gives me a competitive advantage. **"**

> — **Darren Finkelstein 'The Boat Guy'**,
> Bestselling and Award Winning author
> *Honey, let's buy a BOAT!, Honey, let's go BOATING!,*
> *Honey, let's sell the BOAT!*
> www.theboatguy.com.au

" Andrew Griffiths and Bree James are at the forefront of small business thinking - I am addicted to their Business over Breakfast podcast and I read everything they write. As an innovative business owner keen to learn and stay ahead of the curve, they are my 'go to team'. They just make sense. **"**

> — **Kate Christie**, Author
> *Me Time, SMART Time Management for Doctors*
> www.timestylers.com

" When I am looking for practical business advice or have issues that require soft skills to solve, I always know I'll find the answers with Andrew and Bree. Pragmatic and wise, you don't get better business guidance than from this duo. **"**

> — **Tracy Angwin**, Author
> *The Payroll Revolution, Profit from Payroll, In Safe Hands*
> www.payrollhq.com.au

" Andrew Griffiths – we salute you. **"**

> — **Weekend Sunrise**

" I have never felt as uplifted and inspired as I have with spending time with Andrew and Bree. Their ideas, insights and methods are second to none and they are true thought leaders in their fields. I can honestly say that my business is far better as a result of knowing and working with Bree and Andrew. **"**

> — **Katherine Maslen**, Author
> *Get Well, Stay Well*
> katherinemaslen.com

MEET THE AUTHORS

So you've picked up this crazy kind of book, encouraging you to think about your business whilst downing strong coffee and eating Coco Pops (or drinking organic vegan kale smoothies, mmmmm nice). Why on earth should you listen to anything that Bree James or Andrew Griffiths has to say?

OK, we can give the formal, we've been in business for, like, a gazillion years, been successful, written a pile of books, presented to hundreds of thousands of people around the world script, which is true. But really, the reason we hope you listen to the advice we offer is because we give a damn.

We give a damn about you and your business. Why? Because we know just how much you invest into your business, (and money is the least of the investments), and we want to help. We are what is commonly called, "Street Smart Entrepreneurs" (some people may say Sesame Street Smart). This means we've had to learn as we went along. We've made many mistakes, but been smart enough to get better from them and then open enough to share what we've learned with others (that's you).

We've known each other for a long time and in the last few years we decided to get serious about working together. We've got huge plans to write more books, do more business programs, create piles more content, basically take everything we are doing now to the world. Sounds ambitious right? Sounds kinda scary? Sounds like we are dreaming? Yes, yes and yes. But isn't that what life is all about?

Our approach is really simple. We don't preach. We simply share what works for us as we know it will work for you. All we ask is that you keep an open mind whenever you read, watch or listen to any of the material we share.

— **Bree James and Andrew Griffiths**, Authors
Business Over Breakfast Volume 1.

ACKNOWLEDGEMENTS

We want to acknowledge the business owners out there, and there are millions of them around the world. They toil, day and night, often for little money, with crazy amounts of stress, with not a lot of support, because they are amazingly passionate about what they do and they want to change the world in their own way.

Please know there are many of us who understand the journey you are on. We know the challenges you face, the sacrifices you make every single day. We know the questions you ask yourself in the darker moments as much as the joy you feel when everything goes right. And we know that what drives you is not money.

You are not alone. We respect and admire each and every one of you. Never think for a second that what you do goes unnoticed or that the impact you make, in any shape or form, is not important. It most certainly is and we admire you for it.

Business Over Breakfast Vol 1 - first published in Australia in 2017

Andrew Griffiths Enterprises Pty Ltd
PO BOX 1170
Cairns QLD 4870
Australia

Telephone 61(07) 4031 8888
Email - info@andrewgriffiths.com.au
www.andrewgriffiths.com.au

This book is not meant as a substitute for a healthy breakfast and the authors in
no way endorse Coco Pops - but we do like them as a treat from time to time.

Authors: Griffiths, Andrew, 1966-, James, Bree, 1980-

Title: Business Over Breakfast Vol 1, Bree James/Andrew Griffiths.

ISBN: 978-0-9874066-6-8

Subjects: Small Business, Business

Author photograph: Veronica Sagredo, Blueclick Photography
Creative Design: Lise Mardon Smith, Grand Publishing
Editing Services: Gabriele Schindler

CONTENTS

INTRODUCTION

We started "Business Over Breakfast" with the daunting quote by Mr Alvin Toffler, author of the book Future Shock, "The illiterate of the 21st century will not be those who cannot read and write, but those who cannot learn, unlearn, and relearn". And we think this is the mantra that anyone in business needs to follow.

There has never been a more exciting time to be in business, there has never been a more challenging time to be in business. Just when we think we've got something figured out, everything changes and we have to go back to the drawing board. The smallest of businesses now has access to the world, technology has most of our heads spinning, being an entrepreneur has been made sexy and opportunities are everywhere. But so is competition. In fact has there ever been a more competitive time to be in business? We don't think so.

We've been in business for a long time, we've both managed to survive, avoiding going bust (just), for many years. How have we survived when so many don't? The answer is simple, the solution is not. We've both constantly evolved to not just survive, but to thrive as the world around us changed. We've stayed relevant in industries that have become less relevant, we've embraced new business practices, chased new markets, learnt many new skills - and been bold and brave enough to believe in ourselves.

The real key though is that we need to challenge the way we do, what we do, all the time. Complacency is without a doubt the biggest enemy to business owners, now more than ever before, because the world is spinning much faster.

That's why this book is designed to not only challenge your thinking but to also provide some really cool ideas for doing things differently. So it's a combination of hard core brain work, some Zen like thinking, followed by some nicer, try this today stuff. We think this approach works.

So to get the most out of "Business Over Breakfast", grab it in the morning, sit down with your Coco Pops and open the book at an idea that catches your eye (or start at the beginning and work through an idea a day for 100 days). Take a moment to read the idea or concept we are discussing, read Bree's suggestions for implementing it and then ponder, think, percolate, ruminate and absorb. Can you apply this idea to your business today? Can you apply it to yourself?

Put enough of the ideas that we cover in this book into practice and we think your business will noticeably change, as will you. Remember, complacency is the enemy, doing nothing is dangerous, status quo is not a good thing (but they were a good band) and be curious enough and brave enough to push your own business and personal beliefs, especially those that if we are honest with ourselves, are holding us back. Enjoy the ride ahead, it's going to get a little crazy.

BREE &
ANDREW'S

100 day business challenge

100 breakfasts

X

 100 new ideas

=

a new level of success

#bobchallenge

SECTION 1

THE WAY YOU THINK WILL EITHER
MAKE YOU OR BREAK YOU.

One thing we both agree on, without a nanosecond of doubt, is that the success of a business is absolutely tied into the attitude of the person running it. Now of course, there are always a pile of external issues that influence a business, but often we use these as excuses for why something goes wrong or doesn't work.

As business coaches and mentors, we spend a lot of our time trying to help people to overcome the negative thought patterns that hold them back, the limiting beliefs that have somehow become gospel, and the fallacies that are now seemingly unequivocally true.

We need to foster the right attitude to business and life every single day, yet sadly, we rarely give the way we think, the attention it deserves. Start your day with the right thinking and you might be surprised how good a day you actually have.

1

Do you have days when you feel
like an absolute imposter? Rest assured,
you are certainly not alone.

I was mentioning to a friend recently that I felt like I was really just coming into my
own as an author and speaker. Her jaw dropped and she looked at me with disbelief
and asked "with all of your books, all of your presentations around the world, all of
your media, all of your success, how can you possibly just be coming into your own?"

Well, the truth was that I felt like a fraud or imposter for many many years.
Everyone else seemed to be more successful, know more, be more skilled, the lot.
I had to have my public "mask" on to feel confident because I didn't really feel like
that's who I was.

The more my public profile grew, the more I felt like an imposter who wasn't as
good as other people. I found it exhausting going through life this way, but one day
I woke up and I didn't feel like an imposter anymore. That was a good day.

I think a lot of people struggle with this concept. We bluff our way through life in
our business wearing our public mask, undervaluing what we do, the skills we have,
and the difference we make. It isn't really a bluff at all, but often we are measuring
ourselves against people with better marketing teams as opposed to people who are
perhaps more skilled or capable.

The following strategies certainly helped me to overcome my own imposter syndrome. They might help you too.

1. **Talk to others about it.** It's amazing how much better we tend to feel after admitting that we feel like an imposter. Generally people will laugh and say something like "Are you serious?" And often they will admit to feeling the same way. An enormous load will be lifted from your shoulders simply by opening up and sharing your feelings with someone you trust and respect.

2. **Look at the facts.** We need to turn off the emotions for a second and turn on the factual part of our brain. Look back at what you have achieved, overcome, mastered, delivered and accomplished, and acknowledge every single thing. Make a list of what you can claim to own as your own successes and be immensely proud of them. The more you do this, the more your brain will start to acknowledge that you are actually very good at what you do and there's no way you are an imposter.

3. **Ask people what they think of you.** This can be a hard one, but if you are brave enough, reach out to people you trust, tell them you are working on a personal development program and you would really value them sharing what they see as your three greatest strengths. Interestingly, most people will say the same thing. It's hard to ignore this kind of evidence.

4. **Stand up and share your flaws (proudly).** As a presenter I used to spend a lot of time being scared to admit the things I'd gotten wrong, my failures, fears, and insecurities. I found as soon as I started talking about my inner insecurities on stage, they didn't seem to be as powerful. Especially when I shared what I learned from them and where I am now. In fact, my authenticity created very real engagement. Many people come up to me to this day to share their own perceived faults and failings, often for the first time in their life. Once you expose yourself fully, the power of the fear of being "caught out" is taken away. I wrote an entire book about my mistakes and deep dark secrets, so there is nothing that anyone can find out that isn't already in a bestselling book. This is very liberating and makes me feel very authentic.

5. **Don't tell people what to do, tell them what 'you' do.** I think this is a big one. If you are a person that tells everyone else how to do things and what they need to do, often without them asking for it, you put yourself under a lot

of pressure to be perfect. So for starters, stop doing that (yes, I get the irony). Instead of telling people what to do, may I suggest you tell them what you would do and why? The rest is up to them. You don't have to be the person with all the answers.

6. **Put your hand on your heart and commit to being the best person you can be.** What more can we do than this? If you really are committed to being the best person you can be, that is good enough. If you get things wrong, you have proven you are human. But at least you've been brave enough to do something. It's easy to snipe from the sideline, but getting in the game is a little tougher.

7. **Learn to laugh at yourself, but don't put yourself down.** It's exhausting hanging onto the feeling of being an imposter. Once you can let it go and laugh at yourself, either in public or in private, it starts to lose its hold on you. Think about what it would mean for someone to find out that you are not as good as you say you are about something? Is it really the end of the world? I seriously doubt it.

I spent so many years of my life feeling like an imposter in what I did. I waited for someone to call me out, challenge me on what I was saying, get up at the back of a room and tell me that I had no idea what I was talking about. Now that the mask is off, my life is much easier, richer, and far more fun. My business is more successful than ever, and if people don't like what I have to say or what I do, that's OK with me.

BREE'S TAKE

Imposter syndrome hits us all at some point. We are all in a space where there are lots of voices wanting to be heard. If you start sounding the same as everyone else and not being authentic to whom you are, then you will not only feel like an imposter, you will be behaving like one too. So how do we combat that? I think that we need to do a success audit. A success audit is an opportunity for you to list all your successes to date. This can include things like:

- Awards you have won

- Milestones in your business (time, financial etc).

- New products or services you have created from scratch

- Peer acknowledgement of some form

- Getting through a difficult situation

- Personal or business changes you have made where you have achieved results

- New skills that you have learnt

- Perhaps even how you handle certain situations now compared with how you used to handle them

- Travel (one that I love to measure for my own success)

And so on. Don't be shy, put everything on paper that you really should be proud of. Look at that list, and I mean, really look at it. Do you still feel like an imposter? I really hope not and I really hope you take a moment now to acknowledge exactly what you have achieved.

2

Once a week I ask myself one simple but important question.

Every week on a Friday I ask myself a simple question "how have I made my business better this week than it was last week?" As simple as it sounds, this question is a powerful part of a bigger philosophy known as being committed to constant and never ending improvement.

Any business that is constantly trying to get better at what it does is way ahead of the pack when it comes to being successful. This positive attitude is one that any customer notices the minute they walk into the business, just as they notice a business that doesn't care.

Businesses that are being driven by a passionate and enthusiastic business owner have an energetic feel about them. There is always something new and exciting going on and as a customer, it is good to be a part of this.

So how does a business constantly improve? We can improve the way we communicate with our clients, we can make it easier for people to buy from us, we can keep working on the appearance of our business, ensuring it is always clean and tidy but also fresh and modern, we can train our staff better, we can keep our product knowledge up-to-date. You get the point.

When you are committed to constant and never-ending improvement it really does show. This attitude rubs off on staff who start to look for ways to do things better as well. Customers are more likely to come to you with ideas to improve your business because clearly you care. Suppliers note this attitude and are more likely to want to help you grow your business. Competitors will respect you.

But the most important thing that needs constant and never ending improvement is the business owner.

As business owners, we need to learn new skills, look for ways to do what we do as individuals even better, to research our industry and be a leader in this industry, to read and broaden our knowledge on a range of subjects that will help our business grow, to be trained in ways that makes us better leaders, and to always be open-minded enough to find new ways of doing things.

With this learning and improvement comes an open-minded attitude that is a key to success. Any business that is too rigid, too lazy, or too bored to change will not survive. Committing to constant and never-ending improvement adds an air of passion and excitement, which is the fuel that sets a business apart, and in my opinion guarantees that it will succeed in a spectacular way.

BREE'S TAKE

I completely agree that we need to be constantly improving our business and ourselves as business owners. One of the big challenges for business owners can come when we hit a bit of a wall and it feels like we are stuck in groundhog day, same stuff just a different day. A great way to overcome this is to measure our progress, and by reviewing and acknowledging our successes. Hopefully most of it is forward progress as it's nice to be able to say, "wow, I've come a long way".

Here are nine questions that will take you ten minutes to answer. Do them every Friday afternoon before you clock off for the weekend (because as business owners we do that right?). Put this weekly task in your diary now.

1. What is one way my team improved my business this week?

2. What one thing did I do that made me a better person this week?

3. Name one person I really helped this week?

4. What is one lesson I learnt this week?

5. What was the one lesson I taught others this week?

6. What is the one thing I loved the most about this week?

7. What was my one biggest success this week?

8. What one thing did I not do as well I would have liked this week?

9. What is the one thing I really want to focus on next week?

You will learn a great deal about yourself by doing this and you will certainly make great progress. This is also a very cool exercise for your team to do on a weekly basis, and if you are really brave, get everyone to share his or her answers in a round table discussion.

3

Why it's ok if you don't want to build an empire.

Here's why you shouldn't feel bad if your idea of achieving greatness is different than Mark Zuckerberg's.

There is a lot of discussion about entrepreneurial start-ups going from zero to billions in a few short years. In many ways there is an expectation that all entrepreneurs should be building an empire. But what if that isn't what you want? What if you are happy to keep your business small and enjoy the lifestyle that comes with it? Does this make you any less of an entrepreneur?

Obviously not, yet there is without a doubt, a sense that if you aren't building an empire, you're not a serious entrepreneur? In my view, entrepreneurs that don't want to build an empire need to give themselves permission to build exactly the kind of business they want, not what everyone else expects of them.

Success means aspiring to achieve something and actually achieving it. What you want to achieve is up to you. Build an empire or don't, both are significant achievements.

The moral to this story is that you get to define what success means for you. You get to set the goals, the dreams and the aspirations and you also get to give yourself a pat on the back when you achieve them. If success means building a small business that you can run from home, that generates enough income for you and the family to have a holiday once a year, that is fantastic.

Often as we get older we get a little clearer about what we don't want in our life. Perhaps clearer than the things we do want. Think about this before you decide on the kind of business you want. There are many pros and cons with both kinds of business, making it vitally important that we are clear on what we want our life to look like with a business slap bang in the middle of it.

Big or small, empire or not, I think we should acknowledge anyone who is brave enough to venture out and into the wide and challenging entrepreneurial world for doing something pretty darn cool.

BREE'S TAKE

Repeat after me, "Regardless of whether I am an entrepreneur that is building an empire or building a business to suit my lifestyle, I am brave, and it is one hundred percent my choice, as to how big or how small I make this business."

There are pro's and con's with both as Andrew identified. The key is working out what your ideal business looks like from a lifestyle point of view. For me, I want a business that I can do from anywhere in the world; I want it to help people; I want it to make a difference; and I want to earn enough money so that I can have a big enough team to support me.

Often it's hard to figure out exactly what you want your business to look like. In fact most of us are far better at working out what we don't want our business to look like. Ask yourself the following questions and see if they help you to get some clarity.

1. Do I want my business to impact the community I live in, my state, my country, or the world?

2. Do I want my business to be able to be run from anywhere, or do I want to have face to face contact with my customers at all times?

3. How much money do I really want to earn this year, and in the next five years to sustain the lifestyle I desire?

4. Do I want to grow my team? Do I like managing people?

5. What would happen to my business if I died or if I got very ill? Could it survive without me and if not will this be ok?

6. How do I want my business to end? Will I sell it? Will I close it? When do I want this to happen?

7. Does my current pricing, structure, and business support these answers?

8. Will my customers still want to buy what I'm selling today in ten years? If not what will my business need to look like then?

Remember, it's your business – no one else's. Sure, those closest to you are impacted by your business, but I would like to think they also benefit from it. Try and get clear about what you want your business to grow into and you are far more likely to stay in control of it, as opposed to building something you don't really want.

4

Keep those people who bring you down at arm's length, and those who inspire, encourage and nurture, close by.

We all have friends who make us wince when they walk in. We know that within five minutes they will have us completely depressed, and feeling that there is nothing we can do about it. Their lives are desperate, sad, tragic, bored or whatever, and odds on, you have a sympathetic ear, so you listen and they keep coming back to tell you more.

Do you know why? Because it makes them feel better. However, they make you feel like you want to jump out of the nearest window, whilst they leave whistling and smelling the roses. This is crazy!

If people like this surround you, it's not going to be hard to change-it's going to be near impossible. It may be hard to get them out of your life because they're your biggest customer, a relative or your business partner. But you really need to draw a line in the sand. If most of the people you mix with are more negative than positive, you have a problem, which will only get worse over time and keep you trapped in the cycle of feeling overwhelmed.

I made a very conscious decision a number of years ago about the type of people I would have in my life. I want to be surrounded by energetic, enthusiastic and positive people who are getting on with their lives. I don't care what they do for a living, how much money they have or who they know. All I care about is their zest for life. These people inspire me and motivate me to be the best person I can be; they are supportive of any decision or change that will help me to achieve this goal. If I fail, they are the first people to support me, and say, at least I gave it a go.

If I listened to the negative people, I wouldn't do anything. Because life is clearly so damn messed up that there is nothing I can possibly do, that would make it any better. There is no malicious intent in these people, it's just a reflection of where they are at in life at the time, and that is sad. But we all need to decide if we want to be equally sad. I made the decision not to and that was that.

I suggest that you develop a way of keeping such people at arm's length. Some of them won't like you for it, and they will tell you so. Be prepared for some repercussions, but stay resilient because the pay-off is big.

BREE'S TAKE

As the old saying goes, we become like the five people we spend most of our time with. So I agree with Andrew that we need to be mindful of who we have in our lives. And most importantly, we need to keep negative people at arms length. Sometimes this is really hard, especially if they are relatives.

Maybe it is time for a people audit? People audits are hard, because we tend to find people who are close to us, occasionally need to put at arms length. I'm sure you already know people in your life that need to be distanced.

So where do we start with a people audit? Take some time out to define the character traits of the ideal people you want in your life. How do they act? How do they think? What is their attitude towards life and business? How do they treat those around them? How do they treat themselves? How do they grow as human beings? And how do they learn and grow?

Now you know the kind of people you want in your life. So how many of the people currently in your world fit the bill? And an even bigger question, how do the five people you currently spend most of your time with, fit these qualities?

People that don't fit into your criteria need to be encouraged or inspired by you to meet this criteria, or you need to invest less energy into them. I know this might sound harsh but if you want to achieve things in life, the people closest to you will have a big impact on whether or not that happens.

Sometimes we have to take a business approach to our relationships. Would you invest a pile of time into someone who isn't good for your business? Perhaps a staff member with a really bad attitude or even a terrible customer? If not, then why do you invest a pile of time into that negative person who doesn't align with your own values and expectations?

Invest your time and energy into relationships that are going to increase in value over the years.

It's hard at first to slowly remove the negative investments, but once this shift occurs, your world will be a much happier place. And of course remember, if you are looking to those around you to live their lives to a higher standard, you have to do the same.

5

We need to be really good at seeing other people's pain, frustrations and irritations - and providing solutions to all of them.

How good are you at identifying what causes your prospective customers pain, frustration or irritation? It's a skill we need to develop and be working on every single day because the future of our business may ultimately depend on it.

To use a well-worn example, Uber has come along at a time where there was a perfect intersection of technology and frustration. People were well and truly ready to use an alternative to taxis after years of frustration. When one came along, Uber was embraced around the world and became a multi-billion-dollar company in a few short years.

The same concept applies to virtually any business. It doesn't only work for the famous ones. Many businesses slowly become irrelevant, because they are providing solutions to pain, frustrations or irritations, that are no longer relevant to their target market.

The key here is to get really good at identifying, pain, frustration and irritation with your target market. Then constantly staying in touch and connected with our market to make sure we don't become irrelevant. We need to know their struggles and be the solution.

The problem is that many businesses have become too inwardly focused, making it all about them not their customers. Even worse, some companies simply don't care.

For a while I was working with a large newspaper on a range of advertising campaigns. I had six sales representatives to work with because that's what worked best for them. It drove me crazy, six meetings, six lots of emails, and six people to track down. I begged them to give me one rep, but their response was "that's not the way we do it". In the end I stopped using them, because it was simply too hard. Their inflexibility cost them hundreds of thousands of dollars when all they had to do was provide a simple solution to my pain.

In any business, a major key to long-term success is being super vigilant, super connected and super aware of what is going on in the world of the people who buy your products or services. We need to be talking to them, researching them, building relationships with them, asking them better questions and constantly be on the lookout for anything that causes them pain, frustration or irritation.

Of course identifying these issues is one thing, but then we have to make sure we find solutions and tell them about these solutions. This is an ongoing cycle and every member of your team should be involved. Sometimes the people in accounting hear about a client's pain more than the people in the dispatch area. If no one speaks up, or if no one asks them to report back on client issues, they might not, and a small easy to fix problem becomes a deal breaker.

We also need to look at what is happening in other industries. What problems are arising and how are companies within that particular industry solving them? Studying innovators and start-ups is a smart way to find this information out. Whilst they are often really impressive, we need to look deeper at the pain points they are solving, the frustrations they are helping to resolve and the irritations they are ending.

So what causes your potential customers pain, frustration and irritation and what can you do about it? Understand their struggles, and be the solution, and your business will flourish for a very long time.

BREE'S TAKE

Yes, we need to look at what things are causing our customers pain and look for solutions. But we also need to look at what we are doing and hand on heart, ask if we are making it harder for our customers to do business with us.

From my experience, here are my top five most painful things that businesses do:

1. **They don't have a website.** A Facebook page is not good enough. You must face it that digital is here to stay and every business needs a good website so invest in one.

2. **They make it hard for customers to communicate.** People communicate in various ways, some want to talk to you, some want to email you, some want to visit you. You MUST have a phone number, email address, and physical address if you work somewhere people can visit you or at least a postal address.

3. **They don't have a business card.** Kissing phones to swap details is not cool. You need to have a professional business card, print is not dead. I know we live in a tech-based world, but the number of people I try to do business with that don't have a business card is just plain wrong. They are easy to forget.

4. **They don't do what they say they will.** If you say you are going to do a quote do it. If you say you are going to be somewhere, be there. Don't be all talk and no action.

5. **They take people for granted.** Whether it be your customers, your team, your family and friends make sure everyone knows how much you appreciate them and what they do for you before they stop doing it.

So we all need to do a bit of soul searching and make sure we are always bringing our "A" game to our own business and how we treat and interact with our customers.

6

If you don't ask these nine questions often enough, your business can easily go off the rails.

Every business owner needs a simple checklist that they can spend a few minutes reviewing on a regular basis (at least weekly), to make sure that their business is on track (and being on track is not just about the money).

This keeps us focused, it ensures we take action early if one part of our business is not being given the attention it deserves, and it increases our chances of being successful.

1. **Am I focused on where my business is heading?** From my observations most entrepreneurs share one common challenge, they are butterfly chasers. This means they are incredibly easily distracted to run after the newest opportunity or idea that happens to flutter by. Sure, the very nature of being an entrepreneur means we look for opportunities, but if you are not careful you can spend all of your time chasing new opportunities and not realising any of the ones under your nose. So be focused on your core business and stay focused.

2. **Are you on top of money that you are owed?** We all need to keep track of the money we are owed. One of the best ways to monitor this is to watch your average length of receivables. Put simply, this means how long it takes you to

get your money in. If this is starting to take a while you could be headed for trouble.

3. **Are you actively marketing your business?** Successful businesses never stop marketing. When times are good they market, when times are tough they market even more. Because they understand that the marketing you do today generates the business you need tomorrow. Every business needs to be committed to business development every week, ideally every day.

4. **Are you charging enough?** From my experience, many businesses simply don't charge enough. This is generally due to their own state of mind around self worth. One way to benchmark your charge out rates is by how many jobs you win. If you get every job you quote on, you are too cheap. If you get less than a third, you are probably too expensive. I like to sit somewhere in the middle, around the sixty percent mark I know then, that my rates are about right.

5. **Are people referring others to your business?** If you are not getting referrals there could be a problem. So clearly you need to make sure you are asking people how they heard about your business and ideally, the number one reason will be, they were referred by someone. It is always good to do an online search as well, to see what people are saying about your business. Even if you don't like what you read, you can at least do something about it. Putting your head in a bucket is a sure fire way to failure.

6. **Are you up to speed with trends in your industry?** We all need to stay abreast of what is happening within our industry. I spend at least an hour a day researching online to see what people are doing in the entrepreneurial space. It is the best hour of my day and it has huge returns.

7. **Are you investing in yourself and your staff?** To put it simply, if you're not growing, you're dying. From my experience really successful entrepreneurs always invest in growing their own skills and knowledge, and they do the same with their staff. This is not just a once a year retreat. This is a daily investment through books, online research, seminars, workshops and so on.

8. **Are you contributing to your community?** Now more than ever, businesses are under scrutiny to show that they play an active role in the communities

where they operate. This means stepping up and giving time and money (if you can) for good causes. And make certain that you tell your customers what you do in your community, most businesses don't do this very well.

9. **Are you driving your business or is it driving you?** There's no two ways about it, being a workaholic may bring short-term success, but it is not sustainable or enjoyable. We need to have a very clear life outside of our business, one where we do the things we really enjoy doing and also recharges our batteries.

BREE'S TAKE

I love these nine things. So let's do a quick check.

1. **Am I focused on where my business is heading?**
    TIP- Have a one-page document that has your yearly goals for the business on it. Read it every day.

2. **Are you on top of money that you are owed?**
    TIP- Ensure you are getting a list of debtors given to you monthly (especially if you are not in charge of the books). Make changes to your invoices to make them more personal, if you are up for it, a photo of your family with a sad face and caption saying "We can't pay our bills if you don't pay yours" works a treat.

3. **Are you actively marketing your business?**
    TIP-Sending an electronic direct mail (EDM), or putting up a Facebook post is not enough these days. Have a marketing plan, a list of must do's and a list of like to do's and make time daily to execute. Marketing is planting seeds-every single day.

4. **Are you charging enough?**
    TIP - Take some time out and research what the market is charging. Check out your sales conversion rates and see if you sit around the 50% mark. If not,

fix it. Winning every quote doesn't mean you are awesome, it means you are too cheap.

5. **Are people referring others to your business?**

   TIP - Train your team to ask the very simple question "how did you hear about us?" and "we would love to have more customers just like you, do you have any friends or colleagues that you think may benefit from working with us?"

6. **Are you up to speed with trends in your industry?**

   TIP- Spend time every week looking for ideas, list them in a book and when you need inspiration check your list and implement one.

7. **Are you investing in yourself and your staff?**

   TIP- Make a list of things you would love to be trained in, do a list of things that you would love your team to be trained in. Then find an expert who looks for grants, you would be surprised at how many grants there are out there to help you gain more skills.

8. **Are you contributing to your community?**

   TIP- Pick one cause in your community and support it. This makes it much easier to say no to other charities and saves you a lot of wasted time screening calls from other charities. You can simply say, "we only work with one charity per year and we've already chosen for this year." Change it yearly if you like, get the charities to submit applications for support and then get your team involved in choosing which one you would like to work with.

9. **Are you driving your business or is it driving you?**

   TIP- Develop a plan for your ideal workweek. What does it look like? Does it have some family time, "me" time, and learning time on there? If not, put it on there and try and stick to it. If you want to be a high performing business owner, you need to be a happy one.

7

Seriously, it's time to lighten up, it's only business.

I recently went into a business to buy a few things for my car. I was a little overwhelmed by how miserable everyone in this store looked and how serious they acted. There didn't really seem to be a good reason for it, but I was desperate to get out and I will never go back.

Fortunately, there aren't too many businesses like this but there is no doubt that some businesses suffer from what I call terminal seriousness. There hasn't been a smile cracked on the premises for quite some time and there is no real chance of one occurring in the foreseeable future.

Unfortunately, terminal seriousness has crept into workplaces, and many business owners wanting to lighten up the place a little don't know where to start. They can't remember why things got so serious and why the laughter stopped but they want it back.

So here are ten simple ways to encourage your team to laugh a little more often and to take things a little less seriously. I know that some of them might sound a little corny, but that's part of having fun.

1. **Develop a Fun Committee.** The committee's job is to come up with ideas for making your workplace a whole lot more fun. (People need to volunteer for this, and ideally need a good sense of humor).

2. **Joke of the day.** Share the responsibility around and get everyone to take turns at coming up with a joke of the day.

3. **Ugly shirt day.** While many businesses already look as if they are holding this competition every day, make it a special event.

4. **Baby pictures.** Have a pin-up board with baby pictures of every member of your team and you!

5. **Have a fun zone.** This can be where people go when they need to laugh. It can have a few silly toys, some joke books-anything that can raise a smile.

6. **Baking day.** Have a rotating roster for everyone to bake something and bring it into work. There must be guidelines to make it equal and everyone should at least try the end result.

7. **Have a weekly buddy system.** Everyone gets allocated a buddy for one week, and the buddy has to look after the 'boss', get them tea and coffee, buys their lunch, and so on. But the catch is, the next week, you swap.

8. **Introduce spontaneity.** Take your team out for coffee, bring in a treat or just do something out of the ordinary.

9. **Success Board of Fame.** Have a notice board with staff successes for the month. This can be any success, not just work related so that it raises all kinds of interesting awards.

10. **Have a 'something you didn't know about me' day.** Every member of your team tells the rest of the team one thing that no one at work would know about them.

Start having more fun at work today. If your workplace is a little humour-challenged, give it time, don't try to turn it into the local comedy club overnight. Start small, work your way up, but start today. And remember that laughing is also an excellent form of rejuvenation. Fifteen minutes of laughter has the same relaxing effect as meditating for eight hours; ten minutes of laughter has the same relaxing effect as two hours' sleep.

BREE'S TAKE

Ok, so you've read this article over coffee before heading to your business. Today I want you to observe your team and give your business a score out of ten for happiness.

Is there a sense of playfulness in your workplace?

Is their any laughter in the workplace?

Are people smiling and light hearted?

Are your staff engaging positively with customers and with each other?

Are your staff open and forthright in coming to you with issues?

So give each of the above a score out of ten, then average them out. This is your "Business Happiness Score" and whilst it's really just a simple way of getting some kind of measurement, it can be something that you do on a regular basis, just to check in with your team. If you find it isn't a very happy workplace, Andrew has made some great suggestions to make it happier.

8

Are you letting your competitors' run your business?

I have encountered a lot of business owners whose entire business is based on what their competitors are doing. Every decision they make is the direct result of something the competition has done or is planning to do. They have spies checking on the competitors, they watch them like hawks, and they are totally obsessed with everything they are doing.

Business owners like this often come across as being totally paranoid about their competitors. In many ways, their competitors are running their business, because they are the main consideration in all of the decisions being made.

Clearly, this is not a healthy way to run a business. Being obsessed with every move our competitors make tends to be a sign of other issues. Often this obsession, is the result of insecurity, inexperience, and lack of confidence, and as a result, the reactive steps taken by the business reflect these negative traits.

This is how price wars start and no one wins a price war. Pricing is not determined in a sound and logical way; it is more about being cheaper than the competition, regardless of whether the business is making money or not.

It is a fear-based way to run a business, and from my experience, it rarely, if ever, proves successful. Essential day-to-day considerations like delivering a high level of customer service gets forgotten, as the business owner is too busy looking at what the competition is doing rather than what is happening within their own business.

By all means have a healthy awareness of your competitors as I think this is essential to being truly successful in business. Be aware of what your competitors are doing and evaluate their actions, but don't make their business the center of your business.

I think a much better approach is to be good at what you do, to lead in every way, to be different, and to focus on what makes your business unique. Then you can set the pace for your competitors to follow. This takes a wonderful level of maturity and confidence, which radiates from a smart, proactive, and successful business.

BREE'S TAKE

What we focus on is what tends to happen, so make sure you're focusing your energy on the things that will improve your business in a positive way. A good old SWOT analysis really helps when you have competition in the marketplace. Get a piece of paper, break it into four squares and put an S for strengths, W for weaknesses, O for opportunities, T for threats and then do your own self review for your business (stuff I'm sure you've done before).

But something I like to do is a SWOT analysis on my competitors. It's very good to be able to identify how I see the strengths, weaknesses, opportunities and threats of my competitors. This really helps me to work out my own strategies in every part of my business from marketing to product development.

9

Is playing victim stopping you from being successful?

I have a friend who was very successful in business and he made a lot of money by a relatively young age. Then, through a series of misfortunes, his business failed and he went broke. At the time of his misfortune he was quite young and easily had the ability, the resourcefulness and the ideas to start again, but instead he turned into a bitter and angry man who blamed the world for his loss.

Holding on to past failures and mistakes takes a lot of energy. One of the best lessons I have learned, not only in business but also in life, has been the power of letting go. The quicker we learn to let go the better. And whilst it does take considerable effort to let go, especially a situation that has really upset you, the more you do it, the easier it gets.

A long time ago I had a business partner who took literally everything I owned. He left me with a pile of debts and a battered and bruised ego. I spent a year feeling really angry with him and feeling sorry for myself.

Then one morning I woke up and realised how much energy it was taking to hold on to this anger so tightly. I was physically suffering from my rage. I had boils all over my body, I wasn't sleeping, I was short-tempered and unhappy. That morning I decided to just let it all go, to learn from the situation, and to put a little faith in the universe and the law of karma. The change was amazing. My boils cleared up within a few days, I started to sleep like a baby and my whole disposition lightened so I could enjoy life again.

Identifying the issues you are holding onto that are draining you of energy is the first step to letting them go. Then you have to ask yourself two questions:

QUESTION 1
What have you got to gain by holding on to this issue?

QUESTION 2
What have you got to gain by letting it go?

In a business context, if a member of your staff steals from you, it's easy to decide that you will never trust another employee again. Worse still, you might start to imagine that everyone is trying to steal from you. You will become paranoid and spend all of your energy worrying about this issue. But how can you grow your business if you don't empower people and trust them to do the right thing?

If you have a bad experience with a client, don't assume that everyone is going to be same. If you try a marketing initiative and it doesn't work, don't classify all marketing as useless and a waste of money.

From my experience, businesses that are stuck in the victim mode, regardless of the reason, tend to struggle to prosper. It is only when they let go of past experiences or mistakes that they can actually move forward.

BREE'S TAKE

Ok people, if your business or life is making you ill (boils ewww Andrew) then it's well and truly time to do something to fix it.

DID YOU KNOW:

1. Stress can cause hair loss. After stressful situations, hair loss can start and last for up to three months afterwards.

2. Stress changes the neurochemical makeup of the human body. It is estimated that stress is the cause of approximately 30% of infertility problems.

3. Too much stress can result in physical problems, high blood pressure, an irregular heartbeat, heart disease, and even chest pain.

My advice is simple but effective. Write a list of all the things bothering you. Have a long hard look at this list, and make a decision as to which ones can be offloaded or resolved once and for all. You can offload by writing a letter and binning it, talking to someone about it, trying to solve the problem so it is off your mind, or giving it to someone else to solve.

Some things are not going to be able to come off that list, but think about how you would like them to turn out. For example, the business is not making money at the moment, so think about exactly what the business will look like when you have got it all sorted. Then work back and figure out how you are going to get to this point. I know that sounds simple and kind of dumb, but how does that solve anything? The reality is, that being successful is really a mind game. We have to figure out as many ways as possible to solve problems, deal with our own issues and generally cope better on a day-to-day basis.

Often the issues that we are really worried about just need us to draw a line in the sand and say "I'm going solve this issue today – right here, right now". Unsurprisingly, we then solve it, whereas it's been on our mind for months, taking up emotional space and not paying any rent.

10

Five reasons the word 'success' should send shivers up your spine.

Every entrepreneur strives for success. But be careful: achieving it comes with its own set of problems, problems that can doom a business. Indeed, over the years I have seen way too many businesses go under about a year after they finally become financially successful.

Why does this happen? In my experience, there are five habits that successful business owners fall into that might signal the beginning of the end.

1. **We spoil ourselves.** After making the sacrifices necessary to make your business successful, surely you deserve a nicer car, a better house, some new clothes, and a business class trip to somewhere exotic? Absolutely. But you need to be super careful that your new luxurious lifestyle doesn't become an addiction that breaks the bank. By all means have a splurge-but go back to instant noodles on a regular basis to keep you anchored to reality.

2. **We lose the hunger that made us do whatever it took to become successful.** Think about what it took to succeed. The crazy hours, the people you chased, the countless times you went above and beyond the call of duty to get the deal or ensure that a customer was happy? All too often success leads to a general lessening of that hunger and drive. We need to be conscious of this.

Perhaps not alarmed, but certainly aware enough to know when we need to get fired up enough to stay successful.

3. **We stop spending quality time with our customers.** As a business becomes more successful, it employs more staff. From here the business owner starts spending more time in the back office. We grow too busy to serve customers (after all, we have people for that now.) Whereas a loyal customer used to be greeted by the owner with a hearty welcome, they are now just downgraded to the rank of "just another customer". From here it isn't long before customers stop feeling the love altogether. No matter how big your business or how busy you get, never lose touch with the people who pay your bills.

4. **We lose our reason "why?"** For most business owners the big "why?" in the early days is less about success and more about survival. Once survival ceases to be an issue and we move into the success zone, we can actually start to feel lost. The urgency that propelled us to be successful is gone and now we find ourselves struggling with motivation. As business owners, I think it is vitally important to always have our next challenge mapped out before we conquer the current one. This moving target ensures we always have a place to aim for that will hopefully keep us motivated.

5. **We start to believe our success will never end.** I don't think we need to live in fear of imminent failure-in fact quite the opposite. But believing your own hype puts your business in peril. So by all means embrace your success. You earned it. But be aware of the nasty habits that can accompany success and be prepared to take serious action.

BREE'S TAKE

We should all be striving for success in some way shape or form. Whether it is success, from baking a cake that we never thought we could bake, or running a multimillion-dollar company. If we aren't striving for something we are kind of stuck in suspended animation and I think this is the danger zone that Andrew speaks about.

So my tip for you is to start a "Business Bucket List" and a "Personal Bucket List". These are two lists of things that you want to achieve personally and professionally. Be creative, your business list can have business ideas for your current business, or business ideas for a new business. Your personal bucket list can have things from learnt to be more present, to learn a language or sky dive.

If you need reinvigorating, or you are looking for that next challenge, you can pull out your list and work on the next bucket list item. Success is never ending in my opinion. It is a non-stop journey to learning and mastering new things at every chance that you get. For those lucky enough to realise this, and passionate enough to make it a way of life, rather than a clichéd poster on the wall, extraordinary things really do happen. chance that you get. For those lucky enough to realise this, and passionate enough to make it a way of life, rather than a clichéd poster on the wall, extraordinary things really do happen.

11

Six reasons women make better entrepreneurs than men.

Writing an article like this is clearly fraught with danger. I have to generalise in a world that is already full of gender-based land mines, but I feel qualified to do it in this instance. For many years I have worked with entrepreneurs around the world, big and small, male and female. So up front, I want to apologise if my article offends, stereotypes or just plain makes you grumpy; it is certainly not intended to do that. I am simply sharing some of my own observations and realisations about women entrepreneurs.

Here are six very important reasons why I think women make better entrepreneurs than men (and these characteristics also make women better equipped for doing business in the lead to 2030):

1. **Women tend to be more honest about business.** If I sit down to a coaching session with a husband and wife business team, the man will generally talk about what irritates him, the women will get right to what the big issues are facing the survival of the business right here, right now. Women open up, they talk about their fears, they are not afraid of sharing their failings because they have less ego attached to the success or failure of the business and they want to address issues not ignore them. In short women are more open and honest about what is going on and that makes it easier for others to help.

2. **Women are much more aware and emotionally intelligent about the human side of the business.** Humanity and business are colliding. We all need to run our businesses with much greater consideration for the people we interact with, our employees, our customers, our suppliers, our communities, the lot. Women seem to get this inherently. They want to make the world a better place; they want to take care of those around them; and they sincerely treat people with respect (and expect to be treated with respect themselves). They understand the more emotive aspect of doing business and that is why they understand their customers. In an era where connecting and engaging are highly sought after by customers, women have a very distinct advantage, over men.

3. **Women are fairer negotiators.** Without doubt I find women much better negotiators than men. Why? They don't try to win a negotiation, because this implies that someone has to lose, they tend to go into a negotiation with a win/win attitude. To me negotiations with women are always tough but fair, the way a negotiation should be.

4. **Women are better at getting to the point.** Women are like Gen Y-they don't really want to beat around the bush too much. They will have a few moments of pleasantries, and then it's down to business. Men can talk about sport, politics, sport, the economy, sport, the weather, sport and then in the last five minutes of a meeting try to hammer out a deal. Women also make better networkers for the same reason. They don't really want to sit around talking about the canapés at a networking event, they want business. So either help them get some business or get out of the way.

5. **Women appreciate the value of creativity.** We live in a world where creativity is a very important commodity. We need to be creative in every aspect of running a business and I think that any business that has a creativity shortage will find it very hard to survive in the coming years. Women tend to be more open minded, in touch with the creative aspects of life and they see value in creativity. As men if we can't fix it, sell it, win at it or do other things to it, we are not interested.

6. **Women value relationships and wellbeing more than the business.** Generally, women will always put the health and wellbeing of their spouse and family as their main priority. If they have to choose between the business

and the family, the family will always win. Now I am not saying that men will choose the business over the family, but for many men, myself included for a very long time, the idea was to put the business first and build something that would support the family down the line. Sadly, all too often, by the time the business is financially successful the family have moved on, because they got sick of being ignored.

BREE'S TAKE

As a woman that has been an entrepreneur for half of her life, this is a nice read, thank you Andrew. I agree with all of Andrew's points, however I would like to add some things for you to think about when it comes to supporting female entrepreneurs. Entrepreneurship is not an easy road for anyone, but women, especially those with children I believe, have a lot of issues that men don't have to worry about.

You see, I grew up with a mother who is a feminist, and I often had to do the "man" type work around the house to help her. I was raised to believe a woman can do anything they set their mind to, and in fact we should never rely on a male. I guess that this is the main reason why I've taken on a role in life that is unusual. I am the breadwinner, I am the business owner, and I am a woman that can do anything she sets her mind to.

But the thing is, I'm also a woman who doesn't feel like she fits in with her own gender at times. I'm also a woman that ponders how life would be if she was a man. Now don't freak out, I'm very happy to be a woman, I'm also someone that loves and admires men, most of my closest humans are men. The last thing I want anyone to think is that my thoughts here are "man bashing". Nothing could be further from the truth. So the men who read this, please know that I'm sharing my perspective on life as a woman and wondering how things would be different if I was a man.

So this leads me to post 5 questions. These are based on my own experiences, and direct conversations that I've had with people, including conversations I've overheard when others are sharing their thoughts on how a woman should act, from both men and women.

1. **Would I be judged for working hard?** If I was a man, it would be expected and accepted that I work hard to provide for my family and make sacrifices to do so. Men who work hard to provide for their family are celebrated. Women who work hard for their family are admired, don't get me wrong, but it is admiration with judgment that we are being less of a mother or partner in doing so.

   It's funny, I often get two reactions from people after I hop off a stage from doing a presentation. The first one is "wow, what you are doing is so inspiring, you've made me want to try harder", which is really nice. The second one is "I really admire what you are doing, but I wouldn't want to be married to you". It's hard to imagine a man getting this kind of feedback and in asking some of my high achieving male friends, who present like me, they have never had anyone make this comment.

2. **Would I be judged for working out of town?** I've never witnessed a man being asked "so who is looking after your kids?" when they travel for work. Yet I'm constantly having the conversation with people who ask me "how can I leave my family to do what I do?" I'm sure that if I had a willy, I wouldn't be asked this question as it's much more socially acceptable for a male to travel for work than a woman, and no one questions his love of his family. It's just accepted that he is doing, what he has to do.

3. **Would I ever be accused of sleeping my way to the top?** If a man is doing well, it's because of merit. If a woman is doing well, it's because she is sucking up, a ball buster, or she does a lot of "sleeping around" to get there. This is the most insulting accusation and completely diminishes a woman's hard work. I'd prefer to be broke and homeless than use my body to get something from someone and I am sure that the majority of women would agree.

4. **Would I ever be hit on during a business meeting?** Once I had a meeting with a male client over a beer in a busy bar, as that is unfortunately how business was done in this particular town. This married man then asked me "so are we going to have sex now or what?" It was one of the most degrading moments as a business woman that I have ever experienced, and it made me

realise that I have to be careful when meeting men for business. How terrible is that to have to consider. Fortunately, it's a rarity, but I'm sure there are plenty of other women who have had the same experience. If I were a man, I wouldn't have been put in this degrading position.

5. **Would I be personally judged as much?** From what we wear, to our weight, to how we look, women are constantly being judged on their physical appearance, and I'd like to extend that to basically their whole life. Yes, men do some of the judging, but I think a huge proportion of it is lead by women. Women can be judgmental monsters and it really needs to stop.

As women we need to stop judging others for what they are doing (and of course the judgment is generally a reflection of our own inadequacies, saying much more about the person doing the judging than the person being judged). We also need to celebrate others more, instead of being jealous of what others have achieved. And this means being serious about celebrating and acknowledging the success of others, not just giving it lip service.

Men, today I ask you to celebrate the women in your life. We know we are crazy at times, we know we are challenging. Please understand just how hard we try to be all things to all people. We need you to be amazing, incredible and strong and not threatened by women who are the same. And when you are working with a woman, ask yourself "if she was a he would I act this way?"

Ladies, I beg us all to be better. I truly believe that women set the emotional tone for the world. So please, let's stop being nasty to each other. Let's stop being jealous of each other. And let's stop judging each other. Let's stand tall, be powerful, deeply loving and authentic with every other woman and make our world better in every way.

SECTION 2

ACTIONS SPEAK FAR LOUDER
THAN WORDS.

When it comes to doing business there is no shortage of advice. In fact, you're holding a book full of it right now. But we all know the reality is, ideas without action, are pretty much a waste of time. Getting motivated enough to seek out ways to do business better, and to grow as a person, is certainly a giant step in the right direction, but we need more.

The concept of the Business Over Breakfast book is to put some serious thought into the bigger issues and opportunities for business and then implement them. Hence the reason why you'll notice Bree's excellent advice at the end of each idea. Whenever we read, watch, listen to or discuss an interesting idea, we always need to be asking ourselves the question, "How can I implement this to get maximum benefit?". Master this and you will really start to get some serious progress in every part of your life.

12

There is an old Chinese proverb that says 'a man without a smiling face must never open a shop'.

This sounds like pretty solid advice, if you can't smile and be friendly you probably shouldn't open a shop. When I am presenting I quote this proverb often, and I am always surprised at the response.

The audience collectively bursts out laughing, which in itself is kind of fun. But I don't quite understand why it's funny. In fact, I think it is deadly serious.

In the past many purchases were simply transactions-money was exchanged for a product or service. In many ways there was not a lot of emotion tied to the exchange, it was more about convenience and necessity.

Today, we make many, if not most of our purchases with a much higher expectation of emotional connection and one thing that stops us connecting is miserable people. Sadly way too many businesses have a lot of miserable people working in them (and owning them).

Of course the real issue is why are people miserable? Generally it is a lack of engagement of some sort in the workplace. But even this starts much higher up the food chain. The person at the top, the CEO, the business owner, the manager, whoever it may be, will always have a dramatic impact on the mood of the business. These are the people who have "opened the shop" and if they are miserable, the overall mood of the company tends to follow suit.

The bottom line is that we all need to have a lot more fun when it comes to doing business. It is very easy to dismiss this as being all hippy dippy, however I see more evidence daily that successful organisations encourage a playful culture. One great example of this is Virgin Airlines. The sense of fun starts at the top with Richard Branson and works it way through the business like a playful virus.

What are the videos that go viral? The ones where the business is being fun playful and the staff are having fun. As consumers, this appeals to our thinking and our desire for emotional connection.

Some businesses tend to think that a sense of fun is unprofessional. Do we think Virgin is any less professional or safe as an airline because of their playful attitude? Absolutely not.

Now of course, there are some businesses that need to maintain a more solemn approach. It is hard to imagine a funeral parlor being a place of huge amounts of fun. Generally though, most businesses can certainly encourage their staff to lighten up, to relax, to engage and be more human.

As the business owner, CEO or manager, you need to ask yourself if you have become way too serious?

Bringing a more playful approach to doing business has to start from the top and for many people, this means relearning how to have fun. From here, we need to let our team know that it is OK to lighten up, to connect and engage with our customers in a fun, but respectful way. And collectively we all have to learn how to laugh a whole lot more.

BREE'S TAKE

There is something heartwarming about seeing a business owner that is so passionate about their business that they nearly burst. Business is like a marriage, you are going to have your ups and downs, and to help us get through the downs we need to be the best version of ourselves possible. And believe me, I've certainly had those days when I've found it very hard to smile, so please don't think I go through life riding my unicorn and giving away puppies.

Sometimes I ask people if they are happy in their business and they give me a puzzled look and respond with, "I don't really know". I guess it's like the relationship metaphor, hopefully you are happy more often than you are not. So here is a little quiz that I use to determine how I'm feeling about my business with a simply happy scale.

Score yourself a point for every yes answer and a zero for every no answer. Then add up the total out of ten to see how happy you are in your business. If you're under 5 on the happy scale, maybe it's time for a divorce...

1. Most days I jump out of bed excited for the work day ahead.

2. I love talking about my business in a positive way.

3. If someone asks me "How's business?" I tell them more positives than negatives.

4. If I had a choice between running a business and being employed, I'd choose my business.

5. My business still has potential I want to reach.

6. If I sold or shut down my business overnight, I'd be really sad.

7. If I was given a million dollars, I'd still continue my business.

8. I love what my business stands for.

9. I enjoy being at my business and have fun most days.

10. The people in my life, my team and family all love my business nearly as much as I do.

This is a great little exercise to do on those days where you find it hard to smile.

13

Have you got the customers you want or the customers you've ended up with?

If you're anything like me, when you started to build your business you were grateful for any customer who would walk through the door (or contacted you online). In the early days that's generally how a business starts, being selective feels like a luxury.

The problem is that if we don't start to get selective and targeted with our customers, we get whoever comes our way, for whatever reason. This means we can end up with the customers we deserve, but probably not the ones we want.

One example of this is when we sell ourselves as being cheap. Now we attract customers who are looking for cheap. They in turn tell their cheap friends and before you know it, you have a business that struggles to make money because all of your customers are cheap. And cheap customers tend to not be overly loyal. They are demanding at a level far higher than they are prepared to pay for.

We need to reach a stage where we are clear on the type of customers we want to attract into our business. Making an "ideal customer avatar", is a great way to paint a clear picture of the exact type of customer you want to attract to your business.

Figuring out who your ideal customer is can sometimes be a little challenging. Here are a few ideas that might help you get more clarity:

Go back over the last years' worth of figures and see which customers have been the most profitable (not those that have spent the most, but those that you have made the highest profit margins on). Clearly we want more of these people or businesses as customers.

Think about every project you did in the last year; which ones were perfect? The customer was great, they paid well, they respected you and your team, in fact everything was perfect. Who were they, what industry were they in, what made everything go so well? Ask these questions to paint a picture of your ideal customer.

Think about where your business is heading - your goals and dreams. Are your existing customers going to help you achieve these? If not, what are the characteristics of the customers who will help you to get where you want to go?

What products or services are the most profitable for you and the easiest to deliver? Who are the ideal customers to buy these?

What is going on in your industry and what trends are emerging? You need to do some serious research or you may wake up one day and find that you no longer have any customers. Generally there is a lot of information available about trends, big data is churning this information out all the time. Use it wisely and plan your future.

Once you are really clear about who your ideal customers are, and you can define your niche, you can develop your messaging. Start to write content for them, develop your online presence accordingly, develop products and services that they will want, and generally tailor your business to suit, and whatever it is that they need.

When this happens, you develop a wonderfully competitive advantage, you enjoy your business much more and you generally make more money. Three wonderful outcomes that simply come from knowing who you want your customers to be.

BREE'S TAKE

Activity time. Grab some paper and let's work out who your ideal customer is. So many businesses don't work it out, put yourself ahead of the game and let's do it.

Step One: Think about your customers. You may have one type of customer, or you may have six types of customer. What I'm trying to get you to do is think about the different groups of customers you have.

EXAMPLE: Your business as a web developer means you could have customers like; Millennial start ups, Mum & Dad start ups, 60+ year old start ups, and small businesses who have a website but need a new one. These are four different customer types, each having very different needs and expectations.

Step Two: Once you have your list of customers, it's time to give each of them a piece of paper. Split the paper into four parts and write headings on each; Strength, Worries, Opportunities, & Language.

Step Three: Now it's time to put yourself in your customer's shoes. What do you perceive as their strengths for your business? List them. It could be, high disposable income, creative flair, more likely to pay on time etc.

Once you know their strengths you can work to them, and you can also ascertain the most valuable client when you compare your other clients.

Step Four: Now it's time to list what you think they worry about when working with you? Will their $10,000 investment in a website with you work? Will you get it done in time? Will it function as promised? Will they pay what you quoted or will more pop up? These questions will help you have solutions to their problems, which will help you with your sales approach and marketing.

Next, write down what you have to worry about working with them. Will they be organised and meet the deadlines to get this website happening? Will they change the brief once we start, etc. These questions will help you determine what processes you need to put in place to combat this.

Step Five: Now it's time to work out the opportunities, especially the marketing opportunities for each of these customer avatars. Could you market yourself at start up workshops, could you do a flyer drop to current businesses in a set location, could you offer to speak or sponsor a local business event?

Step Six: We are nearly there. You now have who your ideal customers are, you know their Strengths, Worries, and the Opportunities, now it is time to decide what Language you will use for each of these customer avatars.

For the 60+ start ups you will use language that may need to be more layman's terms, that is reassuring, helpful and confident, where as the Gen Y's you may need to use language that is more technical. Write out a couple of sentences or dot points covering the tone and type of content you are guessing you will have to use.

Step Seven: Well done! Time to hand this scribble over to someone to design for you with the key information that you think is important. Then put this up on a wall and discuss with your team so you are all on the same page.

Now, you might realise a few things as part of this exercise (well I'm sure you will realise a lot of things). But one big thing might be that you have customers that you don't really want. Trying to meet the needs and expectations of such a diverse group of customers can be challenging. It might be time to narrow down your business focus by targeting specific niches that you are really good at working with and most importantly, great at getting results for.

14

Ninety percent of businesses fail to do this one thing (which means it's a great opportunity for those of us that do).

I often meet with business owners who are trying desperately to increase their income. They spend a lot of money on marketing and advertising, they invest in great websites, they do everything they can to get more customers in the door or online and they succeed. But they have one major problem that lets all of that good work down - they are terrible at following up with their potential customers.

This means that they might submit a quote to a customer, which they supply, but then they do nothing else to follow the quote up. Often they don't even check to make sure that the customer has received it. In this age of email, it is surprising how many quotes end up in junk mail or spam boxes. Because we are so used to businesses not following up, we get frustrated, assume they didn't follow up and we contact someone else.

I reviewed an article recently that stated that almost ninety percent of small businesses failed to follow up quotes that they send out. This is a staggering figure when you think about it. Another report that I reviewed indicated that sales could be increased by up to 40% simply by giving a customer a follow up call to make sure they have received the quote and to answer any questions that they might have.

Now this doesn't apply to every kind of business I know, but it does apply to a very large proportion including trades and services as well as businesses that sell higher priced products. When was the last time you had a tradesperson ring you to see if you received the quote or to ask if would like to proceed with a quote?

Of course the problem is that most people are busy, especially small business owners. But let's be honest, who is too busy to get another sale simply by making a phone call? I believe very strongly that any business that is extremely good at following up on quotes is going to get far more than their share of new customers.

If you are too busy, why not pay someone else to follow up on your quotes? I think that this is perfectly acceptable, as long as the person doing the follow up has some idea regarding the service or product so that they can answer a few simple questions. In fact today there are numerous businesses springing up who provide this exact service.

Getting in front of a customer and providing a quote or proposal means you are very close to the sale, but only if you do the right things from that critical time on. Become relentless and thorough when it comes to following up and your bank balance will reinforce that this is a smart move for your business.

Now one word of warning, if the customers you want are vastly different to the ones you have, it may take some time to change the mix. You have to go through the "losing the deadwood" stage and that can be scary because all we see is lost revenue, not the transition into something better. So be prepared for things to dip before they rise and become far better than before.

BREE'S TAKE

What causes terrible follow up? Generally it is a lack of systems and processes. So my advice is simple, get yourself a sales process. Take ten minutes and think about the ideal way your sales process would work. Here is an example process for you to work through.

Step One: Initial lead (build rapport with client, establish their wants and needs)

Step Two: Qualify the lead (budget, timing)

Step Three: Offer solution (that satisfies their wants and needs)

Step Four: Send the quote for the solution

Step Five: Call within 24 hours to see if they received it. Ask for feedback on your quote.

Step Six: Deal with any objections until sale closed.

Step Seven: In every interaction agree on the time and expectations for the next contact.

Step Eight: Make contact at the agreed time and in the agreed way – no if's and no but's.

Step Nine: Follow up after sale to see if they are happy and if they can refer any of their friends.

Once you have your sales process complete, you can then train all your team to follow the process. This will not only improve your bottom line, but also improve your customer service. Being great at sales is really about being organised.

15

The art of the bluff.

I bought my first business when I was eighteen, a SCUBA diving school and retail shop (some thirty miles from the ocean I might add). I knew how to dive and how to teach other people to dive, but I had absolutely no idea how to run a business. It didn't take me long to realise that if I was going to survive I had to learn the art of bluff.

The simplest of tasks were alien to me. I didn't know how to manage money, stock, staff, customers or any basic business function. On the other hand, I looked the part, I spoke with confidence, and I spent a huge amount of time learning new skills and getting good at finding answers in a hurry. No matter how insecure and afraid I might have been feeling on the inside, I managed to hide it all behind a super confident, capable, "can do" exterior.

That was some 30 years ago and I always remember people at the time saying how impressive it was that this young man had somehow gotten a loan, bought a business, and was running it successfully. If only they knew how much pedaling my legs were doing under the surface. Yet somehow I survived and moved onto other businesses.

My good friend bluff came along for the ride.

I soon realised that I wasn't alone. Most of us bluff our way through business in some way. We might know our own area of expertise, but that certainly doesn't mean we know every aspect of running a business. We have to bluff it or risk that important people will lose faith in us, which of course can spell disaster.

A bluff can make a small business look like a giant corporation. It can open doors and create opportunities. In many ways, bluffing helps you do what others won't, which in turn gives you a significant competitive advantage. In the business world of today, we are all desperately looking for a competitive advantage.

In my experience, the best bluffers are hugely passionate about their businesses and are going to do whatever it takes to make them successful. It isn't just about making money; it is about building something of substance.

So when is it dangerous to bluff? When you know you can't deliver.

Bluffing without substance is the best way to develop a reputation as someone who can't deliver. Telling someone that you can deliver a million-dollar project tomorrow, simply to get the job, when there is absolutely no way that you can make it happen, is a sure fire path to disaster. We all know businesses that fit into this category. They rarely last.

For this reason, it's important to very clearly identify the line between a bluff and a lie. Bluffing is not about saying something that isn't true; it is more about showing that you are more than confident and capable than you actually feel on inside.

Likewise, if there is a time for bluff and bravado, there is also a time to have deeper, more open and transparent conversations. Bluff can get you in the door. But then you have to prove that you can back your claims. To me this is the winning combination, a healthy dose of bluff combined with real capability.

The moral to the story, don't be afraid of getting your bluff on. Even though you might not have all the answers, say yes now and figure them out later-but only do it if you know you can deliver. Stand tall and proud. Just don't let people see your knees knocking.

BREE'S TAKE

Over time we have to be getting better at "bluffing with substance". However, here are some things we must never ever bluff.

1. Anything integrity related; i.e. saying you have worked with a company but you haven't, saying you have a qualification that you don't.

2. If you know that you absolutely can't deliver in any way shape or form, then don't say you can.

3. Don't bluff on anything that could affect the health and wellbeing of others, or someone's job or business.

As you become more experienced in business and have more proven track records you won't need to bluff quite as much. You will speak confidently from your past successes and experiences. Till then, bluff, but bluff with integrity.

16

Don't do business angry - if you do, there is always a price to pay.

We all know someone who is always angry and doing business with them is not a lot of fun. If you're doing business angry, ultimately it will cost you. Of course we are all under a lot of pressure these days, but we need to deal with the issues that cause us to be angry as opposed to simply reacting to them.

I've had sales people who are angry because they aren't getting sales, who then got angry with me because I wasn't buying. I've had invoices issued when the person was clearly having a bad day and they've been very heavy handed with their billing out of frustration from someone else not paying. I've seen presenters in a bad mood telling off an audience. And of course the list goes on.

Let's be honest - we all get a bit grumpy from time to time. And sure, lots of people get downright angry. But most of the time they tend to take out their frustration on the wrong person. Instead of confronting the person or the situation that has made them angry (or even better, letting it go all together) they tend to lash out at those around them who did nothing.

I remember talking to a lawyer who said that he got so frustrated with slow paying clients that when he was invoicing he automatically put himself into a rage and charged for every second of time and then some. Change your policies and procedures, hold a credit card on file for minimum fees, charge up front, do whatever it takes but don't take your anger and frustration out on those customers that do the right thing.

I think there are a couple of morals to this story. The first is that if someone is making you angry in the daily course of doing business there are probably some significant issues in the relationship and surely you would have to ask if that customer is worth having?

Secondly, if, for whatever reason you are getting frustrated by a behaviour from some of your clients, perhaps deal with them as opposed to taking out your anger and frustration on everyone else, especially those great customers who are the backbone of your business.

Finally, if you are finding yourself getting angrier in the day-to-day course of business, perhaps it's time to step back and reflect a little to figure out what is really going on. You might not think anyone else has noticed your new behavior, but I guarantee that they have.

People don't like doing business with angry people - if you don't do something about it, ultimately you will pay the price.

BREE'S TAKE

Grab a piece of paper and write a list of everything that is making you angry. Take a good hard look at this list and ponder the following:

- What are the things you can fix if you took the time right here right now to fix them?

- Are there any that you need to simply let go?

- Are there any people that you need to have a good chat with so that you can sort it out?

- Are there any that are purely ridiculous and you can't believe you are getting angry about them?

- Are there issues that maybe you need to get a third party to help you? Perhaps a mutual friend or even a counselor of some kind?

You'd be surprised how doing the above will shift your anger. It's ok to be angry sometimes, but if it is ruling your life and you spend more time than you should being angry, then you need to do something about it. Remember, nobody likes doing business with someone who is angry all the time.

17

Sometimes it's the things we've stopped doing that can bring our business undone.

I recently met a lady who was experiencing a major financial hiccup in her business, in fact her revenue had virtually halved in the past two years. This decline had been gradual, but the end result was her business was now in big trouble.

We sat and chatted about the things she had been doing over the past couple of years, trying to get a grip on what was going wrong. Sure, we could blame some of the impact on the economic conditions, but nowhere near a drop of fifty percent. This lady had built her business up to a very successful level over the previous five years and then she got a little bored and started to look for other opportunities. She started to expand, setting up some satellite offices and even two franchises in other cities.

This expansion started about two years ago - you guessed it, the same time that her main office started to go downhill. Of course, it is easy to see that her focus was on the other new and exciting business opportunities, not on her core business and that is what caused the problem.

Once we had figured out the lay of the land and where she was right now, it became clear that we had to put some serious effort and energy into the main business, and we had to do it fast.

I started to rattle off a list of things that I would do to get the cash register smoking such as increasing communication with existing clients, develop more targeted and inspirational promotional material, follow-up sales religiously, instigate- "a refer a friend" campaign, get out in the community and tell the network what is happening in the business, do some media releases and so on.

As I worked through this list my client was shaking her head somewhat forlornly and I asked her why? She said she used to do all of the things I was suggesting back when she was first building her business, but she stopped doing them a while back, actually about two years back, because she got too busy focusing on her expansion.

Sadly this is a common story that I hear on a regular basis. Businesses often struggle financially not because of what they are doing, but because of what they are not doing. Chasing other opportunities distracts the business owner and as a result, their main business becomes compromised.

In this case the lady I met went from having a highly profitable, successful and easy to manage business, to having six troublesome, struggling businesses that had created a world of stress, financially and personally.

As we stop doing the things we should be doing, the flow on affect is not immediately clear. The impact is often gradual and it can sneak up on you, just as it did with my client. I know that it is hard to keep going, to keep putting energy into your business day in and day out, but it is easier to do a little every day as opposed to having to do a huge amount to save the business if things start to go seriously wrong.

I have two very simple and straight forward questions for you: firstly, what have you stopped doing in your business and secondly, how much is this costing you?

Entrepreneurs chase opportunities because that is what we do, but the most important rule to always follow is to never pursue an opportunity at the expense of your main business.

BREE'S TAKE

I have been victim to this situation myself. As Andrew says, entrepreneurs by nature chase opportunities, we just need to make sure we are always treating our primary business with the respect and attention that it deserves.

That aside, I also advise everyone to have a rainy day plan for their business. Strange things happen that we are not prepared for and having a rainy day plan that you can action straight away is a great insurance policy.

List ten things you could do should your business be hit with a downturn (whether it be a result of something you've stopped doing or something out of your hands). This is a list that you need to keep handy, up to date and ready to implement at a moments notice. It really is about being ready to take action.

At the same time, it's important to go through life with our eyes wide open. Look at your competitors and the companies you like and admire (they can be from the same industry or from a completely different industry). Is there anything that you could emulate in your business? We need to keep a balanced mix of fresh ideas coming into the business whilst making sure everything else is being attended to and nothing is slipping between the cracks.

18

Are you an opportunity addict?

My name is Andrew and I am a recovering addict. My weakness: Opportunities. For more years than I care to remember, I have been addicted to chasing opportunities.

This is a problem for many entrepreneurs. You chase every opportunity that comes your way-like a dog chasing a butterfly, with the same result. A 12-step program could help, though I suspect most entrepreneurs would lose interest with that many steps. Instead, I have developed a six-step program designed to cross all language, cultural, political, and geographical borders to help opportunity junkies everywhere find their way to recovery.

STEP 1: Create an "Opportunity List"

One of the biggest fears that opportunity addicts share is the fear of missing out. A common, obsessive question: "What if I have the best idea in the world and I forget it?" So every time a great idea comes your way, the first thing you must do is add it to your opportunity list. Then, do absolutely nothing further about it. This way it is recorded and you don't have to worry about losing it.

STEP 2: Develop your own "Opportunity Evaluation Process"

In other words, devise a checklist of criteria that any opportunity must meet before it can graduate from the wish list to the potential list. Make sure your checklist is rigorous and honest. That way, the opportunities you pursue will truly be worth the effort.

STEP 3: Dismiss any opportunity that requires you to act immediately

If I had a dollar for every time I dropped everything to chase a once-in-a-lifetime opportunity… let's just say I would be a very wealthy man. I have since learned that most time-sensitive opportunities are a waste of time. In fact, you'll be surprised how often these opportunities come around again (and again).

STEP 4: One opportunity at a time

Get into the habit of having just one opportunity as your priority at any one time. This means you have to choose wisely and be disciplined enough to stay focused. Don't worry, the others are still there, but you are not allowed to move on those until you nail the one at the top of your list.

STEP 5: Find yourself a brutal opportunity gatekeeper

Your job is to pitch every opportunity to this individual for approval. Their job is to push back, in order to make sure you aren't chasing butterflies again. If you can't sell the opportunity to the gatekeeper, then it doesn't make the cut.

STEP 6: Avoid the places where opportunities lurk

They might not be down darkened taverns or red light districts, but rest assured, opportunities lurk all the same. You need to know the places where we tend to get piles of ideas and avoid them. Don't worry, when you are running low on opportunities (as if) you can revisit some of these locales, but do not go there to chase butterflies.

Rest assured, the world will never run out of opportunities, there are new ones being created every minute.

BREE'S TAKE

I'm pretty certain that most of us can relate to the concept of being an opportunity addict. Often it's a fear of missing out as much as a love of anything new. Whatever the case, opportunity addiction can have some serious problems.

My advice is to start an opportunity list. On it add all of the opportunities you have on your plate right now. As new opportunities come along, add them to the list. This helps eliminate the "fear of missing out" or losing the idea, as you have now got it clearly documented.

Now you need to develop your own criteria, or simply adopt Andrew's process and make sure that every opportunity that comes your way gets processed accordingly. This will eliminate the butterfly chasing and make it more of a business process to follow.

19

Is your business at risk of being left behind by your fast-growing customers?

There is an old saying that if a business isn't growing it's dying. I believe this to be true. There are many ways to measure growth, it's not always just about turnover. It can be about expertise, technology, skills and capability. When dealing in the business to business space, if you have clients that are growing rapidly, you have to keep up with them or face the risk of losing them forever.

I have certainly experienced this in the past. Several years back I worked with a medium sized company that underwent a rapid growth spurt, increasing annual revenue from $35 million to $150 million in two very short years. As a small business supplying marketing services to this company, it became very clear that as my client grew, my business needed to grow with them. If I didn't, I would be left behind and they would end up using a bigger marketing firm and that would have been devastating to my business.

I made a very strategic decision to ensure that I invested in my business and my staff to ensure that we were more than capable of meeting the needs and expectations of this rapidly growing company. This meant:

Investing in technology: I was determined to ensure that my business had the latest in computers, printers and all of the related technology and hardware.

I also made a point of investing in training to make certain that we could use this technology to its full capacity.

Investing in our skills: within the business I made a point of up-skilling everyone, including myself. This investment was in training, coaching, personal development products and specialised consultants, all of which ensured that our internal capability kept growing at the same pace as our big client.

Investing in research: I made a point of investing financially in research, to ensure that the advice we were offering was at the forefront of our industry. In other words, my researcher was charged with finding case studies, new industry practices, and new resources that were available etc.

The end result of this was that although my business was relatively small (we had less than ten people on the team) the services, skills and capability we could offer were on par with much larger marketing firms.

This ensured that we retained our rapidly growing client for many years. We were able to bat above our weight, doing work for larger companies who traditionally wanted to work with bigger marketing firms. Clearly a good outcome and a good model.

BREE'S TAKE

Our customers want to work with the best and if they get the slightest hint that you and your team are not keeping up, they will probably start to look elsewhere. To be the best, we need to have the best. Think about the following – what implications could a negative response mean for the future of your business?

1. Do the members of my team have all the skills they need to do their work?

2. Is everyone on my team really, really good at what they do or do I compromise because it is easier?

3. Does everyone have all the right equipment to do their work to the best of their ability?

4. Do we have the right resources to help people manage their time, their work and their relationships, either with other team members or customers?

5. Is our office somewhere we are proud to bring clients?

6. Is our office of a standard that is on par with our clients?

7. Does our business have an appropriate digital presence?

8. Is our branding fresh and relevant and at a level that our customers would expect?

9. Do we have a well-developed training program to ensure that we are growing as both individuals and a team.

20

How much business is your language costing you?

A few years back I was going through a particularly stressful period in my business. I had plenty of work, in fact I had way too much work, trying to manage it all was leading to me spending ridiculously long hours chained to my desk. During this time I developed a bad habit that cost me a lot of money.

During the course of the day, if anyone asked me how things were going I would go into a tirade about how busy I was, how stressed out I was, how crazy my life had become and so on. Without realising it this outburst had become an automatic response whenever someone asked me how I was. It didn't matter whom I was talking to, I did the same automatic response to anyone who would listen.

Then something strange started to happen, my business died. My company was built on word of mouth referrals, and these had suddenly stopped in their tracks. Clearly something major gone wrong and I needed to do something about it straight away.

I bit the bullet and started to call each and every one of my best referrers to find out what we had done wrong. I assumed that the clients they had referred where not satisfied with the work my company was doing and this had in turn caused the referrer to lose confidence in us. But what I found out was actually much different to that.

The first conversation went something like this:

"Hi, Bob! Andrew Griffiths here. I notice that you have stopped referring new clients to our company and I was wondering if there was a problem of some sort. Perhaps we failed to meet your client's expectations. I am terribly sorry if that is the case."

Bob' response was "Andrew nothing could be further from the truth. We love to refer people to you because we know the advice you provide is always spot on. But you're right, there is a problem. Every time we catch up and I ask how you are, you tell me how busy you are, how stressed out you are and how overwhelmed you are, and I really don't like to see you like that. So I made the decision that I would not refer any more business to you until things calm down in your world."

Now after making about a dozen more phone calls, I realised that most of my referrers had made the same decision to stop sending me business as an act of kindness. Their kindness almost sent me broke, but the real culprit was my language, my words, and my automatic script.

Fortunately, I was able to resurrect my referral network relatively quickly, but it cost me a lot of money and I could easily have gone broke. From that point on I needed to be very careful about the language I use. So I changed my script into something a little more proactive and a little less sad and sorry:

"Hey, Bob! Great to see you. Yes, business is very good, we have a lot of exciting projects underway. Everything is working well and we are always looking for new, high caliber clients exactly like the ones you kindly refer to us."

This new script is my response, regardless of how busy I actually am. It took a while to reprogram my automatic response, but I am very glad I did.

With the realisation of how my old script had impacted so dramatically on my business I became much more aware of other scripts that I blurted out without any real thought to the damage they could be doing. I also became much more aware of other people's automatic scripts and the damage they were doing to their businesses.

I think a lot of people in a sales role turn on their automatic script and the minute they do we sense it and disconnect. Any repetitive situations tend to create the same scenarios.

We all need to be considered with the language we use. It might just be costing us more than we could ever imagine.

BREE'S TAKE

Here are the most common lines I hear out of small business owner's mouths that I'd suggest reframing if you are up for the challenge. They address the most common issues of turning away business without realising it, questioning your businesses credibility and being guilted in making a commitment that you don't really want to make. It takes time, but opens up conversations in a positive way both personally and professionally.

OLD LANGUAGE	REPLACE WITH
Hi how are you?	Really nice to see you, how is life treating you?
Really busy!	Really busy, but always looking for new opportunities and new quality projects to work on.
Things are tough.	Business isn't as good right now as I would like it to be, but we are working really hard to improve things.
My staff are driving me crazy.	My staff are great at what they do, but as my business evolves there are always challenges and opportunities.
Are you available to….	That sounds really interesting, but I need to check my calendar and other commitments first.

21

What's the one thing that lets your business down and why haven't you fixed it?

Most businesses seem to have one thing that constantly lets them down. In fact I'm sure if we all did a bit of soul searching we would have a pretty good idea what our own Achilles Heel is, but the issue is not so much that we have a problem, but more importantly why don't we fix it once and for all?

From my experience this problem tends to fall into one of two categories: either it is an irritation, that if we fixed it our customers would be happier and perhaps refer more of their friends to us, or the second type of problem, an absolute deal breaker. As much as we love everything else about the business, this issue is simply too much of a problem for us to keep doing business with them, so in frustration and disappointment we move on.

Clearly if ours is the second type of problem, we need to do something about it and fast. Here are three examples that really could be solved, if some lateral thinking was applied, and perhaps some common sense.

I work with a great printer. Their print quality and pricing is second to none, but the problem that constantly lets them down is delivery. Now in fairness to them, this is outsourced to a specialist delivery company, which for some reason, can't seem to deliver when they say they will. But the buck stops with the printer.

This has been an issue for years-why isn't it fixed?

I used to stay at a great hotel, right in the middle of the city, the rooms were nice, the price was good, everything met my expectations, but they insisted on cleaning the rooms between 4pm and 6pm. So you get back to your hotel after a day of meetings to find the room still not cleaned, and you know that you will get a knock on the door shortly asking to make up your room, which in turn means you have to leave, when you want to be relaxing or finishing your day's work.

Last but not least, my favourite coffee shop was for many years the place I did business. I would spend a lot of time there, conduct countless meetings and buy a lot of coffee. I liked everything about this place, until they bought a new sound system. From that day on, I constantly had to ask them to turn down the music so that you could hear and be heard during meetings. I asked, and asked and asked, then I left.

Now as specific as these issues may be to me, I know for a fact that many other people stopped using the printer for the same reason, colleagues of mine stopped using the hotel, for the same reason and many friends and business associates stopped using the coffee shop because they got sick and tired of yelling at each other in meetings.

Think about your own examples. What are the businesses you use but find frustrating? What is their one thing? And think about the businesses that you really wanted to keep using, but they just made it too hard, what was their one thing?

Sometimes we can get it ninety-nine percent right, which might be close enough. But it depends what the one percent is, that we get wrong. Fix the one thing that lets your business down and make it easier for people to do business with you and they will.

This can be the difference between a business doing OK and a business soaring.

BREE'S TAKE

It's amazing how "one little thing" can impact our business. Andrew gave us some great examples, and the funny thing is, to the business owner they probably don't think the issues he has raised are that big a deal, thus they don't fix it. That is what is scary about this.

We all need to be able to honestly look at our business from a customers point of view and accept that maybe the things we don't think are important are actually very important to them.

My advice to you is this, ask your current clients if there is anything you can do better to keep them buying from you? How you ask is really important. People are hesitant to open up and be critical, mostly because when they've done it in the past, they haven't had a good response from the business owner. So explain how genuinely you want their feedback and how you are committed to making any changes that you can, to ensure they are totally satisfied.

I'd also love it if you can join us in being "Improvement Ambassadors". What that means is when you see something a business can improve on, write it down and ensure your feedback makes it to the owner or manager. Your feedback could make a huge difference. If they do nothing with the feedback that's up to them.

22

Nine signs you are dealing with a "douchepreneur".

Over the years I've met a lot of entrepreneurs and I've always loved and admired their passion. But in recent times, there has been a rise in one very particular kind of entrepreneur commonly known as the "douchepreneur" and it seems that I'm not the only one who has noticed.

According to Urban Slang, the definition of douchepreneur is "an unemployed douche that loves bragging about the dozens of start-ups he/she had a role in." And I think we've all met this kind of person. The minute your eyes lock you can almost feel the pitch coming, and as the words fly, it is pretty clear that there is no real substance.

Now I think it is important for us to be able to identify douchepreneurs fast, because this gives us the chance to end the conversation and back away as quickly as possible. It is also nice to do a little check in, to make sure we are not turning into a douchepreneur ourselves.

So how can you tell if you are on the receiving end of a conversation with a douchepreneur?

1. They are really intense close talkers who never seem to blink.

2. They immediately start bragging about the dozens of start-ups that they've played a pivotal role in developing and the money they generated (yet you have to pay for the coffee).

3. They never miss a chance to pitch their latest idea (even at funerals).

4. They take it personally if you question any of the assumptions they make (like is there actually a market for Apple Watches for cats?).

5. They have a huge (but meaningless) social media presence-all purchased.

6. When asked their job title, often it is vague and nebulous, for example "I make dreams come to life".

7. They have wonderful acronyms, metaphors and woohooo phrases that are generally delivered in a condescending way, something like "individually we are one drop, together we are an ocean".

8. They know everyone and shamelessly drop names and act as if Richard Branson is their best buddy.

9. They normally wear at least one very distinctive piece of clothing.

The moral to the story here is that whilst it is great to be passionate about our business and proud of our achievements, we need to be an entrepreneur of substance, not a douchepreneur.

BREE'S TAKE

Ahhhh the Douchepreneur, these guys actually make me laugh and they are a good reminder on how not to behave as an entrepreneur. The one that frustrates me more is the "Wantpreneur" the people that really *want* to be an entrepreneur, have an idea, but never act on it. Some of these ideas are fantastic, but they are too scared to back themselves and give it a go.

Everytime you see them they haven't done anything since the last time you spoke to them. They are still just "thinking about it". You spend thirty minutes giving them ideas, encouraging them and putting a fire in their belly. They leave your company all revved up, then months down the line you see them again...nothing.

Wantpreneurs- for the love of God, please just give it a go. If you have an idea for your business, today is the day, stop talking about it and start actually doing something.

23

Seven things you absolutely, positively should never do at the work Christmas party.

If it's that time of year, the dreaded office Christmas party is upon us or some other work function. We've all heard shocking stories around bad behavior, mostly fuelled by alcohol, with the post party walk of shame on the Monday morning, where embarrassment is shared and humiliation is complete.

Don't let the festive season be something you regret. Here are seven things you absolutely, positively must not do at your work Christmas party (or your partners work party or any party), especially if you are the boss:

1. **Don't start the party badly**
   At this time of year it doesn't take much of an excuse to start a party early but resist the urge to start your work party early. First impressions count, especially with your regular colleagues. Don't turn up drunk, late or dressed inappropriately (you might be really proud of your new piercing and have a strong desire to express your individuality, but the work party is not the place to launch it for the world to see).

2. **Don't act like you have never been out before**
   The bottom line here is simple, if you wouldn't do it sober, don't do it at the party. Make sure you follow this rule of thumb, and you won't go wrong. Don't

drink everything in sight, or eat everything in sight, or be inappropriate in any way with anyone. Rest assured, people are watching and their opinion of you will be impacted, either in a good way or a bad way, based on your actions.

3. Don't talk business

There is nothing worse than a party where everyone stands around talking about work. Use the work party to find out more about the people you spend your days with, be interested in them and what they are doing, not what projects they did or didn't finish. Go prepared with a few topics of discussion if you feel awkward in these social scenes.

4. Don't tell anyone that you love them

The words "I love you" should never be uttered at an office party. The internet is littered with the remains of careers that have been destroyed by a Christmas party romance gone wrong, so don't become that cliché.

5. Don't initiate drinking games

Sure, who doesn't like a good shot of tequila? But there is a time and a place. Don't be the person who starts calling for tequila shots to be drunk out of someone's belly button. Drinking games of any sort should never be initiated at the work party simply because they spell the beginning of the end when it comes to behaving in a sensible way.

6. Don't use the Christmas party to express your true feelings to your co-workers

Work parties are notorious for people deciding to tell others exactly how they feel. To say that this is dumb is the understatement of the year. The work party is not the place to tell the boss what a jerk you think they are. And if you are the boss, it is not the place to tell an employee the same. Keep those personal feelings to yourself.

7. Don't go looking for the microphone

There is a strange connection between alcohol and microphones-the more people drink the more they want to use a microphone (the entire karaoke industry is built on it). Avoid, at all costs, the drunken speech. Everyone has a smart phone, and someone will gladly record your performance for all to see. Best to make speeches early, get them out of the way and then make the microphone a no go zone (in fact get rid of it all together). Leave the entertainment to the professionals.

BREE'S TAKE

Work functions have taken on a whole new risk these days and less businesses are offering them to their team for the above reasons. Gone are the days when workplaces encourage their staff to get really drunk and act crazy, simply because there is too much at risk. Think about the following scenarios:

Scenario 1: A drunken employee wraps their arms around another employee and gives an unwanted kiss.

Scenario 2: An employee drinks heavily, gets into their car and crashes on the drive home.

Scenario 3: A frustrated employee, fuelled by alcohol, gives a fellow team member a piece of their mind.

Scenario 4: A high value client is invited to the office party and insulted by an inebriated employee.

Scenario 5: An employee with a mobile phone takes inappropriate pictures and posts them on Facebook.

Simply put a group of people together and add alcohol and these imagined scenarios could very easily become real. As business owners we need to think about every possible risk, because it is the right thing to do. If you are worried about being a party pooper, I suggest it's time to grow up. These issues are real, they have both criminal and moral consequences and if you own the business, the buck stops with you.

We need to make sure everyone on our team knows the ground rules and there are no exceptions. Some of the main ones need to be:

- Sexual harassment is the number one key risk that employers need to be aware of. Ensure your employees sign and understand your Harassment Policy.

- Employees can lodge a workers' compensation claim if they are injured travelling to and from work. This risk goes up with consumption of alcohol. Paying for the taxi home for staff is likely to be cheaper than a compensation claim on a failure to provide a duty of care.

- Have codes of conduct so that your employees know what acceptable behavior is, and remind them before the party. This should also apply to what is acceptable behaviour with customers (do you want your staff sleeping with customers?).

- Ensure your team know your Social Media Policy. Make sure all employees are aware of the consequences of discussing fellow employees, or posting inappropriate pictures online.

- Be a great host, not a party animal. You need to be the most responsible person at the party as the boss, it's your duty of care and even more importantly, it's simply the right thing to do.

SECTION 3

HOW IS YOUR
POVERTY MENTALITY?

Many, many, many business owners have a serious poverty mentality. This often stems from the way they grew up. Rest assured, we understand, we've both had to overcome it. If you struggle with self respect and self worth, it's unlikely that you will ever charge what you really deserve to charge for your products and services. The end result of this poverty mentality is that you will always struggle financially in your business.

This is a topic that is not spoken about enough, but one that we are ridiculously passionate about. Helping people to see the value they bring, and being secure enough to charge accordingly, is a big step for many people. Instead it's easier to under charge and make all kinds of excuses about "what the market is prepared to pay" and so on. In this section, we challenge some of this thinking, and offer some ideas for you to make peace with the "poverty mentality monster" that lives within many of us.

24

Four clues that you are probably not charging enough for what you do.

Most of us struggle with charging what we are worth. We tend to look at pricing as a number plucked out of thin air, perhaps based on what we think our customers can afford to pay, or even worse, we base our prices on what our competitors are charging, with no idea at all as to what they are basing their costs on.

Get your pricing right, and your business will succeed. Get it wrong, and you might have a pile of business, but you will never make any money.

Here are four tell tale signs that you're probably not charging enough for what you do:

1. **You win most of the projects you bid for.** Winning every project sounds great, but it probably means something is wrong. I used to pat myself on the back because my business got ninety percent of the jobs we pitched for. We had periods in there where we got every single job. My ego told me it was because we were awesome, but in reality, and with hindsight, we got them because we were too cheap. And whilst the business was busy, it never made any money.

    Then I changed my pricing structure dramatically, virtually doubling what we charged. Our conversion rate on projects dropped to fifty percent, but we started making money. From that time on, I have always used this as a measurement of how my pricing is working in a particular market, if I am winning too many jobs, I'm too cheap, if I'm not winning enough then I'm getting too expensive.

2. **You are really busy but there is never any money in the bank.** Sure, there can be other reasons why there is never any money left even if you are really busy. You might be spending too much, taking too long on projects, not managing your team properly, but most of the time it comes back to simply not charging enough.

   I have encountered businesses that could never make money, even at full capacity, simply because they are not charging enough for what they do. They haven't taken the time or sought help to understand exactly how much it costs them to run their business, and by association, how much they need to charge to break even and more importantly, make a profit. They have plucked a number out of thin air that is on par with their competitors, without knowing what model their competitors use to work out their prices.

3. **Your entire marketing strategy is based on being the cheapest.** This is a strategy that is pretty much doomed for failure. Sure, the odd company can be built on it, but over time, it's very hard to sustain. As simple as it sounds, a business with a tiny profit margin is not resilient. They are incredibly lean, they feel the impacts of changes in the economy immediately and they are always susceptible to the next new business that comes along and bases its pricing on being the cheapest.

   If your business development and marketing strategy is based entirely around being the cheapest, there will come a time when it will stop working.

4. **You find it really difficult to talk about money with your clients.** We should be able to have very open and honest conversations with our clients about money. This means being able to talk openly and honestly about costs, or more specifically issues that could affect the cost, payment terms and expectations, what happens if there are payment problems and so forth.

Any business where the business owner struggles to talk about money, tends to be on the receiving end of not getting paid what they are worth. They can even develop a reputation as being a push over. Who wants that?

If the thought of having these kinds of conversations makes you cringe, it's really something you need to come to terms with. Start having these discussions early on in the client relationship. Make it as normal as talking about the weather. When there are problems, bring them up straight away, don't stew on them or let them fester.

BREE'S TAKE

Most of us tend to struggle when it comes to talking about money. Here are five "money one liners" that can help make your money conversations much easier:

1. **Can you tell me what the commercial arrangement is?** This one liner will help if you are asked to provide a service like consulting, public speaking or entertaining when often there is almost an implied "we might be asking you to do it for free" undertone. It's a very reasonable question to ask, and it takes the "FREE" undertone out. It's a lot softer than asking "how much are you paying?"

2. **Do you have a budget in mind?** This is a great question to ask if you have to quote a price on something. This question may seem brash, but it helps you establish a ballpark dollar figure, which can make it easier to talk about money. This is a very reasonable question to ask, and in fact, when working with larger organisations, it's almost unprofessional not to ask.

3. **Do you have any feedback on my proposal/presentation/quotation?** If you have presented a proposal with pricing, instead of asking "what did you think" asking for feedback is a lot more open-ended. It allows the conversation to flow and gives a softer way to get feedback on the prices you have quoted.

4. **What are your payment terms?** This question will help you find out when you can expect to be paid, for the products, or services provided. Knowing means that you won't have to sheepishly call when you haven't been paid.

If they don't pay by the agreed time, you can more confidently call, stating that they haven't met the payment terms that were agreed on.

5. **How would you prefer to pay?** This question is basically you asking for the money, but it's a helpful question allowing the buyer to think about the best way to pay, cash, credit, or bank transfer to name a few.

Money isn't an easy topic to talk about, but the more you do it, the more comfortable you will be. Try out a few of these, say them with a smile and you'll find that it isn't so bad after all. From my experience, people will respect you more if you are able to have money conversations in such a simple, open and forthright manner.

25

Next time someone wants you to do something for free, consider this.

We all have to deal with people wanting us to do things for free. There are those who blatantly ask for it, those who try to negotiate on price because that's what they do and those who are just plain cheap.

What does it mean when someone wants us to do things for free or cheap? It means they don't value what it is that we do. And in some ways, that is kind of insulting. Over the years the projects that have caused me the biggest grief have always been the free ones or the cheap ones.

I suggest you take a moment right now and think about the following. How many hours have you actually spent learning about what you do? How much time have you invested in educating yourself? How much money have you invested in your chosen business? How much has getting to this point cost you?

So as an example, I'm an author. How many hours have I spent learning to write books, publish them, promote them and leverage my knowledge? Easily 10,000 hours, in fact many more. How much have I invested in learning to be an author, promoting and leveraging my books? Easily $250,000 dollars over the past 20 years. Clearly that's a big investment and clearly I have accumulated a lot of information, knowledge and expertise, through a lot of trial and error, that is highly valuable. This means I should charge accordingly.

I'm sure that you are the same - you have invested a lot of time and money to get to where you are today and you are probably still investing time and money. You have to value this investment and have the self-respect to charge accordingly.

Next time someone tries to get you to do what you do for a cheaper price, think back about how much it has cost you to get to where you are today. Consider that, before buckling to take a cheaper price. If you have lots of people trying to get you to do what you do for a cheaper price, you might need to rethink your marketing to build your credibility, and show the value you bring to the table. And perhaps rethink your customers to find more who will value you and your expertise.

BREE'S TAKE

Self worth is a big issue and many business owners struggle with it. I'd suggest looking at your actual hourly rate. Sit down and work out how many hours you put into your business in a year, and how much you pay yourself a year. This is your actual hourly rate.

This can be a pretty scary figure for the majority of us, and it likely falls below minimum wage. Now I am in no way suggesting that you are worth this rate, you are likely worth ten times this rate. But the purpose of this exercise is to show you that you need to stop wasting time and giving free hours away to people who should be paying for your time, so the hours in your day decreases, and your hourly rate increases.

Seeing that you actually earn a lot less per hour than the person asking for a discount, also enables you to remove that guilt of saying "no" to a discount too.

I have worked in some of the most notorious industries for wanting a discount and not valuing the work you do; the music industry, the advertising industry, the consulting industry and the speaking industry. In these industries, many people don't value what you do and you will be asked to do it at a discount, or even worse, for free.

I've been asked to many parties and then been asked if our band can 'please do the music for free', and had many "opportunities" to speak at a conference where "it will be great exposure for you, but we can't pay you". I'm sure you have had many experiences like this too. Now don't get me wrong, I am not one of those people that wants to be paid for everything I do, nor do I want you to be that way. Many of us have special talents and gifts that we should freely donate to the world without any expectations of what we get in return. But if I am going to do something I want it to be valued, and often people don't value something if they don't pay for it.

Here are some tips and things to think about if you are considering giving a discount or doing something for free.

1. How much time will you honestly have to commit if you take on this project? Is it worth taking away time from your business or loved ones to do it?

2. Will giving a discount upset your loyal paying clients? No one wants to find out that they are paying more than someone else, especially if they feel they are more worthy of the discount.

3. Do you have an amount of "free" work that you donate every year? Come up with a budget for free work, and then you can decide if you want to use these hours for a certain project.

4. Decide one organisation you will help for the year, this helps when someone asks for a donation as you can say "thanks for asking for this donation, but we are supporting this charity for the year so we are fully committed". It's a much easier guilt-free way of saying no.

5. I am someone who rarely discounts, I don't believe discounting is good for business as it devalues your product or service. I believe in value adding, this can be extra's you offer to get the sale, or it can be extra's that the client wasn't expecting, which is always a nice bonus.

6. Always let someone know the monetary value of what you have given them. The best way to do this is by adding the amount to the invoice and then putting "Done Free of Charge".

7. Charge what you are worth, but always realise your value over and above the money exchange. This shift in value perception about yourself will tend to get you charging what you are worth.

26

Why is everybody else's business easier, simpler, and more profitable than mine?

Over the years there have been plenty of times when it seemed to me that everyone else's business was so much better than mine and not just a little better, but better in every way imaginable. Whilst I was working crazy hours, struggling to make ends meet, dealing with challenging clients and never really seeming to have more than a buck fifty in the bank (on a good week), everyone else's business seemed so much easier.

These were the times when I would look longingly at the local cafe and think how easy it must be to simply make coffee. Or the local newsagent, surely selling newspapers and magazines, couldn't be hard and they must make truckloads of money right? Or a gardener-how nice to wander around in gardens plucking a few leaves here and there, adding some fertiliser, and generally having a nice old time.

Well after working as a marketing consultant for many years, and having clients in pretty much every industry, I now realise that there is no such thing as an "EASY" business. Each one has its own unique set of challenges. Just because I have drunk an ocean of coffee in cafés doesn't mean that I can run one or that if I did, it would be any easier than the business I have now (in fact if you ask me, food businesses are the toughest of them all).

It is easy to lose perspective and look longingly at other businesses, but I am sure that any business owner you talk to from these "grass is always greener" businesses will gladly tell you all of the challenges they face on a daily basis.

When it comes to money and the feeling that every other business is making more money than us, this is again often an illusion. When looking in from the outside, any business can look super successful-but from my experience, the more expensive the cars, the bigger the building, the more staff, all add up to mean a lot of debt. Don't assume that every other business is making more money than you, no matter how it might appear.

So why am I talking about this? Because I come across a lot of people who have a romanticised view about everyone else's business but their own, and I felt a need to put some perspective around it. They spend a lot of their time, like I did, lamenting their businesses shortcomings instead of appreciating what their business actually gives them.

Whenever we find ourselves in that depressing little place, when things are not going right and we start to feel that every other business in the universe is so much better than ours, think again. We all have parts of our business that we really don't like, but we have the choice to focus on them or focus on the bits that we really love.

I have this conversation with business owners all the time, as they complain that they are not making much money in their business, or they are working too hard, or some other perceived issue. My advice is to focus on the great things your business gives you (and be grateful for them):

- Such as freedom, even if it is a freedom with a lot of responsibility

- Or, not having a boss to answer to (sure we all have to answer to someone but it is a very nice feeling to tell someone that you don't want to work with them and you don't have to)

- The ability to work when and how you want

- Getting to make the decisions

- The satisfaction of coming up with new ideas and making them work

- Having people like what you do enough to pay you for it

- Being able to choose the people you spend most of your working day with

These are all things that I wouldn't swap for a million dollars. Sure, we all have bad days, but when I look down the list of the great things my business gives me, I wouldn't swap it for anything. So whilst it may seem that the grass is greener and every other business on the planet is better, easier and more successful than yours, it might just be time for a rethink.

BREE'S TAKE

We all have moments when we start to resent our business, and it often comes down to not receiving the amount of money or credit we feel we deserve for the time we are putting in. If that hits a nerve for you, perhaps it's time to create a one-page "What my Business actually gives me" sheet that you can look at whenever you are having one of these moments.

Ask yourself these simple questions:

1. Why did I start this business?

2. What does my business give to me?

3. What does my business give to the people in my life?

4. What does this business give to my clients?

5. What does this business give to my community?

6. Why am I good at this business?

7. Why is this business great? What have people said about it?

Type it up, print it out and put it somewhere for when you need that extra little pep up. This might help you realise that your business is not worse than everyone else's. In fact it's probably better.

27

Nine strategies for building a smarter relationship with money in your business.

Without doubt, the number one issue I have encountered with business owners over the years is a poor relationship with money. Either they don't take any responsibility for the money in the business, or they are unrealistic about costs and revenue, or they simply don't know how to charge appropriately.

Here are 9 strategies that if adopted in any business, will have a profound impact on income, profitability and cash flow.

1. **Be 100% clear about exactly how much it costs you to operate your business each month.** Very few business owners know this figure. I think it is the single most important number that we need to know. If you don't, you are flying blind, never really sure if you are making money or not until, you do your tax return at the end of the year. By then it can be too late. Ideally, you need to know how much it costs you to run your business every hour, every day, every week and then every month.

2. **Always be absolutely conservative when it comes to estimating costs. Most people under estimate their expenses.** They forget about certain items, they don't think things cost as much as they do and they are

often unrealistic with spending. It is always best to err on the side of caution and over estimate what things cost as opposed to underestimate.

3. **Review your costs all the time.** Costs creep up over time and what it costs you to run your business a year ago will probably be quite different to what it costs today. We need to monitor all costs in our business closely and often. I review my operating costs every month, looking for changes, anomalies and anything else that catches my eye.

4. **Set a clear sales target each month (and remember breaking even is not the goal, making a profit is).** Like most things in life, if you set a goal or a target, your chances of achieving it are dramatically improved. Set a monthly target, one that ensures you make a profit, and then do whatever you can to reach that target. And when you do, celebrate long and loud.

5. **When it comes to saving money or cutting costs, work out how much you could save in a year not just a month.** To save $200 a month doesn't really sound like a great saving, but when you convert it to $2,400 a year, it suddenly gets significant. Most businesses could save a lot of money simply by spending time actively looking for ways to cut costs.

6. **Adopt a much harder approach to setting budgets.** For many years when I was planning a project I was always overly optimistic with everything and the projects rarely produced the numbers I thought they would. So I developed a seriously tough budgeting model for new projects. I had to double how long I thought the project would take, double how much it would cost and half how much revenue I would generate in the first twelve months and if it still stacked up, go for it, if not, forget it. Now this is a tough model, but I've never lost money since adopting it.

7. **Don't be afraid to put your prices up.** All too often I encounter businesses that simply don't charge enough for what they do. If you were operating at full capacity, meaning you couldn't do any more work, what is the maximum amount of money you could make (less costs). Is this enough? Be realistic about the number of days you could actually work, take out holidays, sick days, weekends etc. If your maximum income potential is not what you thought it was, either your prices have to go up, or you have to reduce your costs (or both). Charging more is generally the first strategy I

recommend and yet most businesses are hesitant to do this out of fear of losing customers. If you have a great business, with excellent service, top quality products or advice, people will accept you increasing your rates if you explain the benefit to them.

8. **If you invoice for your services, invoice quickly.** Way too many businesses are hopeless at sending out invoices. By the time they get around to doing their invoicing they have forgotten half of the things they need to charge for and there will almost certainly be items that simply slip through the cracks. Of course once you invoice you still have to get paid, adding even more time to the money ending up in your bank account. Invoice immediately.

9. **Cut people off who don't pay their bills.** We have to set boundaries with our customers in terms of payment. If payment is overdue, stop supplying them. Now we need to let them know that this is the way the relationship will work from the beginning, don't just cut off their service out of the blue. If they know the rules and they don't pay or ask for an extension of payment terms, don't let the amount get larger. Slow paying is the first sign of trouble with an account and I have certainly extended credit when I shouldn't have, and that has ended up costing me a lot of money. I have learned that people respect businesses that are clear and tough on their payment terms. Don't keep extending credit out of fear of losing the client. If they don't pay on time who wants them?

Imagine how your business would look if you adopted these 9 strategies?

BREE'S TAKE

Time for some positive affirmations that reinforce Andrew's great tips. Put these somewhere and read them every day.

1. Success and money come easily to me.

2. I know what my business costs to run and we make more than enough money to cover them.

3. We meet our monthly sales targets with ease.

4. We are careful with our business profits and put them to good use.

5. My business is a gift to this world and I am compelled to share it.

6. I am building a successful company every day.

7. I create daily opportunities for growth for myself and others.

8. My income is growing every day by doing something I love.

9. I attract my ideal clients and customers with my energy.

10. My business is set up for massive success and growth.

28

What are the nine biggest and most costly mistakes that consultants make?

I've been a consultant for many years and have actively coached and helped a pile of consultants from every industry imaginable to grow their businesses. I have come across the same business blunders time and time again, enough for me to draw the conclusion that the following list really does make up the nine biggest, most costly and sadly the most common consultant mistakes.

Of course any consultant who manages to avoid making these mistakes will build a fantastic business, charging what they deserve to be earning, with a long list of valued clients.

So what are the nine biggest and most costly mistakes that consultants make?

1. **They have a confusing offering.** In other words, it is really hard for potential clients to figure out what services they are providing and what problems they will be able to solve. Being able to sell yourself and what you do is vital to the long-term success of any freelance business. Often the client doesn't really know what they need, but they know that they need a particular consultant to help them, so make it easy for them to buy the services you are offering.

2. **They are poor communicators, with clients continually having to chase the consultant.** This is normally the biggest complaint made against consultants-they are lousy communicators. If you want to build a really successful business as a consultant, become exceptional at following up. Get back to people before they expect you to, even if you have nothing to update them about.

3. **They don't differentiate themselves in any way from their competitors.** In fact, it is even worse, they tend to tell their potential clients how they are exactly the same as their competitors. Check out a range of consultants from the same niche and you will find that they list all of the things they do (like accountants who say they do tax and provide business advice-imagine that?) as opposed to explaining what makes them significantly different.

4. **They are reactive to business development not proactive.** They wait for business to come to them as opposed to chasing it, or even working with existing clients to develop more business over a longer period of time. Business development tends to be done based on need (as in "quick we need more work") as opposed to a strategic business development plan.

5. **They are lousy at asking for referrals.** Often consultants are very reluctant to ask their clients to refer them. Feedback that I've had is that it feels a bit pushy and too much like a sales person. Well I hate to break the bad news but if you aren't selling you aren't eating. Consultants who do a great job should never be afraid to ask for referrals, and they will get them naturally anyway.

6. **They bill without showing details, leading to client dissatisfaction.** I remember a few years back I received a bill from my lawyer-it had a one-line description, "Legal services rendered $25,000". There was no description, no explanation, certainly no sense of value. It just looked like a number was plucked out of thin air. You have to provide itemised and detailed invoices, explaining exactly what you did, including anything you did for free, to show value for money.

7. **The client gets fobbed off to lower level staff.** This is typical in a growing business. In the early stages you get the full attention of the

business owner, but over time, you get passed onto someone else and you feel less valued or important. Not long after this, you change consultants. There is nothing wrong with getting other members of your team to manage a client's work, but explain to the client how it will work and make sure they are OK with it. Stay in touch with them and make sure they know that you are always available to them if they need you.

8. **They provide bad advice, more as a lack of attention to detail than anything else.** This tends to be a problem in a business that has really taken off and the consultant is holding a tiger by the tail, just trying to get through their huge workload on a daily basis. They don't pay attention to the details simply because they don't have the time. Their service suffers, which clients will deal with for a while, but when the advice suffers, the situation becomes unacceptable. As consultants we need to manage our own workloads closely and be honest enough to know when we are slipping, and smart enough to do something about it immediately.

9. **They don't manage their client relationships.** When the client stops feeling that loving feeling with their consultant, they move on. Smart consultants always build and maintain their client relationships. In fact it becomes the backbone of their marketing activity. They communicate, they are proactive with the advice they offer and they acknowledge the relationship and the fact that they value it.

BREE'S TAKE

These tips don't just apply to consultants; I think most of these apply to any business as things we can improve on. I want you to pick one point that made your heart sink, as this is the one that you need to work on, implement it today. Think of how much your business will improve by making this lowest performing task one of your best performing tasks? You can do it!

29

It took a tragedy for me to halve the number of hours I worked and double my income.

A few years back I found myself at a terrible crossroads. I was stuck in my business, working ridiculous hours, making no money, my relationship at the time was ending and then I got a phone call to say that my sister had literally dropped dead of a heart attack at the age of thirty-five.

My world wasn't just rocked it was turned upside down. Apart from dealing with the death of my sister, I realised that the writing was on the wall for me as well. If I didn't make some dramatic changes quickly, there was a good chance that I would also drop dead of a heart attack.

I had fallen into some very bad habits. I was working ridiculous hours in my business (and I mean ridiculous-6am to midnight, seven days a week), I said yes to everything so I was totally overcommitted. I had no real idea if I was making money or losing money, because I was too busy to make the time to figure it out. I was eating badly, having no exercise and I was fairly delusional about my life at the time.

For me it was all about building a successful business at any cost. And in reality, it was only a matter of time till I paid the ultimate cost, so I made the decision to change. I set myself a totally unrealistic goal-to halve the number of hours I worked and double my income. It took me about six months, but I did it and this is how:

1. **I stopped working on weekends.** I drew a line in the sand and I made the commitment that I would no longer work weekends. My first Saturday off I sat on the floor for an hour at 6am, wondering what on earth I was going to do with the rest of my weekend. I had completely forgotten how to have time off. My friends had stopped calling me, because I was always working, I didn't even know what I liked doing when I had time off. This was tough, but over time I learned to relax, to take time out and to enjoy life. This made everything better, most importantly I regained a sense of sharpness that I had well and truly lost.

2. **I stopped wasting time.** Because I was working all the time, I had developed the nasty habit of wasting a lot of time. For example on Thursday's and Friday's I told myself that I would be coming in all weekend anyway, so I basically did nothing productive on these two days. I just turned up and wasted time and paid the price by working all weekend.

3. **I doubled my rates.** The reason I did this was because I finally had the time and energy to look at my business and realise that there was no way I could ever make money, based on the rates I was charging. I sat down with my clients, explained why I was doubling my rates and what was in it for them (better service, better advice and a much bigger commitment from me to them). Sure I lost a few, but most stayed and the relationships grew stronger and I attracted plenty of new clients prepared to pay the higher rate.

4. **I declared a moratorium on doing pro bono work.** At the time, I was doing a lot of free work, helping all kinds of charities by offering marketing advice. Sure this made me feel good, but it was clear that if something didn't change, I was going to need the charities I was supporting, because I would be homeless. I made the call that I would not be able to do any pro bono work for 12 months. Having made this decision, I found it much easier to say no when various charities came calling for help. This in turn enabled me to focus on paid work.

5. **I decided to do a better job**. I knew that I had been 'calling it in for years'. Even though my clients were happy enough, and there seemed to be lots of work, I knew that I was really only giving most jobs fifty percent of the attention they deserved. And that wasn't good enough. Now I had more time, more commitment, and a much clearer state of mind. It enabled me

to take my work to a whole new level, which in turn created many new opportunities, better projects and more revenue.

6. **I stopped wasting money.** Once again because of the crazy cycle I was in, I really had no idea what was going on in my business. When I took a step back, and created the right headspace, it soon became very clear that I was wasting a lot of money in my business. There was a total lack of systems, accountability and even decent record keeping. Any business that fails in these three areas can never make money. By focusing my attention on creating systems, making people accountable and hiring a decent bookkeeper I was able to cut my operating expenses by almost twenty five percent per month.

7. **I engaged two personal trainers**. For me one personal trainer wasn't enough, so I engaged two. They dragged me up and down hills, into pools, beaches, sporting ovals, gyms, as well as Yoga classes. I lost a pile of weight, but most importantly my mind cleared, I had an interest outside of my business and I felt good about myself.

8. **I asked for help.** I knew that I needed help, so I reached out and asked for it. I asked my staff to support me, my family and friends, my clients-everyone and anyone. And they did. Their support and encouragement helped me to change my life forever.

Individually the changes I made were significant. But when combined, they became exponentially more powerful. Everything in my life changed and whilst I still work a lot, I work very differently. I love what I do, I have a great life and my business grows more successfully every year. I have no doubt that it's because I replaced a lot of bad habits with some very good ones. And best of all, when I look down that tunnel and see a light, I know it isn't a train heading my way.

BREE'S TAKE

It's great to take a few minutes, and take a snapshot view of our life, to see if we are where we want to be. Ask yourself these five questions to see how you are tracking.

1. How does my life look now?

2. Is it how I want my life to look?

3. If not, what will I do to make changes?

4. What should I do less of?

5. What can I do more of?

We need to be doing these constant check-ins to make sure we are on track. Remember the point we made earlier, business success really is about self-management more than just about anything else. Taking time to think about where we are right now, and how far we've come, is always good for the soul, but also good to keep us motivated. Your business has to work for you, that doesn't happen by accident.

SECTION 4

IT'S ALL ABOUT ENGAGEMENT
AND CONNECTION.

We live in a world where we seem to communicate more than ever, but say less than ever. We crave for deep, real and meaningful engagement, yet it's getting harder to find every day. When was the last time you sat in a meeting where the person on the other side of the table gave you their full, absolute and undivided attention?

We need to relearn the ability to engage with others. But it will take time, energy and a commitment to achieve it. Is it worth the effort? Absolutely. Especially as more people begin to demand it. In this section we look at ways to conduct fully engaged meetings and building better relationships with our customers, by engaging in a more meaningful way.

30

Thirteen tips for powerful engagement in every meeting.

Are we losing the ability to connect when we are in face-to-face situations? Are we turning up distracted, thinking about everyone and everything else except the person sitting across the table from us? From my experience in life, I would say a resounding yes.

Perhaps being able to deeply connect is a lost art. I really don't think so, because we all know how wonderful it feels to have a deeply connected and engaged conversation with another human being. It's just that we always seem to be too busy, too connected and too distracted with everything else. Such a wasted opportunity.

I'm a passionate communicator. I love being one on one and I take great pride in being a very good communicator. My aim is always to make the person I am meeting with feel like they are the only person that matters right here right now. And to me they are.

When you connect with people like this, you build real relationships, whether it be a business meeting or a personal catch up. Two key considerations to make this work, are the need to be absolutely sincere in every interaction and to be genuinely interested in the other person.

How do we create that deep kind of connection with people, when face-to-face?

Here are thirteen techniques that I have used for many years:

1. **Really connect with your eyes, but don't stare or be too intense.** Remember to blink and look away at appropriate times.

2. **Smile.** Show you are hearing what they are saying.

3. **Listen, which means being fully attentive, not semi attentive.** We know immediately when someone stops listening to us, so don't think you can fool them and check your email on your phone when you are supposed to be listening to them.

4. **Speaking of phones, have all distractions put away.** Show them you are fully committed to listening to what they have to say.

5. **Nod your head.** This shows you are encouraging them to keep talking and sharing.

6. **Don't interrupt them.** Let the other person keep talking, even if you want to stop them. If you interrupt too often, they will expect it and they may stop communicating.

7. **Let the other person choose the pace of the conversation.** Even if it is going slow and you feel a little frustrated.

8. **Keep it about them, even if they try to make it about you.** This means gently steering the conversation back to them when they try to push the conversation to be about you.

9. **Don't sigh.** Even though it can be an innocent reaction from the body calling for more oxygen, it can come across as you being bored. Watch your breathing, be aware of it.

10. **Be sincerely interested in them.**

11. **Summarise what they had to say and use a nice, affirming line like "have I heard you correctly when you say.......".** This gives them a chance to correct anything that you might have gotten wrong, but if you have gotten it right, it shows that you really did listen.

12. **Remember to thank them for being so open and direct.** It is a big deal for a lot of people, so it's nice for them to be acknowledged for communicating so openly.

13. **Make the effort to remember details.** So that when you meet again, you prove that you were actually listening.

BREE'S TAKE

There is no doubt in my mind, that those who communicate the best have more success. Here are some hacks to help you be more engaging in most business situations:

1. Get a Customer Relationship Management system (CRM) in place. There are so many free digital CRM's, or you can get a hard copy card file from a stationery shop for about $30. This means that you can make notes about your conversations and keep important information handy. Have you ever wondered how hairdressers are exceptional at this? They write down points from the last conversation on a card, and will ask you "so how did Sammy go with her graduation" and you will think they are wonderful because they remembered. We can't remember everything, so having a simple CRM to record important details and conversation notes will really help.

2. Do your research before you meet someone. This could mean you jump on their LinkedIn, Facebook or website to have a quick scan of what they have been up to. This ten-minute investigation will show the person that you are interested in what they have been up to.

3. Get a few questions ready in case of emergency and the conversation heads south. If you have done your research prior to the catch up, I am sure you can find a few great open ended questions to ask that will keep the conversation flowing.

4. If you don't have time to do research on someone, there is a free app called Charlie that syncs with your online calendar for appointments you have coming up, or you can simply put in the persons email address and name, and Charlie will give you a report in less than ten minutes. Charlie will comb through hundreds of sources and automatically sends you a one-pager on the person you are going to meet before you meet them. Charlie covers common connections, company stats, hobbies and more. www.charlieapp.com.

5. Think about how you would like the meeting to end. I like to revisit and clarify who was going to do what, the next steps and a deadline for the meeting to finish. I have found the best way to do this is to start the meeting stating the time it must finish by and why, which is usually "I have another meeting to get to at 11am and I am sure you have too, so lets get cracking".

31

Sometimes the most important email is the one that says nothing.

I was doing a project recently where I had to interview a pile of people who worked with loan brokers, mainly for residential loans. I asked them what their number one pet peeve was when it came to working with brokers. The overwhelming response was poor communication, specifically having to chase the broker all the time for updates on the progress of the loan.

When I confronted the brokers about this, their response was that often there was nothing to tell the client, so they didn't see the need to email them or return their call. My response, send them an email to say that there is no update yet, but rest assured you are onto it. This way the client doesn't have to worry or do the chasing.

We live in a world of hyper communication - and it is surprisingly easy to have a communication fail. I come across them all the time. Arguments arise because someone thought that someone was doing something, but they were both wrong. Sitting there waiting for the other party to send them details, that they were never going to send. So clarifying who will do what, by when, is a simple way to avoid that.

Back to this main issue here. If people don't hear from you they will start to make assumptions. Perhaps you've forgotten about the task at hand, or maybe you don't value their business, or you're not professional or any one of a hundred other reasons.

I've seen a lot of business relationships fall apart simply because someone didn't send an email to say that there is no news at the moment. Assumptions are made that end in tears.

Now some people will struggle with this. Surely this is just more email filling our inbox and it is. However, we are all struggling to manage the huge flow of information and communication. Anything that takes stuff off our "to do list", or out of the clutter of the brain, is a good thing, not an inconvenience.

Great communicators always seem to know when to communicate and what to say. They know the value of sending an email that says nothing. The end result will be happier clients, more engaged suppliers, more productive members of your team and you will develop your own reputation as a great communicator.

BREE'S TAKE

I have fallen victim to poor communication many times and it has cost me. We all get busy, and we all have a million excuses for our poor communication. If you are like me, you hate the absolutely ridiculous amount of expectation people have about the need for instant responses. But the reality is that people do expect a high level of communication and if you can't give it to them they will find someone who can – simple as that.

So how do we become better communicators? Well my approach has been to get automated. You can automate a lot of your communication. But be very careful, it's pretty obvious when a robot is doing the talking. Here are some things that you can automate, to save you some time.

Most email platforms have a huge number of features, all designed to help you to be more organised and to communicate better. Everything from automatic responders (which are great for adding personal messages and things like "I only check emails twice per day, between 9am and 10am and then between 3pm and 4pm, so I will respond to you during these times". Which then lets you get on with getting on, through to calendar invites, and all other kinds of goodies.

Take the time to learn your way around your email platform and you might be surprised by just how much it can do automatically that will save you a great deal of time and also dramatically improve your relationships with your customers and staff.

32

Fear of missing a call could be a sign that you need to build better relationships.

Could this be the year of the digital detox? It's something I am certain is going to happen at some point. Over the years, I've had quite a bit of feedback from people saying that they need to have their phone on all the time, "just in case". My question is "just in case" of what?

I can certainly understand the need for surgeons, emergency workers and in fact anyone on standby where a call may literally mean the difference between life and death, needing to keep their phone on, but how many of us are really in that space?

I've had sales people say that if they miss a call, they might miss a sale so they had to have their phone on all the time. Really? My view on this, having been in sales for many years, is that if you have a client who will take their business elsewhere simply because you aren't accessible every second of the day, either you are doing something seriously wrong or you need to find new clients in a hurry.

Sales is a relationship business. It requires intelligent communication, consistency, reliability, honesty and integrity. You build a great sales relationship by always exceeding the expectations of your client. This happens over time. A mature sales relationship is one where the client understands that you are a busy professional and that if they miss you and leave a message, you will get back to them as soon as possible.

In the message they will let you know if it is urgent, or any other relevant details. Because over time you have developed trust and built a relationship, they will wait for your call. If they choose to buy from someone else simply because you weren't able to take their call, you never really had them as a client in the first place.

The problem with many sales people is that they are always waiting for the sales call or email from the client, instead of proactively building the relationship. This means reaching out and engaging the client, looking for ways to help them, save them money and educate them about new products and services. Once again, if your relationship is a good one, they will want to know all of this, if it isn't, they won't want to know any of it.

What is my point? If you are a sales person, and you live in fear of missing a call from a client, or fear contacting a client outside of trying to sell them something, it might be time to rethink your approach to selling overall.

Now more than ever, we live with a world of choice and sales people in particular are competing in ways we never even imagined. Success or failure will come from deep and highly communicative connection and those relationships that are constantly evolving.

It might be time to put your hand on your heart and ask if fear is driving your sales behavior. Fear that your relationship with your clients is not as strong as it should be. Fear that if you do the slightest thing wrong they will dump you. Fear that at any moment you could lose them and their business. Who wants to live like this?

If fear is driving your sales, you need to look at every single relationship and look for ways to create that deeper engagement. To have more meaningful conversations with your clients and to show your commitment to them and at the same time ask for a commitment from them.

Fear is just a sign that you need to build better relationships and you need to do it now.

BREE'S TAKE

Building strong relationships with your clients takes a genuine approach. You have to truly want to help them, support them and solve their problems. Most importantly we need to make them feel valued and this needs to be genuine. Here are five easy ways to make your customers feel valued. Now I understand that you can't necessarily do this for every customer, but perhaps you can do these things for your VIP customers.

1. Remember important dates and send a gift (and not a pen with your company logo on it).

2. Random acts of "Thank You". Send a handwritten card, or a small gift saying how much you appreciate their support.

3. Send them interesting articles that you have read that will be relevant to them.

4. Start a VIP club that has exclusive offers for your most valued clients.

5. Create a special event just for your VIP's as a way to say thank you.

In reality, we should all be having better conversations internally, discussing how we can better engage with our customers. Sadly these are not common conversations but they need to be.

33

There is one phrase guaranteed to make people seriously dislike you.

So what are the three words and why are they so toxic? They are "you are wrong," and if you use them, I guarantee there is a trail of resentment following behind you. This resentment can be from co-workers, staff, peers, and even customers.

Every time I hear someone utter these three words, I can almost feel the anger rising and the resentment growing from the person on the receiving end. It might not be obvious to the person saying it, but it can cut someone to the core in a heartbeat, especially if it is said with a hint of aggression behind it.

Saying "you are wrong" breaks pretty much every rule of quality human interaction. No one wants to feel like they are wrong, and even worse, to be told that they are wrong adds insult to injury.

If people are saying this in the workplace, well that is just wrong. Personally I think people who have this phrase in their "personal feedback" repertoire tend to look immature every time they use it.

For starters, in their opinion it might be you who is wrong, which doesn't make it fact-it is just an opinion. Second, even if someone is clearly wrong, pointing it out so blatantly doesn't do much except make that person feel small. Of course, this is what someone needing to feel big hopes for.

And finally, telling someone "you are wrong" makes that person want to prove he or she is right, which can lead to arguments, or even worse, a resentful mission to prove the accuser wrong. The cycle continues and everyone loses.

Next time you see someone utter the words "you are wrong," take a second and see how it makes you feel, even if the words are not directed at you. Likewise, if you use these words, after they have left your mouth, feel the mood of the conversation change and get dark. It pretty much ends the conversation.

This is just one phrase, of course, and there are others that have considerable impact and not in a good way. The world is moving towards greater connection and engagement and how we talk to others is becoming increasingly important; we need to be very considered with every interaction.

We all have words that were said to us years ago that we never forget. Having someone in a position of authority and respect pointing a finger and saying "you are wrong" is certainly one of those experiences that will stay with you for a long time.

BREE'S TAKE

I am going to add to the list of things that really shouldn't come out of your mouth in a business setting (or to anyone really, even your kids)

1. "Because I said so"

2. "But this is the way we've always done it"

3. "I don't care"

4. "I told you so"

5. "As I just said a minute ago"

6. "You can't do it"

7. "It's not fair"

8. "I don't get paid enough for this"

9. "That's not my problem"

10. "That's not my job"

If you or anyone in your business uses language like this, it's time to stop.

34

Is it time to cut your customers some slack?

I was standing in a line waiting to order a coffee at a cafe yesterday and the lady in front of me was having some difficulty placing her order. She wasn't that fluent in English and the man taking her order was not helping the process.

In fact he started to mutter under his breath, raise his voice at the lady and then he started complaining about her to other staff standing close by. The lady was very embarrassed and she literally ran off, visibly upset. What did the man behind the counter do? He laughed.

When I got to the counter I told him what I thought of him and his business and stormed off. But in reality if you stand around any business for long enough you are likely to hear one of the staff (or even worse the business owner) complaining about their customers.

Let's be honest, we've all been guilty of moaning about customers that drive us crazy, but maybe we need to change our attitude and be more empathetic with our customers.

We are all customers at other people's businesses and often making a purchase is not as easy as it should be. Sometimes things aren't that clear when you walk into a shop or a restaurant. Sometimes our mind is elsewhere. Sometimes we just have no idea what we want and we need some help.

Of course this is the very fundamental meaning of customer service-offering to serve customers to give them what they want and need.

We need to make sure that we always have absolute and total respect for our customers, even when they are challenging or uncertain or indecisive. Developing a desire to really serve our customers and to be committed to helping them in any way we can is the sure fire way to build an incredible business.

And best of all, very few businesses actually have this desire to serve-which makes it even easier for a business that does to stand out from the crowd and attract many more appreciative customers.

If you are a business owner, think about your own attitude towards your customers, because your staff will reflect and project your attitude. Lousy service starts at the top not the bottom.

Next time you are faced with a customer that you find frustrating, remember that just like you, they are simply human. Cut them some slack, put your own issues and ego aside and help them.

BREE'S TAKE

If someone has made the effort to complain about your business to you, you should really be grateful because they are giving you an opportunity to fix it. So many of us don't complain to the person or business we actually have a problem with. We complain to everyone else instead which is very damaging to a business.

My advice to you is, make it easier for people to complain, or as I'd prefer to word it, give you feedback.

Have surveys, feedback forms, or simply ask your customers for feedback. Come from a place of "we always want to be improving our business, have you got any ideas or feedback for us?" Some of what you hear will hurt, but at least you can take steps to improve your business, which is something that we should all be doing daily.

35

Have you become a lazy communicator?

Often I do work that requires businesses to send through follow up material, proposals, quotations and so on. I am amazed at how lazy people have become. Simply thinking that attaching something is all it takes to actually sell something.

What are the most common mistakes I've noticed:

- They got my name wrong (and I assume it was still addressed to the person they had sent it to previously).

- They got the dates wrong (three proposals required me to respond several weeks before I had actually contacted the business).

- All bar one virtually ignored my questions and just sent me an electronic brochure for me to try and figure out the details (one brochure was 86 pages and the part that was relevant for me was buried in there somewhere).

- Most didn't even personalise the message in any way, it was simply a perfunctory "Dear Mr Griffiths, here is the information you requested". Even if it wasn't the information I requested.

- The longer it took them to respond, the more mistakes and lack of attention to detail seemed to sneak into the email.

My point here is that people are getting lazy when it comes to communicating and I see that as an opportunity for those of us who are prepared to do the work. The bottom line here is we need to make it easy for our prospective customers to buy from us and that means we have to put a little extra work in.

If you are prepared to go the extra mile, I'm sure you will see it reflected in sales conversions and word of mouth referrals.

The following tips will show prospective customers that you have heard them and that you want their business:

1. Acknowledge that you understand what they want and need by making reference to the conversation or earlier email, detailing or even better, summarising what they have asked for and even posing the question - "Have I understood you correctly?"

2. If you are attaching brochures/documents - make reference to the relevant pages for them. For example, "the information you requested can be found at the top of page 6".

3. Don't get into an "attachment frenzy" - just give them the information they have asked for, but when personalising your email, let them know you have more information available.

4. Don't just give prospective customers a link to your website - I'm pretty sure they would be able to find that without you. Give them the link to the specific pages that will be relevant to them and explain why.

5. Get a little creative - I've been adding an MP3 file to any complex enquiries for a few years and I've had a great response. So in the email, I simply say something along the lines of "rather than write a really long email, I've recorded an MP3 file and attached it to this email that will explain X, Y and Z".

6. Always check documents for file names (nothing worse than sending out rates for 2016 and the file is called rates for 2012), any required personalisation, names, prices etc. Anything that can change and should change, needs to be checked and rechecked. Even personalising the name of a standard document will be noticed by the recipient. Little things make all the difference.

7. Take note of just how often people send you information - and how badly they do it. By being aware of what lazy communicators are doing you can avoid making the same mistakes. Forward this to other members of your team at the same time, just to bring attention to the blight of lazy communication.

8. Speaking of teams, I suggest that you double check what your team are doing in terms of communication. Have you set guidelines for them to follow or do you assume they will go the extra mile (bad assumption) with their communication? They might not like it, but ask them to forward you their last ten enquiry response emails and see what they are doing.

9. Take the time to write a short but intelligent email. Think about the subject line, think about how to formally acknowledge the person, break the copy into paragraphs, avoid shouting by using capitals, make sure that your email is clear especially with what steps need to be taken from here for the customer if they would like to proceed.

BREE'S TAKE

Start observing others when you are buying things, when you are on the phone, when you are in meetings, when you are in a restaurant, when you are getting served in a shop. Every interaction others are having with you, observe and learn. See how it makes you feel? By becoming a better observer of bad communication you will actually start to improve your own communication.

36

Seven strategies for building a seriously tight network.

I have absolutely no doubt that anyone who has achieved any degree of success will attribute a large proportion of their success to the people in their network. Specifically those who have supported them, encouraged them and provided inspiration and wisdom during the good times and the not so good times. There is an old adage that says it isn't what you know, it's who you know, and this rings more true today than ever.

The reality is that we all have the opportunity to build a network of contacts who can help us to achieve our goals. This network can be local, national and international, thanks mainly to the incredible communication opportunities that we can all take advantage of. A network is something that we have to continually invest in to keep it healthy and to keep it growing and developing.

So how exactly do you invest in your network?

1. Be a giver not just a taker

If you are part of a network and all you do is take, take, take, people will soon grow weary of you. To be a valued member of any network you need to give more than you receive. By taking this approach you will enjoy many rewards. When building networks, it has to be a win/win scenario for all involved. Always ask yourself the question "how can I add more value to my network and the people within it?"

2. Become a big referrer and a quality referrer of others

I have found that one of the best ways to build my network has been to become a big referrer. I love to refer business and I look for ways to refer every day. Now I don't expect people to reciprocate, but they generally do and I always find that if I refer 10 people in a week, I get 20 referrals back (and not from the people I have referred - strange but wonderful I know). The second part of being a big referrer is to only ever make your referrals to others what I call quality referrals. Do some screening first, don't use referring as a way to get rid of people you don't want to work with. I always ask myself, is this person or business one that I would want referred to me? If it isn't, I certainly wouldn't be referring them to a valued member of my network.

3. Make it easy for people to refer you

Just as it is important for you to refer others, if they can't refer you back, that becomes frustrating and awkward for them. So my strategy is to ask better questions and give better advice. I always ask people in my network how can I refer them? I ask what their ideal client looks like and what kind of projects do they really love taking on. This way I can refer business that is perfect for them. Likewise, I explain to them what I do, what parts of my business I am growing, what my perfect client looks like and the projects that I love to do. This creates a high degree of clarity and everyone wins.

4. Don't just sell to your network

A lot of people join a network and all they do is sell to everyone in it. They bombard their network with emails, every meeting is trying to sell them something. The other members of the network soon grow tired of this approach. My test for this is to ask a simple question, if an individuals telephone number comes up on my caller ID, do I want to take the call? When it comes to people who do nothing but try to sell to me, the answer is no. The same applies to emails, if I know it is just another sales email, most of the time I simply delete them and that person goes from being a part of my network to someone on the outside of the inner circle. The real key here is to offer value to your network. Give them things for free, make suggestions, offer advice and ways to make their life easier or to increase their income, but don't just try to sell to them.

5. Protect people in your network

I protect my contacts fiercely. As mentioned above, I won't give them crummy referrals and I certainly won't give my database to other people to sell to those on my email list. If people want me to pass on a contact, generally I ask my contact if this is OK before doing so and if they say yes, I cc them in on my introduction email, just so they know exactly what is said. The moral to this story is that if you don't protect people in your network, they won't protect you and you will get inundated with people who are probably going to try to do nothing more than sell you things you don't want.

6. Be there in good times and bad

We all go through good times and bad in business and there is nothing worse than a fair weather friend. We all know them, they are only around when times are good and they have something to gain. For me, people in my network are trusted friends, if they are going through a tough time in business I will do what I can to help them. A fully functioning network should be like this. If you find that when you go through tough times and your network seems a little light on the ground, you haven't got a very good network. Remember though, how you treat people during their tough times says a lot about you and people of significance will remember that much more than they will remember how you acted when times were good.

7. Work on your network daily

Spend time working on your network every day. It might mean writing a few "how are you" emails, making some calls, or catching up with people for coffee. I spend at least one hour a day doing something related to my network and it is a great hour, one that I not only enjoy, but one that reaps enormous benefits.

In conclusion, take a strategic approach to building your network. Be proactive, not passive about it and invest a generous amount of time and energy. Put in more than you get out of your network and you will soon start to enjoy the benefits. If you have been neglecting your network, or taking the people within it for granted, do something about it today.

BREE'S TAKE

I used to be a great networker, but a big blow to my confidence one year meant I ran away and hid from the world for a year. I hid from my network, I stopped communicating with them. I made myself super busy and started avoiding people. Has it affected my relationships? Yes, but who it has affected the most is me.

We all go through times at some point when we lose faith in the human race and need to take a bit of a sabbatical to get back on track (well I hope you don't but if you do, take the sabbatical). During this time you are likely to find out who the important people in your network are, and it's time to have a bit of a cleanse. I found I was surrounded with four types of people.

1. The ones that need me to lift them up.
2. The ones that want to drag me down.
3. The ones that want to hold me in place.
4. The ones that want to lift me higher.

I think we need a variety of these four types of people in our network, and I'd encourage you to work out what percentage of each that you would like. For me, I'd like:

1. The ones that need me to lift them up about 30%
2. The ones that want to drag me down about 5%
3. The ones that want to hold me in place about 15%
4. The ones that want to lift me higher at least 50%

Now I'm sure you are thinking that wouldn't it just be better to have people in your life who lift you up? And I used to think that too. But I've grown to realise and appreciate the role that the other types play.

Why we need to lift others up:
To me this is often where I learn the most. Teaching others, helping others to achieve their goals, pushing them, not buying into their negative stories or victim mentality. It can be tough love, but if they want it, I will do my best to help them

and my reward is that I learn a lot about myself. Find someone to mentor, be a public speaker, write books, share your knowledge freely. The more people are out there trying to lift others, the better the world will be.

Why we need to be dragged down:

This type of person can be really challenging. And who wants someone like that in their life? Well I think we all have them, whether we realise it or not, but to me, I won't let them drag me down. But I do use them as a good measuring stick for where I am in life, and what I do and don't want in my life. They give a different perspective, they challenge my way of thinking and pretty much everything I stand for, but in a strange way that also keeps me on track. The key here, as you can tell by the percentage split, is not to have too many of them in your life.

Why we need to be held in place:

These are the family and friends that will challenge you and your dreams. Be wary of these ones though. Sometimes this "holding you in place" means that they are actually disguised as someone who is dragging you down, and their own fears are driving their agenda. So you end up having to drag them with you. That is seriously draining and is usually a spouse or business partner, or worse, both. We do need people in our life like this to slow us down, keep us grounded and remind us we aren't invincible.

Why we need people who lift us up:

We all need to be lifted up, in particular those who are constantly doing the lifting of others. Finding people in your network who lift you up can be rare. So if you are someone who feels like you don't have anyone lifting you up in your network, it's time to take some serious action. Location is not an obstacle anymore. Join interest groups online, watch TED talks, invest in amazing conferences, read books, find a mentor and generally start searching for people to inspire you and act as role models in your life.

Take a look at your network today, is it supportive of where you want to go? If not, what kind of people are missing? How are your percentages? What kind of people do you need in your life? You will soon get very good at working out the different kinds of people in your life and hopefully learning how to manage them accordingly.

37

Twenty-One ways to overcome networking awkwardness.

If the thought of going to a networking event makes you cringe, you are not alone. But you can do something about it.

For many people, the thought of going to a networking event is akin to getting a tooth pulled. They know they have to do it, but the prospect of standing around in a room full of strangers, feeling awkward and making small talk is a nightmare.

Of course the problem is that networking is a major part of growing a business. You need to meet new people, expand your contacts, and be actively prepared to go and chase business.

For those who struggle, or perhaps simply want to get better at networking, here are 21 tips that have helped me not only get better at it, but also enjoy it.

1. **Do your homework.** Find out who is going to be at an event and make sure they are the kind of people that could be prospective customers for you. Network with intent.

2. **Don't arrive too early.** I don't like to get there too early, when there are only a few people standing around. It is a little awkward, and the conversation is always distracted as new people arrive.

3. **Don't judge a book by its cover.** Keep an open mind when it comes to meeting people. Don't fall into the habit of assuming anything about anyone simply on the basis of his or her look.

4. **You are not going to an execution, so remember to smile.** Often people at networking events forget to smile (they are generally the people who don't like networking). Remember to smile often and smile sincerely.

5. **Read today's newspaper.** I always take some time to read the local newspaper before an event to find five or six current topics I can bring into a conversation. Asking people their opinion is a great way to get the conversation flowing.

6. **Don't just hang out with people you know.** This is the single biggest mistake: We find someone we know and we clutch onto the person for the entire event. Move around the room, introduce yourself, and meet new people. Sure, it is a little challenging, but the more you do it the easier it becomes.

7. **Learn to ask open-ended questions.** Ask better questions and you get better answers-avoid questions that can be answered with a yes or a no.

8. **Drinking does not make you more networkable.** I hate to break the bad news, but hitting the sauce at a networking event is really not cool. We all know the people that do, and they are the ones eroding their credibility with every drink. Sure, a drink or two is part of networking, but getting drunk is not ideal.

9. **Take plenty of business cards and don't be stingy.** I'm amazed at how many people go to a networking event without business cards. Take plenty and dish them out. I have two versions-one with my mobile number on it and one without. I don't necessarily want everyone to have my direct contact number.

10. **Always have a pen.** I write down notes on the back of business cards after I meet a person. I don't do it in front of the person-that's a little rude-but afterward: what action to take, what potential there is to do business, etc.

11. **Wear something distinctive.** This helps people remember you and it makes you stand out from the crowd.

12. **Hang out near the food.** People are always much more relaxed near the food, sharing guilty treats and laughing while they do it. This is the perfect place to meet people (and carrying extra napkins can make you very popular).

13. **Look for groups of people rather than individuals.** It can be easier to sidle up to a group that is in a discussion than it can be to approach an individual. Approach a group and someone will hold out a hand to introduce themself.

14. **Enlist the aid of others to introduce you.** If you want to meet someone in particular, find a friend who knows the person and ask your friend to do a personal introduction.

15. **Offer a compliment and be sincere when you do it.** We all like someone to say something nice to us but make it genuine. It might be something someone is wearing, something you may have heard about the person, their business, or even their industry.

16. **Focus on the person in front of you.** One of my biggest pet peeves is a conversation in which the person you are talking to keeps looking at everyone else (or their phone) totally distracted from what you are saying. Don't be that person. If the person in front of you is not your target market, politely excuse yourself.

17. **Go with a specific outcome in mind.** Set a specific objective for the networking event for example, "I'm going to meet five prospective new clients tonight."

18. **Use the other person's name in conversation to help you remember them.** When you first meet someone, use their name straight away and keep using it in the conversation.

19. **Be enthusiastic about your business when asked.** When people ask you what you do, be excited and passionate about it. It you aren't, don't expect anyone else to be.

20. **Thank the hosts of the event on your way out.** Always find who is in charge of the event and make a point of personally thanking them before you leave.

21. **Fast follow-up gets the best results.** The best networkers are the people who actually work at networking. By this I mean they meet people, they take notes, they follow up the next day, they build relationships and they get the business.

BREE'S TAKE

I love Andrew's ideas on how to network, I am going to take it one step further and suggest some things not to say in these settings. These are some of the worst conversation killers in social settings that I have witnessed.

- "How's the job hunting going?" If someone has lost their job, don't ask them this question as it just rubs more salt in the wound.

- "You look great, have you done something different?" Firstly, it sounds as if the person looked like a donkey before, make it more "I love that dress" or "I love what you have done to your hair" something more specific shows that you have really noticed.

- "When are you due?" Unless a woman tells you she is pregnant, don't assume she is. I congratulated a woman once and it was a tumor, since this awkward moment I never assume anymore.

- "Let me pick your brain", this one automatically puts the person who is going to get their brain picked in "NOOOOO" mode.

- "How old are your grandkids?" I have also done this to an older mother once, always assume they are the person's parent not grandparent as it's tough being an older parent. It's then a lovely compliment for the person if they in fact are the grandparent.

- "Business must be really tough for you", if someone is in an industry that is getting disrupted they already know that, don't make it worse by putting the spotlight on them.

Your words have power, never forget that, so you need to be very tactful and thoughtful with your interactions, especially in networking settings.

38

Would you like people to take you more seriously?

There is nothing more frustrating than not being taken seriously. In a business environment it can cost you money through lost sales and staff not doing what you ask of them. The number of opportunities that come your way will also be seriously limited if potential partners or customers don't take you seriously.

If you are working in the corporate world, not being taken seriously means that your chances of advancement are going to be limited. Regardless of the situation you find yourself in, when others don't take you seriously, it feels frustrating and hurtful.

Clearly there are many reasons for not being taken seriously. Most of the time it is simply the result of our own actions and without even knowing it, we could be causing other people to think less of us.

The big question is what can you do to get people to take you more seriously?

1. **Don't become a part of the gossipy crowd.** A sure fire way to make those who count, thinks less of you, is to be one of the gossipers. As much as it can make you feel like a valued member of a group, you won't be doing yourself any favors (and this applies just as much if you are the boss or a worker).

2. **Be considered with what you share and where you share.** We've all heard the stories and seen the fallout of inappropriate social media sharing. If you are trying to get people to take you seriously, Facebook pictures of a wild drunken party with you as the star will do very little to help your case. And as much as we think we know who is watching our social media feed, that isn't always the case. Be very considered about what you post and where you post it.

3. **Hang out with people that others take seriously.** Just as we are judged by our appearances, we are also judged by the peer group we are associated with. If you want to be taken seriously, look around you. Are the people in your peer group the kind that others take seriously? Who do you think Richard Branson hangs out with?

4. **Always dress appropriately.** The key word here is appropriately. Right or wrong, we are all judged by our appearances. If you take the time to dress and groom accordingly, it shows that you respect yourself. One of the key steps in getting others to take you seriously, is showing that you have a high level of self respect.

5. **Always be a couple of minutes early and develop a reputation for it.** We all know those people who can never turn up to a meeting on time. Everyone else has to sit around awkwardly waiting for them to arrive. They come in with a pile of hustle and bustle like a mini hurricane, sprouting rushed greetings and apologies that you have heard many times before. This is not the way to be taken seriously. Do whatever it takes to arrive early and become known as the "early bird".

6. **If you make a promise-deliver.** There are a lot of people who talk a good game, but they don't ever deliver. They make lots of promises, everything sounds fantastic, but nothing ever happens. If you develop a reputation for being flaky, no one will take you seriously. So make an internal commitment to deliver on every promise you make, or, have the courage to not make the promise in the first place.

7. **Show respect to everyone you encounter.** I'm a huge advocate of this-treat every single person you meet with absolute respect, regardless of how they treat you. I think we should do this because it is the right thing to do, but at the same time, this is what formulates the core of your personal brand. We all

know people who are delightful to customers but they treat their own staff like dirt. Treat everyone the same, with absolute respect and others will notice.

8. **Let people in-to a point.** Many years ago I used to teach people to SCUBA dive. The instructor who taught me gave me some sage advice. He said you should always stay a little aloof from your students, don't party with them or spend too much time with them, because the more they get to know you, the less they will listen to what you have to say and that might cost them their life. I have followed this advice in all of the teaching and mentoring roles I have had since, and I believe it to be absolutely true.

9. **Do something with your life.** If you want people to take you more seriously, give them a reason to. Show them that you are doing something with your life. You don't need to brag about it, actions speak louder than words. Grow your skills, do something challenging, join a team, renovate a house, have an adventure-do something.

10. **Stand for something but don't push it onto others.** And last but not least, stand for something. Show that you are passionate about something, whatever it might be. But at the same time, don't become a bore by doing nothing but talking about it all the time. Modesty and humility are two attributes of a person that others take seriously, so when asked, share your views and be passionate about them.

BREE'S TAKE

Being taken seriously is something that we all crave. For some reason, it's always been a struggle for me to be taken seriously. As an entrepreneur from the age of eighteen, I was underestimated. As a woman I have been underestimated. The combination of being a young female entrepreneur, I was underestimated even more.

But to be honest, it's been my secret weapon. I love being underestimated, so if you are someone that gets underestimated, yes, it can be insulting, yes you can get resentful as your hard work isn't really understood or being recognised, but try not to feel this way.

Here are some benefits in being underestimated:

1. Being on a mission with a chip on your shoulder of having to prove yourself makes you work harder, it's a great motivator.

2. No one expects anything great from you, so they will be shocked and in awe when you deliver something unexpected.

3. No one is pressuring you, only you.

4. It makes you appreciate your ability and give's you more confidence.

5. It means you can purely focus on the task at hand.

Embrace being underestimated, it's been a great thing for me once I took my ego out of the equation and stopped getting frustrated by it. I made it my own personal game of "you have no idea the person you are playing with, this is going to be fun".

39

Will hiding behind 'stupid' policies alienate your customers?

Recently I had to visit the local pet shop to pick up a few things. I arrived at about 8.50am and the sign on the door said the business opened at 9am. Being impatient, I looked longingly through the window, with my sad puppy eyes, to see if anyone was inside who could possibly open the door a little early.

Inside there were five staff standing around the counter, shooting the breeze and looking at their watches and me in a very strange kind of Mexican standoff way. No matter how sad and pathetic I looked, they were not going to let me in.

At exactly 9am, one of the team walked over and opened the door. On the way in I asked the young man why didn't they just open up a bit earlier seeing that I was waiting and they were clearly ready to open? His response was 'our policy is that we don't open the store before 9am'.

"Sorry, that is our policy" - a phrase we've all heard before, normally followed by a sense of frustration, anger and rage.

Policies are great. They spell out the rules and regulations that add order to our lives and our businesses. Policies take out the grey areas that require us to think.

Sometimes though, we need to look beyond a policy and use some good old fashioned common sense.

The problem with policies is that they can make us lazy. We can hide behind a policy, simply because that's our policy. Our staff can hide behind policies as well. As soon as we are told that something is a policy, it seems that no further justification is needed and in fact, all conversation and negotiation is abandoned. After all, it is a policy.

We live in a time when customers are craving connection and engagement and in my opinion, a lot of policies destroy any chance of either connection or engagement. Instead they put up barriers. They make the customer feel like a second rate citizen and in some instances a criminal.

Policies are normally written for the minority. Shoplifters represent a very small sector of the community, but they determine how many clothes we can take into a change booth, and the fact that we get filmed all day long in shops.

Here are some of my ideas regarding making any business less policy rigid and more customer and staff friendly:

1. By all means have policies in place, but be clear about what the exceptions to the policy are.

2. Encourage your staff to know the policies, but praise them for knowing when to ignore them.

3. Do a review of all of your businesses policies and see which ones are no longer relevant (and do this exercise regularly).

4. Use some imagination when you write your policies. Make the wording clear but have a little fun with it.

5. Incorporate some positive policies. For example, 'our policy is to make sure your stay at our hotel exceeds your expectations. So please tell us if there are any areas that you think, we need to lift our game.

6. Explain the reasoning behind a policy. I saw a sign in a shop in Thailand recently that read 'ninety-nine percent of our customers are absolutely wonderful. One percent steal things from us. Unfortunately, we can't afford to have things stolen so we have to check every bag that leaves the shop. To our honest customers we are very sorry for any inconvenience. To the thieves, shame on you'.

7. When it comes to staff behavior and expectations, get them to write up their own policies. Of course this can be a bit of fun, but helping your staff to understand what is acceptable and what is not helps to clarify why a policy is needed.

8. For the big issues, policies need to be black and white. For example don't drive the forklift drunk. But some topics are not as black and white and they need some discussion and probably some debate. This is very relevant for topics like internet usage at work. The point here is to be a little flexible.

9. Don't let bad policies be an excuse for bad systems. If there is an element of your business that needs to be stream lined or run a little better, don't use a policy as a Band-Aid. Fix the underlying problem.

10. When you are out and about, spending your hard earned money, and you hear those four dreaded words, 'that is our policy', stop and think about how these words make you feel. Then think about how your customers feel when you use the same four words on them.

Policies definitely serve a purpose, but don't let your business be ruled by them. Success in the modern business world is about connection and engagement and we need to do whatever we can to make both of these interactions positive and enjoyable. Whilst I am certainly not saying that we should stop using policies, I am saying to use them wisely.

BREE'S TAKE

I have been in small business for twenty years and I'm embarrassed to say, I have only put in some policies in the past couple of years since my team has grown considerably. It's probably because the word "policy" sounded so formal and something that I thought only "big businesses" needed.

Once I reframed the word "policy" and simply made it "my businesses rules", it made this a simple task. All of our businesses have rules, but most of them are unspoken, so we need to document them and turn these into procedures. There are lots of resources available to help with this – apps, platforms, consultants – you name it. If you want your business to run more smoothly and to be more valuable, make the effort and get your policies in place, but don't become a policy Nazi.

Here are ten policies every small business should have in play. You need to have these printed and in a folder, then read and signed by your staff to state that they have read them. If they impact your customer, you need to have them on your website.

1. **Code of conduct.** Employees should act legally, ethically, and work for the best interest of the business. A code of conduct within the business should ensure employees know how to deal with a wide variety of ethical situations. Think about what theft actually is as well. Today the biggest staff theft issue is information. Make your position on this very clear.

2. **Environmental policy.** Businesses should be committed to minimising their impact on the environment, how is your business going to minimise it's impact on the globe?

3. **A refund policy.** What will you refund for and why? You need specifics in here about timings, quality of returned items, reasons for refunds etc.

4. **Computer and bring your own device policy?** Are you happy for staff to print personal items? Are you happy for them to plug in their own device into your wifi or server where they could download company files?

5. **Internet usage.** Are you happy for staff to use Facebook during work time? Are you happy for them to download certain files and update software?

6. **Drug & Alcohol policy.** As much as you think staff know that it's a big no no to turn up intoxicated, or to get drunk when representing your company, you need to spell it out and the ramifications.

7. **Email policy.** What must never be written or shared in emails, what sort of language can and cannot be used, what is appropriate, what is not.

8. **Social Media policy.** Are you happy for them to post things on the company page, are you happy for them to use social media during work time, what are the rules for what can be shared and what cannot?

9. **Leave policy.** How many day's notice do people have to give you for holidays, do they have to ask for permission before booking the holiday time etc.

10. **Employment policies.** Employees need to understand their position within the business, including how performance reviews are conducted, the process workers go through if they are injured at work, non-discrimination at workplaces, and termination conditions to name a few.

This week set yourself the goal of getting one policy done. Then add another to it every week till you have your very own Policies and Procedures manual, and then have your staff review and agree to every policy.

40

Do you want to capture every audience you stand in front of?

Being a speaker or presenter is a very appealing profession for a lot of people, myself included. However today a lot of people have to present as part of their job, not as part of a jet setting lifestyle. Many business owners find themselves in front of groups to pitch their products and services. In fact the very future of their company depends on how well they get their message across.

Regardless of how you present, or whom you present to, if you can't capture your audience your messages will be lost. Having been a presenter for many years, I've had my fair share of good presentations and plenty where I bombed. The key is to engage your audience, which is easier said than done. These are my seven fundamentals to help capture any audience.

1. **Capture the mood of the room and mirror it to get started (the stealth opening).** I'm a big believer in arriving early to any event where I speak. Not only does this give me time to do some homework on the venue and to make sure that my presentation is good to go. It also lets me assess the mood of the audience. As a speaker you need to know where your audience is at mood wise to engage them early on. If they are flat and you start dancing around on stage, trying to get people to hug each other, it won't work. You have to start a little more slowly and a little more gently and then build up. I have two openings

planned for every presentation that I do - one for an upbeat, energised audience and one for a flat, low energy group. Spending time at the back of the room and chatting to attendees over a coffee lets me determine which opening is appropriate for them.

2. **Start on common ground.** I recently watched a great TED talk by Matt Chan, the producer of the television series Hoarders. He is a great storyteller and certainly someone who isn't afraid of getting down and dirty with his stories. In his TED talk he makes mention of the need to start with common ground with your audience. Start with what they know, not what you know, and I think this is a wonderful piece of advice. As an example, when I'm talking to small business audiences, I open by sharing the story of the first business I bought over 30 years ago and the pile of mistakes I made every single day. They love it, they laugh out loud and they know that I understand them and the challenges they face.

3. **Treat them with absolute respect.** For me this is totally non-negotiable. Any presenter who doesn't treat their audience with absolute respect doesn't deserve to capture them. How do you do this? You respect their time, never be late, you respect what they already know or do, never saying they are wrong but perhaps offering an alternative. You never put anyone in the audience down and you show your respect with courtesy and appreciation.

4. **Make them laugh.** Making an audience laugh is not as easy as it seems. Comedians make it look easy, but it really isn't. What has always worked for me is to use self depreciating humor, in other words I make fun of myself, my own faults and failings (which is generally what comedians do as well I might add). Making jokes about yourself also ensures that you don't upset anyone in the audience.

5. **Make them cry.** What is the best way to really create engagement - be open, be honest, be vulnerable and be absolutely authentic. If you've got some tough stories, tell them. If you've failed, tell that story. If you've overcome adversity, share the journey. Every single presentation I have done over the past 30 years where I have opened up, been vulnerable and shared my own story (growing up as an orphan with a lot of violence) I have created very strong engagement with the audience (hear a pin drop engagement). Sometimes as a speaker you

need to be brave enough to share your stories, particularly the personal ones, but if you are serious about wanting to help people, do it.

6. **Make them think.** Having done a TEDx talk myself, with my topic being "Imagine if we were 33% less angry" I understand completely that a great presentation doesn't just make people laugh, or cry, it also makes the audience think. Perhaps it makes them question their beliefs or the way they do something or react to something, or challenges their point of view. Or maybe it just shows them a whole new world that they didn't know existed before, and that in its own right is thought provoking. It doesn't really matter how we make people think as long as we make them think.

7. **Live up to the story you tell.** A little while back I was at an event, waiting my turn to present. The man on stage was doing a great job talking about the importance of treating people with kindness and respect and not letting the inconsequential things bother you. He departed the stage to a rousing applause, walked past me without acknowledging me and then set about abusing the audiovisual controller because he felt that his microphone wasn't loud enough. He really let the poor fella have it - and as I was being clapped onto the stage I could actually hear the speaker starting to yell.

The message here is that once you leave the stage, you still have a commitment to your audience and that is to live up to the expectation of who you were on the stage. A lot of speakers forget this, and sadly they develop a reputation for being insincere, shallow and two faced.

Live authentically, present authentically. Never give your audience a reason to be disappointed with you on the stage or off.

BREE'S TAKE

Andrews tips here are fantastic. If you are someone that wants to be a public speaker, here are a few more tips to get you going.

1. Start a speakers group or join an organisation like Toastmasters. This is a great way to get experience with a group of people who also want to be speakers. It's hard to get in front of an audience enough to gain experience, so this supportive group is a great option.

2. Start a stories and anecdotes book or list. When you speak and write it's important to have stories and lessons you have learnt to share.

3. Speaker topics, in this booklet also start detailing what topics you could speak on for a keynote or a workshop. You will constantly have ideas, and it's a great idea to store them for your future use when you need some inspiration.

4. Take a look at your wardrobe, ensure you have some great outfits to wear that shows your personality and professionalism. The outfit often also needs to be able to hold a microphone pack.

5. Observe other speakers and performers, how they stand, how they present and write down what you like and don't like, so that you can emulate it or remove it from yours.

6. Get some great graphics and headshots done. Professional slides and imagery of you makes a big difference to your credibility.

7. Always think about how you want the audience to feel after your presentation and ensure your content enables this to happen.

SECTION 5

LEARNING FROM THE PAST.

We are all going to make mistakes in business, we've certainly made plenty. In fact, it would be hard to believe anyone who has achieved any degree of success not having a very long list of "ooopsies" that they lament about from time to time. Without these mistakes, we wouldn't have had the wonderful learning opportunities, that at the time almost killed us, and the harder it would be to grow.

We think there are many opportunities to learn, not just from our past mistakes, but from the past mistakes of others. What we want to encourage is getting away from beating ourselves up over the things we get wrong and instead, acknowledging them as part of the overall experience that is leading us to be the most successful version of ourselves possible. If you want to beat yourself up over something, beat yourself up for making the same mistake time and time again. That's not very clever.

41

Seven valuable lessons I learned from selling newspapers in a seedy part of town.

I was very young when I got my first real job, about 8 years old. It was selling newspapers on a street corner in what was at the time a rough suburb for a young child to be alone. I often think back about the things I learned as part of that job and I realised that a lot of my later success was due in no small part to my career as a paper boy.

Every day after school I would ride my bike to the depot, pick up a pile of newspapers, and hit the streets. Where I sold them was up to me. I kept whatever money was left over above the cost of the newspapers and I was paid $2 a week for 10 hours' work. I thought it was fantastic.

I learned a lot about people and selling things that has proven very valuable to me throughout my life.

Here are the main realisations as an 8-year-old boy:

1. **You have to go where your customers are, not wait for them to come to you.** At first I didn't really know where to go or what to do. So I stood on a street corner, waiting forlornly for people to rush out and buy newspapers. Very few did. One day an old lady came by, she bought a newspaper and gave

me a nice tip - not a financial one, but some advice. She suggested I walk her home, helping her with her groceries along the way and she would introduce me to all of the shop owners that she knew. From that day on I knew everyone, I started going to where my customers were, rather than waiting for them to come to me. Sounds kind of obvious, but a lot of businesses still get this wrong.

2. **Remember your customers and their likes and dislikes.** As a newspaper boy you quickly learn that some people like their newspaper folded, some like it rolled, some people like two copies, for whatever reason, some want certain change, some don't want the one on top and so on. Who knew? I learned quickly that when you took the time to understand and remember what your customers liked or didn't like - your tips got bigger.

3. **Be consistent.** I learned very quickly that with newspapers, people wanted them delivered at the same time every day. I had to be extremely consistent and figure out when people wanted their newspaper so I could always make a point of being there a few minutes early. Lots of them laughed when I walked in the door, saying they could set their clock by me turning up. Today I know how important this is.

4. **Look for people to partner with.** At the start I was intimidated to go into the bars even though I knew they would be good for business. I would look in the doors and be too scared to go in. One Friday afternoon, I noticed a charity worker walking through the bars, and I started to follow him around. I noticed that when he walked through, all of the drunken men would stop being loud and scary and they would drop coins into his little collection box. As I followed him they all started buying newspapers and giving me great tips. The man I was following realised what I was doing and he very kindly took me under his wing and led the way. At the end of every shift on Friday, we would sit and have a lemonade together. This was my first successful partnership, but I suspect I got more out of it than my benefactor.

5. **Never judge a person by their looks.** My best customer was a very old man who sat quietly on a seat in a park every day. He was very frail, his clothes were dirty and he didn't smell very nice. I would sit and chat to him, bring him chocolate bars from time to time and give him a newspaper because I thought he couldn't afford one. One day, just as I was leaving, he pulled a crumpled

ten dollar note out of his pocket and gave it to me. I didn't know what to do - that was a huge amount of money. He smiled, looked me in the eye and said "never judge a man by what he wears". From that day on, every time I brought him a newspaper he gave me a two-dollar note. Needless to say he became my favorite customer, until one day he simply stopped going to the park and I never saw him again.

6. **Have a sense of humor especially when you are scared.** When my charity worker friend wasn't around, which was most days, I had to battle with my fear and go into the bars. One bar in particular frightened me a lot. It was very loud, a working class bar, with lots of big, scary men who fought a lot, swore a lot and laughed a lot. I was a little fat kid, an easy target for them to make fun of. I learned to laugh off their mean taunts, which at first really upset me. The reason? They were the best tippers. The meaner they were, the more they tipped. I realised it was their way of saying sorry in front of their friends. So I learned to laugh about it - and eventually got cheeky enough to give them a regular serve of their own medicine.

7. **When you get paid, celebrate a little.** Every Friday afternoon I got paid my two dollars and all of my tip money. At the time money was very tight in my household, so I felt like I was contributing. I put my two dollars into the household budget and got to keep my tip money, which of course I spent on kid stuff. It was always the Friday afternoon ritual that I grew to love. It was an acknowledgement of the hard work I had put in during the week.

The big question, what did you learn from your first real job. Think about it and I am sure you will start to remember much more than the job itself. I certainly did.

BREE'S TAKE

I love this story, it made me think fondly about my first real job which was selling Avon at age ten.

Andrew has a very unique gift. He is able to think deeply about every situation in his life (and he has had some amazingly challenging times, far more than most), and figure out the lessons he learned. This means that the most difficult of times have been his greatest period of learning and growth. That's a wonderful attitude that we can all take on board.

So in the spirit of this, I think we all have a great opportunity to learn from our first job. So grab a piece of paper and let's take a few moments to reflect on your first job and see if there are some opportunities to learn. Can you answer these questions?

1. What was your first job?

2. What did you love about it?

3. What did you hate about it?

4. What did you find really hard?

5. Who were your role models in the business and why?

6. What lessons did you learn?

7. What did you do with the money you earned?

8. What could you teach others from this experience?

9. What do you wish you learned?

10. What did you learn from this job that you still use today?

42

How would you cope if you lost your biggest client today?

We all like to win those big accounts especially from the big name companies. They provide a lot of revenue, they can give you a sense of security and there is also a nice nudge to our ego, when a large reputable company wants to use our services. But we have to tread very carefully.

For many businesses losing their biggest client could easily spell disaster. This might sound dramatic but I've certainly seen it happen many times and come very close myself. We need to acknowledge that it could happen and have a plan of attack to reduce the risk.

The bigger the client, the more your business resources will be tied up managing and processing their work. This can lead to other clients receiving less attention and ultimately going elsewhere for their needs.

It can also lead to a false sense of security. A pile of work is pouring in, surely it will never end? But of course one day it does and if we are not prepared for that day, it can turn ugly.

From my experience there are three important and proactive steps that we have to take that reduce the risk of being over exposed to one client. They are:

1. **Never stop business developing.** This is the golden rule and unfortunately the first one to get broken. Especially when we have a big and exciting client directing a mountain of work our way. When we get busy we stop business development. It is vital to continue generating new business and to be thinking about new business all the time. It is also really important to make sure we are looking after our smaller clients and meeting their expectations. Leverage the largest client, use them as your main testimonial and credibility establishing resource, but spend time each week actively chasing new clients.

2. **Always have a plan in place for the day you lose your biggest client.** Many years ago I did lose my biggest client and I didn't have a plan of attack. One day my business was thriving, the next I had lost 80% of my monthly income (this is a good space for the very wise moral about not having all of your eggs in the one basket, another lesson I learned at the same time). I didn't have any plan of attack, so I just wandered around a little aimlessly, till the reality of the situation made me wake from my zombie like trance.

   I sat down, cleared my head and developed a short-term business development plan for my business. I built in advertising, networking, direct marketing, updating promotional material, reconnecting with old clients, updating my website and more. All the things I should have been doing but I hadn't because my big client was all consuming.

   Today I always have a rainy day plan ready to implement if I were to lose my biggest client. Having this plan gives me a sense of security and takes away the fear of "what if?"

3. **If you do lose your biggest client, react quickly.** Sure, losing that big client is tough and as a business owner the long-term ramifications can seem a little overwhelming at first. It is easy to freeze up and do nothing, or even worse, get a little depressed. What we need to do though is feel sorry for ourselves for a little while, but then implement the plan we developed earlier on, regarding what to do if we lose our biggest client. Sadly, I have seen way too many businesses fall apart when they lose their biggest client because they didn't have a plan to implement.

   Of course it is always a good idea to keep your biggest customer happy, that way you can enjoy the benefits they bring. However, you never know the fortune of these larger enterprises. They can be sold, sometimes very suddenly. The new owners might have relationships with other suppliers and you can find yourself out of the loop. Your big client might out grow you and decide to use a larger supplier themselves. Or the very worst case scenario, they might go broke and the first you know about it is a letter from the administrator.

There is a lot of uncertainty around these big client relationships. Having a smart plan of attack is a good idea and doing what you can to reduce your risk and exposure is even smarter.

BREE'S TAKE

I've also had the unfortunate experience of losing a big client through no fault of my company. Sometimes it doesn't matter how hard you have worked on the relationship and that you have done everything right; a change of management, a change of ownership or a change in the economy can mean you get that unexpected phone call or email to say it's all over. The great thing that comes out of it is that you get to learn a lot from the experience (as much as it stinks).

Here are three things that I learned from losing a big client:

1. **That good things can come from bad things.** Sometimes we get too comfortable. Losing a big client means we have to replace them with another big client and this can give you and your business renewed energy and vigor. You start to re-energise your other client relationships, your team gets fired up and we remember what it felt like to be hungry for business.

2. **That if you set something free it may come back.** Sometimes the door is closed on us and another one opens. But sometimes the door that got slammed in our face invites us back with open arms (if we have done the right thing of course). Sometimes businesses think that they should try something new, a new supplier, a new product or service and then they find out that the grass wasn't as green as they thought. So as disappointed as you are right now,

always do the right thing, hold your head high and tell them should they ever want to work with you again you would welcome the opportunity. Schedule it in your diary to give them a call in three to six month's time to see how things are going for them. Sometimes the words will be "oh thank goodness you called, I've been meaning to contact you" will flow out of their mouth.

3. **Tough times will teach you two things - who has your back, and who does not.** Losing your biggest client will mean that your team, your family and friends will all have to be supportive during this tough time. Sometimes a tough time will be made worse because we find out that people who we thought would be there to support us are in fact not there, but then we are blessed to find others, perhaps unexpected people, who are there to help. This is a time when relationships become weaker or stronger and as hard as it is in the moment, we really do come out better from the experience.

43

What can we learn from good businesses that have gone bad?

As much as I love to focus on the positive in life, when it comes to building better businesses, sometimes I think we can learn a lot from the negatives. For example, we can certainly learn a lot from businesses that were once really good (well I'm hoping that they were really good when they first started), but somewhere along the line they seem to have lost the plot.

I call these types of business "Anti-businesses". As the name suggests, they are businesses that seem hell bent on doing everything in their power to drive customers away and they have become exceptionally good at doing exactly that.

Now I believe that there are eight very specific types of anti-businesses out there (and I'm sure you've encountered every one at some stage recently). The key here is to learn from them. Because as much as I hate to admit it, traits from each of these anti-businesses can sneak into any of our businesses and slowly take over. Be warned-if any of the following hit a nerve, now is the time to do something about it.

So what are the eight anti-businesses types?

1. **The "I'm too busy to serve you" business.** These are the businesses that have mastered the art of making the customer feel completely insignificant.

When you walk into the business you will be completely ignored whilst the staff (and often the business owner) are extremely busy doing other really important things (like chatting to their friends on the phone). Generally, they don't acknowledge you with so much as a nod of the head, or a simple smile, instead you have to stand there, waiting uncomfortably for the pleasure of their attention.

2. **The "no, no, no" business.** These businesses are extremely frustrating. The standard response to every question the poor unsuspecting customer asks is "NO". Do you have this? NO. Can you get one in? NO. Do you have something that could do the job? NO. Do you know where I could get something like this? NO. Do you give a damn? NO.

3. **The "that's our policy" business.** I just love these businesses. One day someone made the smart move of developing some policies for the business to follow (and good on them for doing this in the right spirit of running a good business). The problem is that they become totally inflexible and just plain dumb when it comes to enforcing them. In other words "we have a policy and we are not afraid to use it". A lot of BIG businesses fit into this category as well. Logic is completely replaced by policy, which tends to be driven by a pedantic "Policy Nazi" somewhere in the bowels of the business.

4. **The "we hate our business so we hate you" business.** Some people have simply stayed in their business for way too long and it shows. They take their frustrations out on anyone considered to be a part of the problem, in this case the customer. There is a wonderful Chinese saying that I use all the time that goes something like "a man without a smile should never open a shop". If that is the case, why are there so many miserable sods out there that do?

5. **The "school teacher" business.** These are the businesses where you get chastised for being a naughty customer. I have had people tell me to stop talking and to be quiet as they lecture me about how their business works. I recently watched a waiter lecture an 80-year-old man on the temperature that coffee should be served because he had the audacity to say his coffee was cold.

6. **The "we'll get right back to you" business.** Typically, the "we'll get right back to you" business translates into "you will never hear from us again". How

many times do you have to stalk these businesses to get what you want out of them? This is one of the areas of greatest dissatisfaction for customers and tragically it is so easy to overcome.

7. **The "we have no idea what we are doing" business.** This business falls apart the minute one customer walks through the door. They can't find anything, nothing seems to work, and they don't even have a pen. You leave feeling very certain that these guys have no idea at all about how to run a business let alone satisfy a customer and you can't help but wonder what happens when more than one customer walks through the door at any single point in time.

8. **And the "how can we make our website completely un-user friendly" business.** Most of us have visited these online businesses. It feels like no one from the business has ever actually used their own site. It is ridiculously complicated, illogical and hard to use. To make the simplest of purchases involves going through ten pages of questions, then when you press confirm, it goes back to page one and you have to start again.

The moral to the story is that there are many anti-businesses out there. Every time you encounter one, make a mental note of what type it is, how they make you feel and perhaps do a quick internal audit of your own business just in case.

Never miss the opportunity to make your business better by learning from what others do poorly. Remember, most bad businesses actually started out as a good business, the seeds of decay seep in slowly.

BREE'S TAKE

I'm pretty sure we can all relate to the types of businesses Andrew talks about here. And I couldn't agree more, these are the businesses we can actually learn a great deal from. At the same time, we need to do a bit of soul searching to make sure we don't fit into any of the anti-businesses identified. So, in the spirit of preventing disaster, here is some advice that might help:

1. **The "I'm too busy to serve you" business.** Do you have a standard for waiting times within in your business? And how do you ensure it is monitored? What do you do in periods where demand is really high and service tends to drop. Most people appreciate when a business is busy that they may have to wait a little longer. All of your staff should know to acknowledge these waiting customers with something like "someone will be with your shortly, please take a seat, can I get you something to drink whilst you wait?" or something more tailored for your business. That works for a bricks and mortar business, but the same principle applies to online businesses. We need to do whatever we can to let our customers know they are important to us, they are our absolute priority and we are sorry to keep them waiting.

2. **The "no, no, no" business.** It's really interesting to be a fly on the wall when someone else in your business is serving a customer (either face to face or on the phone). How often does the word "no" get used? Start to turn your ear to hearing the word "no" and see just how often it's used. If you get a lot of telephone calls, try recording the calls and playing them back for training purposes (you might want to let your customers know you are recording them). You might be surprised by the language you use or members of your team use.

3. **The "that's our policy" business.** Re-read story 38 about hiding behind stupid policies. Have a process in place that either enables your team to use their initiative to break a policy, or give them a person that they can ask who will authorise the policy to be amended when common sense says it should be. Customers feel really important when a business breaks policy for them.

4. **The "we hate our business so we hate you" business.** If you hate your business, either work out how you are going to love it again or get out. Don't die a slow death, life's way too short to be miserable. You need to determine if you are over the business or just going through a "I've lost that loving feeling rough patch".

5. **The "school teacher" business.** As the old saying goes, the customer is always right. Unless someone is asking for your advice, don't give it. If someone is paying for a coffee and it's not what they expected, replace it. If someone complains to you, be grateful for the opportunity to fix the problem. If they walk away with the problem, you may never get them back, and often you don't just lose them, but their circle of friends too.

6. **The "we'll get right back to you" business.** Do you have a maximum time frame for getting back to people? We all get busy, but a simple call or email of communication letting someone know where you are at is better than not hearing anything at all. I always like to give myself more time than I need, so if someone asks for a quote ill say ill get it to them in a week, and then deliver it early. Be a business that always gets back to people and your business will thrive. If you can't get back to someone on a quote, then you have set the tone for how you run your business, you are pretty disorganised and have little follow through. Set a standard, make everyone really clear on your expectations when it comes to getting back to your customers, and make it fast.

7. **The "we have no idea what we are doing" business.** Starting a business is hard and it takes time to iron out all of the creases. Ensure your staff have "In training" badges when they are new. Have a soft launch with colleagues, close friends and family who can give you advice and ways to improve your new business. Note every time something happens and put it into a weekly training program where your team can role play how they should have handled the situation. Document it and put it into your procedures manual. If people know you are in training and you have your L plates on, they will be more forgiving. But if you are struggling to drive and no one knows you are in training they will think you are a crazy person who should not be driving, so proudly show those L plates until you have things down pat.

8. **And the "how can we make our website completely un-user friendly" business.** Can you find five people who would give your website an audit? Can you ask them to buy something from your website to let you know their experience and gift them the item? If your website is not very user friendly, people will assume that it's the same face to face.

There isn't a business in the world that can't do something better, mine included. But hopefully we are doing the right things to get a bit better every single day. It takes passion, it takes commitment and it takes time, but the end result will be a very cool business, that attracts great staff, with a long line of customers who are prepared to pay you a fair and reasonable price for all that you do. Now that is something we all aspire to.

44

Is your business being held hostage by overly demanding customers?

I once had a client who would call or email and demand that I drop everything immediately to get their new and urgent job done. The problem was that every job of theirs was urgent.

And so, every time I received another urgent call, I would drop everything. My entire business would come to a standstill, and other clients would get sidelined, just to meet the unrealistic and often rude demands from this one client.

The final straw came when she called me on a Monday morning demanding that I get a project done by Friday. That gave me five days to finish a project that would normally have taken three weeks. I worked around the clock, and completed the project by 4 p.m. that Friday.

After some brief celebration with the team, I called to let her know the report was on its way, only to be told by her assistant that she had left for a two-week holiday a few days back.

Then and there, I vowed to get rid of these "urgent, urgent, urgent" customers once and for all.

I introduced a new pricing schedule. I would gladly deliver urgent jobs, but I'd charge a 100 percent premium on top of the normal rate. Semi-urgent jobs would cost 50 percent more.

The results were interesting. Did I lose any customers? Not a single one. But what did change was the way my clients defined the word "urgent."

What was even nicer was that I noticed that my more demanding customers actually became much more organised. They seemed to respect my time, and me, much more. Suddenly I wasn't being taken for granted.

Bottom line: Don't let your business be held to ransom by a few unrealistic customers. It is easy to get rid of them, but surely a better outcome is to retrain them.

BREE'S TAKE

It's time to think about your clients, who are the ones you enjoy working with and why? On the flip side who are the ones you don't enjoy working with and why? It's really important to be clear about this.

So with the ones that you don't like working with - what can you do to fix the situation? Should you sack them and move on? I love Andrew's scaled pricing structure, but this wont work in every instance. Are there others that you can try?

We do need to train our clients to behave the way that is best for our business. Once you work out why you don't enjoy working with certain clients you can work out solutions like Andrew did. Maybe your clients are always late for their appointments or cancel last minute (don't we hate that?). Can you have repercussions for that? I'm sure you can. Be proactive with the types of customers you attract and most of your problems will be solved. Think back to idea #13.

45

Is someone going through
your garbage right now?

I've been the victim of identity theft and crime on a number of occasions over the years. Everything from credit card fraud to stolen company letterhead being used to fraudulently acquire equipment by an ex-employee. I'm not going to go into the details of how it happened, because that just lets people know how the criminals do it, but I will say it was surprisingly easy and the resulting chaos made my life very difficult.

Small businesses are generally pretty lax about security. Sure, we tend to be good at making sure the door is locked and the alarm is on, but there are far more insidious criminals out there, that don't want to steal your computer. They want to access your bank accounts, credit cards and sometimes even your intellectual property.

I don't want you to start looking over your shoulder imagining criminals in every cupboard, but with the soaring rate of cyber crime and identity theft, we need to take it seriously.

So here are some simple steps that we can take to reduce the risks of being on the receiving end of criminal activity:

1. **Make it hard for people to get your information.** It is amazing how much confidential information either gets printed out or arrives in the mail, that simply gets put in the rubbish bin. Documents with home addresses, date of birth, account numbers, utility bills, passwords and access codes all end up being routinely thrown away and made easily accessible for criminals. Shred any and every piece of paper that goes out of your office. All you need is a shredder next to your desk or printer and make it a habit. Put the shredded paper in the recycle bin and mix it up when you put it in there. Even better, avoid printing important documents altogether.

2. **Put padlocks on your garbage bins.** Yes this is an inconvenience, but so is someone accessing all of your paperwork and other documents that often get discarded without much thought as to who could use the information. A good old fashioned lock, can work wonders, and as the police often say, locks keep the honest criminals out.

3. **When you employ staff, spell out what is OK and what is not.** As the business owner it is your right to explain very clearly what is your property, either physical or intellectual and what your expectations are regarding this property with your staff. If a member of staff leaves with a client database, that is theft and needs to be treated accordingly. When it comes to access codes and passwords, you might be very diligent about protecting them but some of your staff may not. Spell out your expectations here as well. Leave absolutely no doubt about what is OK in terms of your property and your expectations in terms of security.

4. **Get a little smarter about the passwords that you use.** I know that remembering passwords is a challenge, but we all need to move way beyond the simple birthday password. Research shows it is still surprisingly common. Plus, we need to change them regularly. I make a point of changing my banking password weekly, but I do have a system which makes this easier than it sounds. I have a word, with symbols and a number and I simply take the last letter/number off and move it to the front. This seems to work for me but I do suggest that you come up with a system of your own.

5. **Get a debit card.** A while back I asked my bank to issue me a debit card. I use this for online purchases and for travel. I only put enough money in for any purchase I am making at the time, or expected expenses. As opposed

to just dishing out my normal credit card number, left right and center. Another added benefit of doing this is that I am much more aware of exactly how much money I am spending.

6. **Unsolicited faxes, emails and calls.** This might sound strange, but millions of dollars are obtained fraudulently by criminals sending faxes or emails demanding money for an unpaid bill that doesn't exist. Even calls made to a business demanding payment of an outstanding account. These fake bills are often paid by the unsuspecting business owner simply because their systems are not as tight as they should be. If you aren't one hundred percent certain about what a bill is for, don't pay it. Never fall for "legal action" is going to commence. For legal action to commence there will need to be quite a few official letters to go backwards and forwards, giving you the opportunity to verify supposed debts.

7. **Use technology to safeguard your information.** I encourage every small business to engage an I.T specialist to ensure that your network is as secure as it can possibly be. This can sound expensive and complicated, but imagine how complicated your life will be if someone hacks into your network, or steals your identity. At a simpler level, ensure updates to software and apps are kept current. Make sure all security features on your equipment are activated and read the manuals to make sure you are aware of any risks.

BREE'S TAKE

I've also been the victim of staff theft from my business and it isn't a nice feeling, especially when you are a small, close team. Why people steal is a weird thing to try and understand. Often the person has simply had a lapse of judgment and they may think they deserve what they are taking, even though they do not.

As a business owner, you need to ensure people who work for you know what theft is in your eyes, and what the consequences will be should they break the rules. I never pressed charges, as a mark against their name could ruin their life and I felt bad about that. However, I regret not doing so now, as these people have continued to steal from other businesses.

Some people don't think they are actually stealing when they give themselves an unsolicited perk; free coffees for their friend that comes to the café, ordering extra stationery to take home, and taking client databases for their next job or own business. But theft is theft, and as business owners we need to ensure our employees know what we deem as theft or unacceptable.

When I have an employee start with me, I make it very clear how I deal with theft, that the police will be called and so on. I also state that I am a very generous person, and if they want something, all they need to do is ask and this gives me the opportunity to gift it to them, rather than them taking it and feeling guilty.

Outline in a document what is considered unacceptable behavior. For example, using company IP or unauthorised use of company credit cards, and ensure they sign the document. My staff are required to sign a confidentiality agreement which ensures they know how seriously I take theft and confidentiality. It doesn't stop people from doing the wrong thing, but it does make it easier to terminate someone when you can refer to a document that they have signed.

SECTION 6

BUILD A MIGHTY REPUTATION.

There was a time when we could hide behind our business and let it do all of the heavy lifting in terms of branding and reputation. Those times are long gone. We are all taking a much greater interest in the businesses we buy from, and the people behind these businesses. If you don't make yourself reasonably transparent, your customers will assume that you have something to hide.

So if we are going to be more open, put ourselves out there, start to build our profile and reputation, we need to be pretty darn proactive about it. It isn't something that can just happen by itself. To be honest, this section really is about one thing - building trust. It's incredibly easy to damage, and it can take a lifetime to establish it, if lost.

46

We all need to be bigger than our business.

Businesses come and go. What you are doing today is unlikely to be what you will be doing in ten years' time. You are the most significant asset in your life and it is important to realise this.

I encounter a lot of people who become their business. It is everything from their waking moment in the morning, to their last thought at night (and often it fills their dreams). When they no longer have this business, their life falls apart. They don't know what to do, their life feels empty and dissatisfaction and depression can set in.

Look at the lives of a few high profile entrepreneurs. Rarely do they have only one business interest. They may start new businesses, sell old ones, go broke in some, do a joint venture in others-they are not attached to one business. They are passionate about what they do but they realise they are the resource and the skill centre, used to make the other businesses work. They are more than any of the businesses that they own.

Whatever you are doing, there is life after your current business. For this reason, you need to be more than your business. You need to have more substance, more interests, more beliefs and more of a long-term view about how you fit into your business life. Don't let your business consume or control you, you are in the driving seat, not the other way around.

Often younger entrepreneurs are caught up trying to build their empire. Every waking moment is about the business, leaving little room for anything else. The key here is to make time to stay involved with interests outside of business, keep connected with friends, have regular breaks and getaways, no matter how busy you may be and establish some rules-like "I don't work on weekends".

This might sound unrealistic, but being successful in business is rarely a sprint, it is more often a marathon, and that means that leaders have to pace themselves. Add to this the fact, that when this race is over you need to be in good enough shape for the next race.

Ponder this thought-what would you do if you got a letter in the mail that said you had to close down your business in 24 hours? How would you cope? What would you do next? An interesting situation to spend a few minutes considering.

BREE'S TAKE

I've had two decades of building businesses, I call one of them my ten-year start-up, as it's a business that requires a lot of attention and still has a long way to go before it's where I want it to be. As much as I've kept up the pace, it's easy to fall into the well of working every spare moment you have, especially when you really love what you do.

Raising a young family and raising a business has made me acutely aware of how precious time is, for both my family and my business. You don't want to work too much as you miss out on time with your children, but you also have to squeeze in work around nap times and times that they are occupied or in care to get your work done.

This is a hard stage in life as it feels like a never-ending treadmill of "doing". Every spare minute you have is filled with one of the roles, so it's a time that many business owners burn out, get resentful or worse, give up on their business because they have no balance.

Andrew says to have rules so that you have more balance, and that is true, but if you are like me, work life balance is a never-ending battle that you will lose if you have children or a business that requires you to be 'on' all the time. So I think you need to embrace work life blending.

Every day you are choosing what is the most important thing for the day. Is it time with the family or time on your business, or a bit of both? It's a never ending juggle that some days I do really well, and some days I don't. But accepting the fact that this is a stage in your life and that you are being the best business owner that you can, and the best parent or partner that you can ensures that you don't feel too guilty.

Andrew is right in saying that you need to build a life and a profile that is bigger than your business though. I've spent a lot of time building my profile and I know that if I decided to change course, I could easily transition to something else, because I am constantly building my profile to be bigger than my current businesses. You take your profile with you, no matter what you do and that's why it's so important.

So how can you do that too? Here are nine things you can do today to build your profile.

1. Get a professional photo taken of you to use as your profile image on everything that requires a photo (sounds so crazy obvious right? Yet look at how many people have terrible images on their website and in their promotional material).

2. Get a nice email signature designed with your image and what you do, so that all of your emails are personalised.

3. Have a great LinkedIn profile, get a professional to help you write about yourself.

4. Buy your name as a domain. Having your own website about who you are, has become a must these days.

5. Get someone to interview you or get a professional video done to show you and your businesses story.

6. Learn the art of public speaking, whether it be the ability to do a great speech at a conference, or simply a presentation to your team or the opportunity to tell your story at a business networking event. Being able to speak in front of a crowd is a great way to build a solid reputation and profile.

7. Start a blog that covers what you think and your areas of knowledge and what it is that you stand for.

8. Write content for magazines, newspapers, and other people's blogs, this is a great way to build credibility and show your expertise.

9. Get a great elevator pitch, you should be able to introduce yourself in under thirty seconds in a way that intrigues people to ask more.

We all need to be building our profile so that we are an authority in our current business, but more importantly, for our future endeavors. At the same time, we need to build a life outside of our business. The two go together in a strange but important way.

47

How can you tell if people really trust you? And does it really matter?

There is a lot of discussion about trust these days. People are generally less trusting, tending to be more reserved and guarded about what they share and whom they share it with. We have seen many very public breaches of trust and deep down that is a fear most of us have.

When working with people, either as clients or colleagues, not being trusted can have dire consequences. It can result in lower client loyalty, less referrals, more client issues around billing, delivery of services and even fairly public backlashes on social media.

Today we see entire industries that struggle with being trusted, due in no small part to their previous actions. Once trust is lost, it is very hard to regain.

So how can you tell if someone really trusts you? Over the years I have found that trust can be determined by the type of information that people share with you. The more personal the information the more trusting the person is of you. This might sound obvious, but do you really stop to consider what those around you are sharing or perhaps trying to share but you are missing their hints.

Sharing personal information is a sign of their vulnerability. This is the kind of information that if shared to outside parties could result in them being embarrassed or even humiliated, or it might even have a direct impact on how their colleagues view them. This in turn could cause problems with career growth or even employment, depending on what information was revealed.

We might share private information because it's in our best interest. For example we tend to trust our Doctor, realising that it makes sense to share information that could ultimately have an impact on our health. But to tell someone we work with, or someone who is advising us, something personal, it is a big step and a leap of faith.

What if someone confides in you, but only to share gossip about someone in the office? Does this mean they trust you? Not really. This is more a conspiratorial move, where sharing gossip is done to build rapport. It is often superficial, and paramount to smoking behind the shed in the school playgrounds.

Personally I use the information that people share with me as a way to measure if I am trusted or not. If they are opening up and being very authentic and vulnerable, airing their own perceived faults and failings, I do everything in my power to respect the trust they have shown and I would never, ever, do anything to betray it.

When it comes to sharing gossip and negative comments about other people, I don't engage. I send a very clear message that I am not interested in that kind of talk. I find that the gossipers soon realise this and they stop gossiping to me and start having far more authentic conversations.

The bottom line is that being trusted enough for others to confide in you at a personal level, is a very good thing in every way. Respect this trust, you have earned it. Over time it can become the backbone of your professional and personal reputation.

BREE'S TAKE

Trust is one of the biggest assets you can ever have, and once it's gone, it's near impossible to get back. In a business setting, it's great if you can build trust quickly.

Here are seven ways to build trust quickly.

1. Always be honest. If you are someone that speaks the truth with people about even the smallest thing, people will trust you more.

2. Be sincere with people. If you ask questions like "how is business going" and listen with care, people will feel heard, the more you listen the more they will share.

3. Don't try to be be perfect. Share some of your mistakes and shortcomings with people as it shows that you also trust them.

4. Take responsibility. If you are ever in the wrong, step up and own what you did and apologise. This shows that you don't run from the truth.

5. Don't be a fence sitter. Have a strong opinion or state that you don't have an opinion on that topic for now and that you will have to think about it. Talking to someone who always agrees with you even when they don't, is really obvious.

6. Look people in the eye. If you constantly shift your eyes, it makes people suspicious of you.

7. Say "I don't know". Admit when you don't know something, you'll often get a lot of credibility for that instead of pretending that you know something.

48

Seven ways to prevent reputation ruin by partnering with the wrong people or businesses.

Today everyone seems to be looking to buy, sell or form some kind of partnership or joint venture. Most of us understand that there is value in being able to share resources, cross promote businesses, market to similar customer demographics and even develop products and services together.

Whilst this might sound like a great idea at the time, we need to be extremely careful to protect our own reputation at any cost. Now more than ever, we are judged on the power of our own personal brand, in many ways more than that of our businesses brand. Partner or joint venture with the wrong person or the wrong company and your reputation and that of your business can be destroyed.

In the past I have made this mistake. As a speaker I have presented at an event where I was sold one thing and the reality was very different. What was promoted as an upmarket professional event was little more than a seriously hard sell to a group of exhausted people who were pressured into buying high value products that in hindsight were of little value.

There were some big names presenting at this event. Richard Branson and Tim Ferris to mention just two. I think we all felt a little betrayed. Fortunately, I learned a lot and I will never make that mistake again.

When it comes to going into some kind of partnership or joint venture or really any kind of commercial arrangement, here are seven strategies to avoid it ending in tears.

1. Treat protecting your reputation as the main priority (the reputation of you and the reputation of your business). Keep asking yourself if this relationship, will be an integral alignment with you, your own values and goals. If not, walk away early.

2. Don't rush to say yes. If you are getting pressured into partnering with an organisation, ask yourself why? Be prepared to let the deal go. There are always other opportunities. The minute I get pressured, with something like "you need to decide by 5pm today"; I make a decision on the spot and say no.

3. Always do your due diligence on prospective partners. It is rare that someone will tell you any negatives, it's up to you to do your own homework. If anything looks fishy, it probably is.

4. Moving goal posts should set off an alarm. If you have agreed upon a certain course of action and your new partner organisation wants to change the deal, be very concerned as to what this means. If they can't stick to the agreement at the start, things will only get worse.

5. Always plan for the divorce - not the honeymoon. Any new venture sounds wonderful in the planning stages and it gets exciting when you kick it off, but what happens if it doesn't go to plan? Fingers start getting pointed, promises get broken and the situation turns ugly.

6. Get it all in writing, even the worse case scenarios. It is surprising how often this is ignored. We don't live in a world where handshakes or even verbal agreements are honored. Get everything in writing, who will do what, by when, for how much and what happens if they don't.

7. Think back to any joint ventures or partnership arrangements that you've had in the past. What have you learned from them and what will you do differently next time?

BREE'S TAKE

Partnerships are very tricky but very rewarding if you partner with the right company or people. Of course there are all kinds of horror stories as well. Here are some tips that I think are important if you are looking to either do a joint venture, partnership or even form a new business with someone else:

1. Seek advice from your accountant on the best set up. Usually it is equal shares, and co-directors. You need to work out the best way according to who is going to do what in the business. Maybe you won't do as much work, so maybe taking less shares and responsibility is a better idea.

2. Seek legal advice. You need to know legally where you stand. If you are partnering with someone and they are married or in a defacto relationship, you may need to get a pre-nuptial or post-nuptial drawn up which states that this company is not to be a part of the assets that they are eligible for should you die, divorce or separate. If you do not have one of these in place, the company can at worse be forced to stop trading until the settlement is complete which can cause major problems for the remaining director of the company.

3. Get your Will updated and state who your share of the company is to go to should you die.

4. Ensure your Power Of Attorney is also updated.

5. Have a plan in play for the "what if's". What will happen with debt, who gets what, who does what, what happens if one person wants out etc?

Partnerships are not something to be taken lightly, you need to treat the partnership like a marriage. You are going to have great times, you are going to have tough times and if you commit to starting a business with someone, be committed. You can't just give up; you must give it your all and try your best every single day.

49

Never underestimate the power of a great testimonial.

It's easy to dismiss testimonials as a little old school, but in reality, they are very powerful tools that can increase a business's credibility in extraordinary ways. In my opinion they are more important than ever, and many businesses don't even bother to collect them.

What are the benefits of having testimonials?

Let's be honest, we are all somewhat cynical. We certainly don't believe everything we are told, especially when it comes to advertising. But we do believe other people. This is the reason that sites such as Trip Advisor have flourished and social media in general has become such a force to be reckoned with.

A testimonial means that the person giving it, is putting their reputation with their own mob on the line. If they give a testimonial and the business doesn't live up to what they have to say, their reputation is damaged. So it is a very significant bond between the business getting the testimonial and the individual giving it.

A business that has a good number of current testimonials, from a diverse group of customers, is much more appealing to potential customers than one without. It's kind of like other members of the mob have tested the business for you and given it two thumbs up, so your risk is reduced.

What is the best way to ask for testimonials?

Many business owners really struggle with asking for testimonials. There is almost a sense of embarrassment around asking for them. Perhaps some concern is that people will think their business is not doing so well. This is the first hurdle to overcome. You have to believe in the importance of testimonials and always be prepared to ask for them.

An approach that I suggest follows this kind of script: "Mary I just wanted to say thank you for using my business. I really appreciate it. In fact, I am really committed to growing my business and I would love more wonderful customers just like you. So can I ask you to refer your friends and could you possibly write me a short testimonial. Here are a couple of examples, just one or two lines would be great. Are you happy to do that now for me? "

This approach engages the customer and asks for their help. It is very persuasive and from my experience, most people are very happy to give a testimonial on the spot. At the same time, you have asked them to refer other people to your business - a double whammy.

Asking people to write reviews on social media sites is a good move too. The best way to do this is to send them an email with a link to the sites, and specific pages, where you want them to comment. Make it as easy as possible for people to write the review, something often overlooked.

What should you ask to ensure it's not a generic response?
Some people prefer to give their customers a short testimonial brief to make it easier. This is a good idea as many people have no idea what to say when it comes to writing a testimonial, so a simple sheet with some suggestions - like "tell us what you like most about dealing with us?", "what would make you come back again?", "what did you expect before you used us?" and "what is one word that you would use to sum up the experience of working with us?" Keep testimonials short and sharp. It is OK to have an occasional longer one, but don't make your testimonials war and peace, who has the time?

Who are the best testimonial candidates?

I find that it is important to collect testimonials from people who really are my target markets. For example, when it comes to my books, I want testimonials from small business owners who can share their own experiences with my books and the advice that I have given them. This encourages other like minded small business owners to buy my books.

To make this work, you really need to know whom your ideal customers are. A lot of businesses aren't that clear on this point and they really should be.

How often should you review testimonials?

If you are trying to build your business on testimonials that are 10 years old, it's time to get some new ones. Consumers look long and hard at our testimonials to see not just who is giving them but also when they are giving them. If your reputation is based on what people said ten years ago, new customers will automatically be suspicious and ask why haven't you got any new testimonials?

I tend to leave dates out of my testimonials on my own promotional material, which makes them timeless, but this is harder to control when it comes to social media.

Collecting testimonials is also a great form of quality control. I think we should be asking as many of our clients as we can for testimonials. If they don't want to give us a testimonial, why not? Perhaps they are not happy with our products or services and we need to know. So if you are asking for testimonials, be certain to have a way of managing the process if a customer says they don't want to give one.

One last point

Getting testimonials is one half of the process. Using them correctly is the other half. We should have our testimonials on our websites, in our printed promotional material, in proposals (I give a list of 10 past clients and their phones numbers, who can be contacted to discuss my work - no one ever rings them, but everyone makes a comment about how impressive this is).

Testimonials are powerful, essential and free marketing tools that have always been important. Today they are vital. We live in a world of incredible choice. Any business that has a legion of raving fans who are prepared to come out and not only share their experience but also recommend that others use this business, has a huge competitive advantage.

BREE'S TAKE

They say there is nothing more powerful than the written word, but video testimonials are certainly becoming equally and if not more powerful in the digital age we live in. It does of course depend on where you are going to use the testimonial. A badly written testimonial is just as bad as a terrible video testimonial.

With modern technology, most of us carry a high quality video facility in our pocket. Taking videos is so much easier – and that's a good thing and a bad thing. It means we are seeing a lot of terrible videos, but with a few simple tips, they can get a whole lot better.

The key is that any testimonial needs to be sincere. Anyway, I'm a video kind of girl, so here are my tips for a great video testimonial.

1. Pick your person. You need to be more selective for a video testimonial for obvious reasons, so pick clients that will be comfortable in front of a camera.

2. Pick a great setting. Do it in as natural a setting as possible, like your actual business. If you do fishing tours, do it on the boat. You don't want it to be in a studio, the more candid and the more 'real' it is, the better. Just make sure the lighting works, so test the spot first by filming for a few seconds to see if you like the look and feel of the place you have chosen.

3. Get a few bits and pieces. Most smart phones are fantastic and perfect for grabbing a testimonial on the go. If you are going to be on camera with the person, have a mini phone tripod or a 'selfie stick' or if you are long armed you can do it without either but you may not like how close the phone is to your face. Try a few things first and get comfortable with how it works best for you before getting that first testimonial.

4. Get a small plug-in microphone for your phone. I have a RODE one that costs about $20 and it greatly improves the sound quality. You pin it to the person's shirt or hold it in your hand to interview someone.

5. Prepare the person, tell them you only want a thirty second video, ask them to look right into the lens (show them where that is) and get them to do a quick practice video (film it as they may nail it first time round).

6. Download free video editing software on your mobile phone if you want to edit the video and add a little bit of background music, text and lots more if you want to get creative. Or keep it as is and simple.

7. Load the video testimonials to your website and social media channels and also get them transcribed.

50

Seven strategies for building a rock solid reputation.

I've spent 50 years building my reputation (yep, it started at birth). My reputation is my most valued asset, something I take great care to develop and nurture and I would never do anything to jeopardise it. It helps me make a living, it lets me work with amazing people, travel to incredible places and make a difference to the lives of many other people.

We live in a world where it has never been easier to ruin a reputation, mainly due to social media and the speed at which news travels. We all need to take care to develop and protect our reputation and make it rock solid.

Having been a lifelong student of this concept, I think there are seven key codes to follow when it comes to ensuring that your reputation will withstand pretty much anything.

1. **Get serious about being empathetic.** We often hear people talking about the need to be empathetic and to put ourselves in the shoes of others, but talk is easy, actually doing it is much harder. I think empathy is a skill that can be developed. It does however take an effort to retrain our impulse to jump to conclusions and make every situation about us not them. Personally I have

found that my life changed in every single way when I fully embraced empathy and being known for being empathetic in business has certainly enhanced my personal reputation.

2. **Make conscious decisions about every interaction.** Many people go through life taking a very passive approach to their interactions with others. My philosophy is to try and make every interaction during my day count, regardless of whom that interaction is with. People notice this and in a lot of instances, the impact is dramatic and sometimes even life changing.

3. **Step up to life in a changing world.** We all understand that the world is changing at an incredible rate, but not everyone is happy about it. Are you one of those people excited about this or are you a doomsayer? People get sick and tired of hearing from the doomsayers and if you are one of them, complaining all the time, being negative about your industry, your city, your world, your reputation will definitely be damaged.

4. **Help people especially when you haven't got the time.** Actions speak louder than words and acts of kindness are incredibly powerful, especially when done by exceptionally busy people. We should never be too busy to do an act of kindness-they should simply be a part of our life and we should be kind because that is the right thing to do, not because it enhances our reputation-that's just a nice bonus.

5. **Grow an extraordinary network. The key word here is "grow".** A lot of people have a "what can I get" out of this network attitude, as opposed to "what can I contribute" attitude. Growing a network means investing time and energy into, supporting those in your network, looking for ways to help others and protecting them. Grow a great network and you will have a ready-made fan club that will protect you and your reputation at every opportunity.

6. **Be brave enough to be authentic.** What does it mean to be authentic? For me it means showing people you are human, you make mistakes, you are vulnerable, you try to do your best and that sometimes you get it right, sometimes you don't. Today we admire and respect people who are brave enough to show their authenticity and we intuitively know when people are not. Open up, share the true "you" and see what happens.

7. **Give people a reason to trust you.** We expect people to trust us, but in reality we have to earn trust. People are cynical and rightly so. Trust is built over many years and you can't have a bulletproof reputation without being trusted. So how to do become trusted? Firstly, never give people a reason not to trust you. Hold yourself accountable before anyone else is even in on the picture. Do the right thing, always. And if you say you are going to do something, do it.

BREE'S TAKE

I love everything here that Andrew has written, and agree we need to be building rock solid reputations. But what if you do the above and still have your integrity questioned? I once had this happened to me publicly. Here are seven brutal lessons I have learnt from this experience.

Lesson One: You can try to be the best person all you like. You can try to always be of high integrity and do the right thing. This is a great way to live life. BUT, if you are going to be in the public eye, there are heartless people in this world who will tear you down. You need to accept this as part of the deal, or don't be a public figure- don't put yourself out there. It's as simple and brutal as that.

Lesson Two: If a person speaks negatively about you behind your back, or online it is often a reflection of themselves. If a business uses their power to communicate negatively about a person online, it shows a total lack of professionalism and ethics. Joining in their behaviour makes you sink to their level. As hard as it is to have no voice and to not respond- hold you head high, don't use your words to fight back, use your actions and prove them wrong. People will believe what they want to anyway, so put your energy into your actions. Always moving your life forward rather than wasting energy on the past by fighting with people who don't deserve your energy or attention.

Lesson Three: The challenging times in your life will make two things very clear. The family and friends who support you, and which family and friends really do not. This often makes the situation you are going through even worse. Not only are you dealing with an issue that has rocked you to your core, but you also feel the pain of loss of the people who you 'thought' were there for you.

As brutal as that is, try to look on the bright side.

Lesson Four: Bullying happens. People watch and join in or they do nothing, which means they support the bullying. Only a very few people, if any, will actually stand up publicly to the bully and say what is being done is wrong.

Lesson Five: The culling of people from your life hurts. Because it's really them culling you from theirs, you just haven't been taking the hint. I have had many tears from the rejection I feel from people that I have always tried my best to help. My business and I supported them and their business and I did everything that I could because I cared about them and wanted to help. Then when you want their help and support they are nowhere to be seen. The sad thing is that you know it is for the best and something that you need to accept. As hard as it is, you need to try and make sure that your heart doesn't get cold and that you stop the people that actually do care about you from being shut out by you too.

Lesson Six: Plan for the unexpected. If you experience an unexpected episode like this, it will totally derail you from your plans. Projects will be put on hold, plans will change, and on the positive; projects you never imagined doing will come to you and will slowly help you to heal. You might just find that the new path you take is much more aligned to where you are going, than the old one was anyway.

Lesson Seven: Your words and actions can help or harm people. You can choose to be productive or destructive. By this I mean you help people grow (productive) or you make people self destruct (destructive). Be very careful and considered with every thing you say and do.

In the end, do the best to build your integrity every single day, and if you ever experience having your integrity challenged, hold your head up high and in time the pain will ease. As awful as the experience was at the time, I am really grateful for it now.

51

How long is too long to bask in the glory of winning an award?

Winning an award of some sort is always a good thing for a business. Of course we are all encouraged to leverage the award, which certainly adds to a business's credibility, gives the team a morale lifting boost and helps attract customers by providing a point of difference. But there are times when promoting an award could actually be doing your business more harm than good.

Recently I came across a restaurant that was promoting an award they had won in 2008 and I found myself asking some hard questions about the value of promoting such an old award.

Now let's be honest, that is a long time ago and begs the question, what have they won since then? Which leads on to another question, if they haven't won anything since then why not? Or an even bigger and more concerning question, has the food gone bad? All are probably wrong, but it does kind of look like they are hanging onto something from the past that has little to no relevance today.

This led me to ask the biggest question, how old is too old when it comes to promoting an award? Surely we can get a few good years out of it right?

Personally I tend to think that two years is fine, three years is borderline and four years or longer is too long. If you've won multiple awards, sure put them all up, leverage them all. But the latest award is the most important one and if it has been way too long since winning an award, I think you need to get a little creative and call yourself an award winning business. Don't have the award logo and the year you won it, plastered all over your website and promotional material.

The moral to the story really is that every business sends messages, some consciously, some subconsciously. Both are equally important and both need to be considered constantly. Sometimes saying nothing is better than saying something, which is certainly the case when it comes to promoting an out of date award.

BREE'S TAKE

Most of us have entered our businesses into awards, but many of us don't personally enter awards. I have entered a few, and here are seven things to keep in mind.

1. Entering awards and doing submissions take time. The awards with the biggest criteria's require a huge effort on your behalf to enter, and these are the ones that you should be looking to take part in.

2. The best part of the awards experience is doing the submission, reflecting on what you have achieved is something we don't often do, so enjoy this part.

3. Ensure you are completely honest with your submission. Also have someone close to you check it over before you submit it to check for spelling and grammatical errors.

4. Be wary of awards that encourage you to get your followers to "vote" for you. Often this is simply a marketing tactic for the business running the awards to build their own database. I find these sorts of awards that are based on popularity, do not carry as much merit as one's that are based with a panel of judges and set criteria. Totally different if your business is up for an award, but not for individual awards.

5. If you make it to the finals, prepare a short speech even if you don't think you will win, it's better to be prepared.

6. Remember that winning an award has a huge responsibility attached to it for the life of your award, do the wrong thing and you may have the award stripped from you.

7. Celebrate. I have won awards and made it to the finals but looking back now I don't think I celebrated this enough at the time. Make sure you really stop, take a moment or a few, to appreciate yourself and how awesome you truly are.

Take some time and research some awards that you can personally enter, and some awards that your business could enter, whether you win or loose you are guaranteed to learn from the experience.

52

It's not you, it's me.
How to avoid a bad business break up.

Recently I had to call a supplier to let them know I no longer needed their services. We had been working together for a few years but I needed to work with a business that could provide a different service. The original supplier had not done anything wrong, it was just time for a change. So I made the call and was very apologetic and sincere, letting them know it wasn't them, it was me. That (I thought) was that.

What happened next was kind of surprising. I received a long and aggressive email from the supplier, along the lines of "how dare you." They made it very clear that to get any of my unfinished projects completed would cost a premium as I was no longer a "preferred client." They attached the latest bill which had their hourly rate tripled as an "end of contract" penalty. What are the chances I will ever use this company again? Less than zero.

There could have been another outcome. We could have parted ways amicably and perhaps even worked together in the future. All business relationships have to come to an end. Companies change suppliers, businesses start up or go bust, new products or services become available, people change roles and change suppliers. We all have to face the fact that at some stage we will get a phone call or email saying we have lost an account. It's what happens from here on that differentiates a great business from a lousy business.

Over the years I have seen terrible behavior from companies that have "spat the dummy" when told they have lost a contract. They take the view that the relationship is over, so what's to lose? They start being rude, stop returning calls, start sending through ridiculous bills, become uncooperative and generally act badly. What they don't realise is that word gets around. We all talk to people within our network and a bad break up with a supplier is a very common topic of discussion. No one wants to take on a new supplier if they have heard rumors that they are bad at break ups.

Here are seven ways to make sure you have a good break-up.

1. Aim to finish the relationship in exactly the same way that it started, with absolute professionalism.

2. Never get petty at the end. Be supportive and help the transition to go smoothly.

3. Don't price gouge; make sure that your final bills are fair and reasonable in every way.

4. Brief your staff and show them how to manage a business break up in a professional way.

5. Don't let the relationship ending become an excuse for poor service. Be as attentive with your client once they have advised you of their decision to break up.

6. Ask for feedback from the client such as, what you could have done to have kept the business.

7. Make a point of sending a letter of gratitude to not only your direct contact but also the CEO of the organisation thanking them for their business.

My philosophy has always been to act as professionally as possible, right to the last moment. Interestingly enough, I have often gotten a client back, simply because the new supplier didn't deliver on their promise. I didn't burn any bridges, the door was left well and truly open and the relationship remained positive, making it easy for the client to come back.

BREE'S TAKE

Andrew is right, no one likes to lose business and most of us want to end a relationship way earlier than we actually do. Here are a few tips for you if you are heading towards a break-up with a client:

1. Don't leave it until it's unsalvageable. Sometimes we want to stop working with a business because they aren't growing with us, but we stay on out of guilt. If you are unhappy, tell them straight away, don't let it fester.

2. Put yourself in their shoes and think about how much notice you need to give them. Your contract could be the end of that supplier's business, so if you can, give them as much notice as possible, ie "we are placing this order and we are giving you one more orders notice". Or one month's notice, or whatever you deem fair. Of course the business needs to be acting in the top seven ways above, for that to take place.

3. Speak in person or on the phone about the break up if you have a relationship with the person, and be prepared to answer their "why" questions. If there is a chance they could save the relationship with you, tell them how.

4. Follow up the conversation with an email stating all of the details you discussed, especially the date everything will be finished by.

53

Three ways to get customers who will fight for your business when you need it the most.

There is a small food processing business called Spring Gully Foods that very few people in Australia, let alone the world, have ever heard of. Started in 1946 by Edward McKee, in Adelaide, the capital city in South Australia, this fourth generation family owned business reached a sad day one year when it released a media statement to say it was going into bankruptcy.

With $11m in debt, an empty bank account, growing costs, a large wages bill and an extremely competitive environment, Spring Gully Foods management had no choice but to call it a day. But then something strange happened. The prospect of losing this iconic business had a big impact on many of Spring Gully Food's loyal customers. Particularly those in the home state of South Australia. Local radio stations started a "Save Spring Gully" campaign, which had a dramatic and immediate impact. Five days after the media release Spring Gully Foods had received orders for $1.5million (when considering that total yearly sales were around $26million, this was extraordinary).

Some thought this would be a last minute flutter of activity, but six months later, the orders were still coming in and getting stronger every month. The company is well and truly back on track financially, making this one of the most remarkable customer driven turnarounds, in recent times.

Here are three lessons you can use to create a similar passionate customer base:

1. **Respect your customers and they will support you.** Spring Gully Management didn't come out kicking and screaming, blaming everyone for their impending demise. They simply said that they had tried their best to overcome tough market conditions, but it wasn't enough. In fact, they apologised for letting their customers and staff down. We are so used to sensationalised headlines and public relations spin, that this approach, actually made people sit up and take notice, and admire this humble business.

    This humility underlies a huge respect for customers which was reflected in their product and service quality. Their commitment was always to delivering the very best products that they could out of respect to their customers and these same customers repaid that respect in an extraordinary way.

2. **Show your passion for your business and customers will engage in the same way.** In the darkest hours, it is easy to give up and many businesses do. As much as Spring Gully appeared to be finished, when the extent of their issues became clear, and the community support started to flow, the management team and all of the staff rolled up their sleeves and worked together.

3. **Let others champion your cause and communicate it.** Sometimes it can be very hard to accept help from others. There is no doubt that at first, the community support shown towards Spring Gully would have been sad and condolence based, rather being all about action. But as the ground swell of support grew, individuals became very vocal and started to champion the "Save Spring Gully" campaign, and it was time to let them do it.

    As momentum grew, the Spring Gully team communicated what was happening very clearly and personally. There was no hype or rhetoric, just simple facts, enormous gratitude, and reports on the extraordinary results being achieved. This open flow of communication helped the campaign to keep gathering momentum.

    The Spring Gully story has ended well. We can all learn from their experience and take the right steps that ensure that if faced with a major challenge, our customers will indeed fight for us.

BREE'S TAKE

I love this story, and it instantly made me think "would my customers fight for my business?" and the answer was a resounding yes; I honestly think that they would if I needed them to. There are literally hundreds of things that we can all do, that show you are a company that cares about your community.

Of course it goes to reason, that if you are a company that cares about your community, your community will care about you. Find a business to admire and treat as a role model. One that seems to always be doing the right thing, always supporting local organisations and encouraging their team to do the same. The company leaders that always seem to be giving their time and resources to help those who need it. Learn from them and model your own business and life around these amazing businesses and the people who lead them.

And remember, it's not all about giving money. Sure, that's important, but it is by no means everything. Write down what you are currently doing to show that you care about your customers and your community and ask if there is anything else you could be doing?

54

Can too much experience be a bad thing?

On a recent trip to the hair salon, my lovely stylist told me about the marketing initiatives she had put into place to help ramp up her business. In particular, she was talking about an advertisement that she had put together for the local newspaper, promoting the fact that she and her partner have more than 30 years of combined experience.

I commented on how impressive this was. Then, in a conspiratorial whisper, she mentioned that they actually have more than 50 years' experience between them. But they didn't want anyone to know.

Now this struck me as very strange, surely the more experience you have the better, right? But as my stylist explained, if she promoted 50 years of combined experience, potential customers might think that the salon was run by a couple of old biddies who were still doing perms and blue rinse dyes from the 1970's and would send anyone under the age of 70 running.

This raises a very interesting point. We entrepreneurs almost always boast about how long we have been in business. We use our tenure to make potential customers feel more confident in making a buying decision. Surely if a business has been in business for a long period of time, that is a good thing right?

Now I am not so sure.

In today's world, it's easy to see how decades of experience could have negative connotations. Are you as innovative as a young, hungry start-up? Are you using technology as much as you should be? Has your service grown complacent? Are you at the cutting edge, or resting comfortably on your laurels? And will you charge more simply because you have been around for a long time as opposed to charging more because you are good at what you do?

Such questions have led me to rethink the idea of tenure as a marketing tool. Of course, there are merits in showing that you have been around long enough to be credible. But spotlighting five decades in business might work against you, especially if you are delivering products and services to customers who are more concerned about what you can do for them today.

Of course, it depends what industry you are in. If I was getting brain surgery to remove a tumor, I would much rather have the specialist who has done this operation a thousand times than the guy who is trying it for the first time.

For any business that has been operating for a long period of time, it is important to be really clear about the message you send to your potential (and existing) customers. What do they want? Are they looking for a business that has been around for a long time, or one that is at the cutting edge of their industry? Maybe highlighting all those years of experience is a good thing. But give the matter some thought before you send a message that sends potential customers running.

BREE'S TAKE

As they say, age is only a number, but I think every year that your business survives and thrives should be celebrated! Being in business is hard work, and we often only celebrate the milestone birthdays, 1st, 5th, 10th, 15th and so on. Now I am not saying that we need to celebrate every year with our customers, that would be overkill.

I do think you need to celebrate your business birthday every year with your team, and your family and friends that have supported you. Or at worst just a private celebration with little old you and your business. You can go as little or as big as you like with this celebration, but you need to acknowledge it and you need to give yourself a pat on the back.

I like to take a look at my business plan at this time, to see how on track I am, and how far I've come from my very first day of business. I also like to reflect on how my business has grown, how different my marketing materials look since the day I started, am I still following my big "why", and am I happy with where I have gotten the business to, to date?

I cringe when I look at where my business started, but it makes me so proud to see where it is today.

SECTION 7

GROWING YOUR BUSINESS MEANS MORE THAN JUST SELLING STUFF.

Generally, business owners are good at selling, simply because if they don't sell, they don't eat. Wonderful incentive really. It's easy to think that the key to growing a business is to simply sell more stuff, and in some ways it is. But turning that concept into a reality is much more complicated than it might sound. There are a lot of things we need to consider if we want to grow our business and there are many ways to get it wrong.

In this section we look long and hard at business growth from a number of directions. Each is equally important in our eyes. We also need to develop many other skills along the way, and also have a good dose of reality and soul searching. So some old favourites come back into play; trust, self review, rituals, routines and communication. We love them all.

55

It's time to stop selling and start proving
we can be trusted.

Up until a few years ago, anyone talking about their business in any shape or form, would go to great lengths to explain how perfect it was and by association how perfect they were. We were encouraged to believe that it would be madness to take our business anywhere but to them. And to a large degree we believed everything we were told, or at least we tried to believe it.

The thought of a business owner talking about their mistakes, their ongoing issues, their insecurities and their failings and then expecting us to buy from them was pretty much crazy talk. But not anymore.

In fact we have gone in the exact opposite direction. We are reading books about vulnerability, we are listening to talks showcasing some entrepreneurs never ending list of faults and failings, and we are being driven by emotive words like kindness, generosity and trust.

A lot of this is because our BS detectors are highly tuned these days. We no longer believe the stories of perfection. And any business that tries too hard to tell us how perfect they are, is likely to be put under extreme scrutiny. If it doesn't stack up, through social media and word of mouth from those within our community, look out.

So what does this mean for business owners today? It means you have to be prepared to write and talk about yourself and your business in a very open and honest way. You need to be able to admit what you are good at, and what you are not good at. Share your story, the good bits and tough bits, and you need to rely on others saying the right things about you, ensuring what you say and what they say aligns.

Most important of all you need to develop a reputation that others will trust, and this isn't something that you can turn on in a couple of days. To really build trust, takes years, in many cases a lifetime, and it can be lost in a heartbeat.

How do we build trust? Here are a few really straight-forward and proven ideas:

- Deliver what you promise-always.

- Treat every single person you meet with respect.

- Play a proactive role in your community-it's not just about money.

- Build a reputation for being fair, which means you don't have to win every encounter.

- Be careful with whom you associate, if you lay down with dogs, you get up with fleas.

- Think before you post-this of course can apply to 'talk', 'write' or 'press send'.

- Proudly support your industry-don't be one of those people who does nothing but complain about everyone else in their industry.

- Act consistently all of the time (ideally consistently nice).

- Be really generous.

- Share your failings as much as your strengths.

Really the bottom line is that we all should be doing our best to make sure we never give anyone a reason to lose their trust in us. Now these suggestions might sound simple, and they are, but we need to treat them with respect because they are powerful. Combine these trust building concepts and you really will be trusted, but you have to do them with authenticity. You can't fake trust.

BREE'S TAKE

Nope you can't fake trust. So what can you do if your business has lost your customer's trust? We've all been on the receiving end of where a business we have really been a loyal customer to, does something, which shakes our faith in them. Here are a few steps which might help to start the rebuilding process.

Firstly, you need to acknowledge what you did wrong and that you are sorry that you have lost their trust. You need to totally own it, no excuses, no blame. Just admit what you have done wrong and apologise in a sincere way.

Secondly, you need to state how you are going to fix it, or ask the person or business how they think you should fix it? Guessing how to fix an issue is always much harder. Direct feedback is great for two reasons; it makes the customer part of the solution which in turn empowers them and helps to take the edge off of their complaint. At the same time, you may find a solution to the problem, that is going to be far better than what you had imagined. I also think that direct feedback like this also tends to pin point other issues that you were simply not aware of.

Lastly, you need to fix it and then some and then put measures into place so that it never happens again. Your team need to be made aware of the issue, how it was managed and what needs to happen to make sure the problem won't raise its ugly head again.

If you handle the situation well, people can be pretty forgiving and everyone can move on from the situation. At the same time, I think we can learn a lot about building trust in general, based on how we handle a customer complaint. So some reflection is always a good thing.

56

How much business do you want and how much business can you actually cope with?

This is the start to any marketing campaign or plan, and unfortunately it is seldom considered in small businesses. You need to ask yourself the question: how much business do I really want?

There are two reasons to ask this question. The first is to give you a daily target to aim for. If you don't know how much business you want, you will never be satisfied. The other reason is to try to eliminate the risk of getting too much business, yes, that's right, too much business.

It is amazing how clear everything becomes when all of a sudden you know how much business you need to survive, and how much business you want to make a profit. Very few businesses take the time to figure these targets out, but successful ones always do.

The second point, generating too much business brings to mind the following stories. A friend of mine was involved in building a large Oceanarium. The launch of the attraction was very big with hundreds of thousands of dollars spent on enticing crowds for the opening day. Well the crowds came, far more than the Oceanarium had allowed for and the result was that the day was a disaster. People were stuck in queues for hours, the crush of the crowds was crazy, the restaurants ran out of food, children were lost, people fainted, you get the picture.

It took a long time for this attraction to rebuild its reputation, years in fact. The grand opening was a financial success, but a complete failure in terms of long-term marketing. The crowds left after a disappointing experience and consequently they told their family and friends not to bother visiting the attraction because it was a shambles.

Another short story that I have found fascinating has to do with smoking. A friend recently tried to stop smoking following an intensive advertising campaign from the QUIT line (a number people could call for advice and support to quit smoking) on television. The graphic blood and gore advertisements were too much and the QUIT line seemed to be a fabulous support for anyone trying to give up the dreaded nicotine. The advertisement worked and my friend made the decision to quit on the spot.

After a week without cigarettes she had a moment of weakness and decided that she needed help quickly. A quick call to the QUIT line and everything will be OK. She called the line, was put on hold for ten minutes and then a rather rude lady said that she couldn't help now, but someone would call back soon.

Seven days later someone called, apologising about the delay and protesting that the extra advertising had made them so busy that they could not cope with the thousands of calls they were getting every day. By this stage my friend had given up trying to quit and she still smokes.

There is a valuable lesson to be learned. If you start to do a lot of marketing, make certain that your business can cope with the increase. All businesses want the phone to be running hot, but few can cope with a sudden increase in business without making at least a few operational changes.

BREE'S TAKE

As a small business owner, we tend to spend most of our time worrying about getting enough business, the concept of having too much business is hard to fathom. But, it is a reality that we need to plan for, especially as we grow our business.

The key here is that we need to know our numbers really well, and for many business owners this is not a priority. It certainly wasn't for me until I realised the issues this was causing. We need to know some basics:

1. How much does it cost a month, a week, a day and even an hour to run your business?

2. What are your breakeven sales targets, your ideal sales targets and your maximum capacity sales targets?

3. How much profit do you make, how much do you want to make and what will it take to do that?

These need to be monitored daily in my view, but as a minimum, weekly. Knowing them is one thing, the other important consideration is what will you do in the worse case scenarios? For example, what will do you if you don't reach your sales targets? Or alternatively, what if you are booked beyond your capacity? How will you handle the overflow? We need to be strategic in the way we run our business and that really just means making sure we have access to the right information and at the same time we have plans in place for every possible scenario.

57

Most businesses go to great lengths to make this mistake.

Recently I was preparing a keynote presentation for a large group of Financial Advisers. I was doing my homework, checking out their websites, figuring out the best message I could give these professionals, and something slowly started to dawn on me.

In doing my research, I realised that virtually every site I visited used the same words to describe what they did and most started off by saying something like "we are different to other financial advisers". Then they went on to explain how they are exactly the same.

This intrigued me as it seemed like such a fundamental marketing mistake. I checked out fifty accounting websites and every single one of them said they do tax (wow, what a surprise) and business advice. And they all offer amazing service because they put their clients first.

The more industries I investigated, the more obvious it became that the vast majority of businesses within an industry don't know how to say they are different. And selling 101 is all about pointing out how you are different, not how you are the same.

I think there is something comforting about being the same, it feels like there is certainty. But the problem is, it also makes you beige and blend into the background. We live in a world with enormous choice, and businesses that stand out, are the ones that get noticed by creating real emotional connection.

So how do you explain that you are different? Stop listing the services you offer for starters. Start telling potential customers why you do what you do, what it is that got you started in this business, what are you passionate about, where is your business heading, what are your greatest successes and what gets you out of bed in the morning?

In other words, let them know more about the people in the business, their dreams, their aspirations, and their goals. Don't tell them what you do, they will figure that out, but tell them how you do what you do, with passion, with energy, with conviction, with integrity.

Many of us have been trained to write about our businesses in the third person, to make it formal. Those days are gone. No one wants to read some stuffy copy about an organisation; they want the down and dirty story, the struggles, the overcoming adversity, the successes and the characters behind them. Talk about your customers, your suppliers, and the charities you support and why you support them.

Put all of this into a great story and share it. It might feel a little exposing at first, but I guarantee that you will immediately get more engagement with your customers; they will feel like they know you and they will do business with you for the real reasons, not some hyped up corporate lingo that no one believes any more.

Now, more than any other time, we need to go to great lengths to tell people how our business is different, not how it is the same.

BREE'S TAKE

Nothing frustrates me more than seeing a business marketing itself with a "spray and pray" approach, and a big part of this problem is not having a targeted message for a target audience. Creating a targeted message to your target audience is crucial to getting your marketing mix right. Grab a piece of paper and let's get started by answering these questions.

1. What product or service in your business do you want to market? Let's say you are a restaurant and you want to market your children's meals.

2. Who is your targeted audience that you want to market to? I would say parents, but to take it a bit further, it's generally the primary homemaker, which is statistically going to be mothers, over fathers who make the decision on dining. So the target market is mothers.

3. Now think of your three major points of difference that you want mums to know about. Is it that the meals are healthy and homemade; that you have a children's entertainer; that kids eat free with every paying adult? They are three great points of difference.

4. Now you need to think about what marketing mediums mums are engaging with that you can afford. Is it TV, radio, magazines, newspapers, social media, flyers, posters, banners, your website etc. the list goes on.

5. Now it's time to develop these points into simple, yet effective wording that you can use for your chosen media. The amount of words and imagery will be dependent on the marketing mediums you will be using. But always make it punchy.

Now we need to take this simple but very targeted approach to marketing all of our products and services. Too many businesses simply try to promote their business far and wide with poor results, instead of targeting a specific audience with a specific message, to promote a specific product or service.

58

Learning to be detached from the outcome of a big sale is very good for your sanity.

There is no simple instruction book that explains every single thing we need to know to run a business. If there was, it would be a mighty big book. Sure, there are certain aspects of running a business that are common to all. Like knowing your financial details enough to be clear on whether or not you are making money. However, there are other elements of running a business that are less tangible and more behavioral, but just as important.

An example of this is having a realistic attitude towards money. To run a business, we need to be optimistic. But there are times when we need to make sure that we are balancing our optimism with a strong dose of reality. I have worked with business owners who go through one long financial roller coaster ride in their business. One of the biggest reasons for this rough ride is because they assume a sale is complete before the money is even in the bank.

By this I mean they get all of their hopes and plans tied up on the outcome of a big job or project. They have submitted their prices, and their mind races ahead to what this will mean for the business and what they will be able to pay off or buy, as a result of winning the project. The more they visualise the reward, the more real it becomes and in their mind the money is spent long before they have even been awarded the job.

Two difficult things start to happen when feeling like this. Firstly, they become almost desperate to win the project, often without really thinking through what it will mean for the business. Is it as good a project as it seems? How will they fund it, staff it, manage it and so forth?

Secondly, they stop all other business development whilst waiting to be notified regarding the project they are now desperate to hear about. And this can spell disaster.

The first issue can lead to disappointment and depression. In their mind they have already won the job, so if they are told they haven't, it can be very upsetting. Even worse, they have already painted such a mental picture about what the money will do. The depressed feeling of loss can take away all motivation and create other problems in the business, including poor morale for the entire team.

The second issue, stopping all other business development in anticipation of winning the big project, is an even bigger issue. From my experience the bigger the project the longer the decision making process can take. This can lead to long periods of time when a business is doing no business development, pinning all hopes on wining the "big" contract.

So how do we manage these issues? My advice is simple, never assume you have won a project, contract or client until the money is in the bank. It is an old cliché, but it has worked very well for me over many years. I remove the emotional attachment from all projects that I am bidding for. If I get it, great, but I don't hold my breath waiting to find out and I certainly don't stop business development whilst I am waiting to hear.

Learning to be detached from the outcome of any sale will keep you focused and driving your business forward. When you get the first payment of a big project, then celebrate and go a little wild.

BREE'S TAKE

We all want those big deals to pull off, but Andrew is right, a lot of us have spent the money before it's a done deal. As they say, don't count your chickens until they have hatched. You need to plan what you will do if the deal pulls off, you also need to plan what you will do if the deal doesn't pull off. For me, the real key is to keep business developing.

We've all sat back thinking a big deal is going to come off, only to face the disappointment when it doesn't. It's a lot harder to get going when we face this, so just make every day a business development day.

59

Do you want it bad enough to drop everything and get on a plane?

Many years back when I was trying to build my business, grow my profile, and get the type of clients I wanted, I developed a strategy that has helped me to build a global business. My strategy was to never let my geographical location stop me from doing a deal. I would drop everything at a minute's notice, book a plane ticket and go and see a prospective client the very next day.

There were times that I had to fly for 4 hours (or more), have a meeting with a potential client and fly back that same day, simply because I couldn't afford a hotel. But my philosophy was that if I was talking to a prospective client and they were interested in talking to me, I had to strike while the iron was hot. I would say something along the lines of "well coincidentally I have to come to your city this week, can we meet?". Then I would get off the phone and book the trip.

Other times I would actually say that I am prepared to fly down tomorrow to see them. This impressed people and they took our meetings very seriously and acknowledged that I was serious about getting their business.

Now, years later, I still take the same approach. If someone gets in touch with me and they are a good lead, I won't hesitate to book a flight, to go and sit down face to face. Wherever they may be in the world.

Of course we can use Skype, conference calls, Zoom and embrace all kinds of technology, which I do, but I still believe that there is something very compelling about a face to face meeting. I believe in what I do, I'm passionate and have enough confidence to believe that if I get in front of a prospective client I will be able to close the deal. Hence getting on a plane seemed like a safe investment.

Mind you, there were plenty of times when I flew home, deflated because I didn't get the business. But I never stopped getting on planes.

Why did this work so well? I think there are a number of reasons:

It showed a high level of commitment on my behalf. Even though I lived in a regional area, I was mobile, I was able to quickly schedule a visit, turn up in a suit and tie and show them that I was prepared to do what it takes to get their business.

I did what other people weren't prepared to do. And I did it with no certainty that I would end up with a paid job. People noticed this and acknowledged the risk. I have created a lot of business from people who said they were impressed by the fact that I would get on a plane and come to see them immediately.

I built a reputation for being a person who would take action, respond quickly and did what it would take to get the project going. I was never the weakest link, even though I lived a two-hour flight away from the closest capital city.

So what did this proactive approach lead to? It helped me to become a very successful author, by being able to spend time with my publishers. It got me work with many large corporations, all of which are based in capital cities. It got me media opportunities and much more.

My advice is simple. We live in a time when air travel is ridiculously cheap. Use that as one of the marketing tools, that will differentiate you from your competitors. If you make the effort others will notice and that will go a long way to you closing the deal.

BREE'S TAKE

Living in a regional area used to be a disadvantage in business, but not anymore. Yes, regional areas don't get the same opportunities; we don't get the big events, courses or speakers coming to our towns. But just as Andrew described what he has done for years to make a business deal happen, we need to be prepared to get on a plane and go grow our brain and our network.

Of course, the same can be said for people running their business in a capital city – perhaps getting out and visiting a regional area will challenge the way you do business and provide insights and perspectives that could help you grow.

Every year I make a point of going to a number of conferences that will help me to develop new skills and expertise, and also help me to grow my network. Getting out of my home town challenges my way of thinking. It enables me to learn new things and bring them back to my team, it introduces me to new people, who help me do what I do, better.

Our view is simple, don't be scared to jump on a plane to do a business deal, to grow your own skill set, and to grow your network. Sometimes we just need to do it, to get an energetic fix that comes from being around a group of motivated, like minded people.

I suggest that you put a budget aside every year that goes to your own personal development and growth. I do – and it's the best investment I make every year.

60

We need to become great at telling our customers what's new (and even what's old).

We live in a world that is obsessed with everything new. I don't think there has ever been a time where consumers crave new as much as they do today. If your business has mastered the art of coming up with new products and services, fantastic, but now might be the time to ask if you are making the cardinal sin of forgetting to tell your customers.

I see this a lot in small businesses everywhere. I literally stumble across a new product or service that a business is offering and it's usually one that I would have bought ages ago if I knew it existed, but the business owner simply didn't think to mention it. They assumed that everyone would figure it out. This is a very dangerous assumption to make in any business.

There are two key considerations here. The first is to make sure you are educating your customers about anything and everything new with every medium possible. The second is to keep educating them, don't assume one email has the problem solved. Remember it is your job to educate them, not their job to automatically know what is going on in your business.

To dive a little deeper, we all have a range of mechanisms to update customers about anything new going on in our business. Off the top of my head here are just a few:

- Social media

- On your website

- On your blog

- Through email (and email signatures)

- Pick up the phone and tell them

- On your invoices

- Signage on your vehicle

- In your waiting room

- Send a letter

- On your phone message

- Signage

- In your advertising

Of course it depends on the kind of business you run, but I think you get the point. Then the question is how long do we need to keep telling people about this new product or service? How long is too long? These are tough questions to answer.

Various research will say that a person needs to hear a message somewhere between 7 and 10 times before it sinks it. I don't think it is that clear. Personally I tend to hear a message much faster when it is relevant to me.

The moral to the story is that these days there is no one single communication mechanism that captures everyone and there are different things that different people are attuned to listen out for (mostly subconsciously). This means that you have to communicate the new products or services often, across all of the various forms of media. Most people don't, and that's the problem and the missed opportunity.

Remember we get sick of hearing the message long before our customers do.

BREE'S TAKE

Let's face it, we all make this error in our business. Grab a sheet of paper and let's list all the things our customers should know about our business (but maybe they don't) and every single thing they can buy from us.

Once you have compiled your list, take a really good look at it and ask yourself these questions.

1. What products or services make me the most money?

2. Am I promoting & marketing the products or services that make the most money, in the very best way that I can?

3. What else could I do to market these high profit products or services?

4. What other products or services do I have that my current clients would love but may not know about?

5. What am I missing off my list? Are there some future products or services that I want to bring in; is it worth market testing these?

Every product and service that you have needs attention. The ones we sell the most of tend to be the ones we give the most attention to. What are the gaps in your marketing? What products or services are you not giving the attention they deserve? And what do we assume our customers know about our business, but in reality they don't?

I absolutely love the point Andrew makes "remember we get sick of hearing the message long before our customers do". So true.

61

A big mistake in negotiating a deal is talking money too early - you might blow the opportunity before it even begins.

I recently had an email from a friend of mine regarding an opportunity that she was finding a little overwhelming. To put it simply, this was one of the biggest opportunities for a joint venture that she had ever had and the pressure was starting to show. A very big and very respected company wanted to buy her business and intellectual property for a global project and they wanted a proposal from her as soon as possible.

My friend was struggling to come up with prices, what did she really want? All of the 'what if's' and 'what could be' thoughts were combining to make her feel a little overwhelmed. Add to this the pressure of an impending meeting with the company, where she felt that she needed to attend with a detailed proposal with all details finalised, things were getting a little out of control.

My advice was very simple. She was trying to get to the dollar value of the deal and address all of the added complications, before she had enough information. From my experience most larger organisations move very slowly, and whilst it may feel like a deal is moving ahead like a freight train, rest assured it will be slowed down the minute it hits the legal department. Then it will go at glacial speed as all risks are assessed and the minute details worked through.

I suggested that she go to the meeting, with some ideas, nothing finalised, and talk to them. Voice her concerns as well as the opportunity as she sees it, and get them to do the same. If it takes ten meetings, or a hundred meetings, take your time. Look at each meeting as a fact-finding mission and a way to get more clarity and at some stage, you will have enough information to start structuring the deal accordingly.

Taking my advice, my friend did exactly this, the deal has proceeded and it is easily the biggest financial opportunity of her life so far. Only when you fully understand the deal and how it can work, can you really put a detailed proposal together, with the right dollar and cents value, and the negotiation can commence.

All too often we feel the pressure to put a price on something before we have enough information to accurately do this. It's far better to get the deal right, rather than get the deal fast.

Interestingly, another friend of mine, a consultant in the field of Neuroscience, always makes a point of doing a preliminary project, free of charge for the client before they commence down the path of a commercial arrangement. This might be a workshop or some coaching with key people. The reason she does this is to ensure that she is the right fit for the organisation - and if the preliminary work indicates that she is not, for whatever reason, she can walk away, with no negative feelings from the client.

Bottom line, take your time to get all of the information you need. Then make an informed decision about where you go from there. Don't get pressured by others to give a price prematurely. If you do, it might just end badly.

BREE'S TAKE

Think about deals and opportunities in the past that you have been a part of. Think about the deals that you went ahead with. Think about the deals that you didn't. Why didn't you?

Think about how the conversation went when the topic of money came up in both situations. Is there a correlation with the deals that you got and the deals that you didn't, when it came to talking money? Did you in fact talk money too soon on the ones that you didn't get?

One of the key elements of being a successful business owner is the ability to constantly review and learn from our past experiences. If we do this in enough area's we can't help but improve. It's not about getting it right all the time, but hopefully as our experience grows, we get it right more than we get it wrong.

62

If you want to make your proposals more powerful and win more work, try this.

When I was a marketing consultant, to win work I generally had to write a proposal of some sort, outlining what I would do, by when and how much it would cost. The better the proposal, the better my chances of winning the project.

I was going through a stage where I wasn't winning as much work as I wanted to (or needed to). I had some testimonials, but I felt that my proposals needed something more. So I decided to be really open and honest, and give my prospective clients access to my most recent clients.

I started to list my last ten projects along with the client's direct contact details, with their permission. I encouraged the prospective client to contact each and every one of them. I explained in the proposal that these are not vetted contacts; the list is simply updated with the latest ten projects done by my firm.

Now, this is much more powerful than testimonials alone. It is a real-time, current and an accessible list of people, prepared to share their experiences of working with me, and I didn't really know what they are going to say.

You can't be selective and just pick those clients that you know will say nice things. Especially if you haven't done work for them for sometime, because any smart person sees through this in a second.

So the bonus here is that you really have to make sure that you are delivering a high level of service and value for money, to each and every client, and that is just good business.

I immediately started to win a lot more work. The value of the work increased and the feedback from the new clients was that they really liked the open approach to sharing my contacts for the most recent projects. Not a meaningless testimonial from a project I did five years ago.

In business, credibility and trust come from putting your money where your mouth is, by being open and transparent.

BREE'S TAKE

I really like this idea of Andrew's, and I am sure his upfront approach actually meant that very few people reference checked this list of business owners. The idea and the list in itself was enough credibility. But what if we aren't a consultant; what if we are in retail, hospitality or another industry that deals with the general public? We still want credibility from our existing customers, but we might need to take a different approach.

This means we need to find ways to encourage people to talk about our business online, through social media and of course in the real world as well. My advice when it comes to looking for ideas, is to once again become a student. Look at those businesses that do it really well and always seem to get incredible engagement with their customers, who are very vocal at promoting them. How do they do it? What campaigns do they run? What social media platforms do they use? What do their customers say about them and why? We don't have to come up with every new idea, but we do need to be smart enough to learn from those going before us who are doing it really well. Then we need to be brave enough to give these ideas a go in our business. What's the worse that can happen?

63

Sometimes the smallest ideas can have a surprisingly big impact.

For those businesses that send out invoices, I think it's time to rethink the opportunity we have here. Invoices are always seen as a perfunctory kind of document, sent with the hope of fast payment in most cases. But I think they are much more.

I see invoices as a great opportunity to build relationships, educate clients, sell your services and generate more money.

Who reads invoices? Well of course it depends on the size of the business you are sending it to. If it is a small business, generally it will go to the business owner, the decision maker and the person you want to influence the most.

For a mid-sized company, it may go to the accounts department, but generally a manager of some sort will need to approve it, and once again we get to influence someone in a positive way.

For a larger company, their systems and resources generally mean that they have a bigger finance department. Your invoice might make it to a manager or someone else of authority within the company, will still have to approve it for payment.

So in short, it is very likely that our invoice will be seen by a number of people, many of whom we want to influence in some way. How do we go about making an invoice more effective as a marketing and relationship building tool? Here are 10 ideas that you might like to give a go:

1. If you do anything for free, put it on your invoice and make a point of high-lighting "NO COST". Don't assume your client knows or remembers what you do for free.

2. Introduce a new staff member with every invoice, make it fun, make it personal and let people see inside your business. Always include a photo to give it that personal touch.

3. Put a customer testimonial on your invoices. Reinforce the fact that the customer you are sending this invoice to has made a great decision.

4. If you support a charity, put it on your invoice. Explain why you support that particular charity, what you do to support them, and be proud of your contribution.

5. Won an award lately? Don't be shy-let everyone know, but if it has been a while since you won the award, let it go. People will question why you haven't won anything since.

6. Make a commitment statement of what you promise to deliver to your customers. This might be in terms of attitude, collaboration, help, support etc. For example, "Our mission is to make your company a market leader by using our products".

7. Educate your customers by telling them about new products and services.

8. Have some fun by sharing some of the most commonly asked questions that are little out of the ordinary (or downright weird).

9. Let your customers know that you value and appreciate their business. You also realise that they have a choice and they chose you. Make this a humble and sincere thank you.

10. Tell a joke, put a smile on the face of whoever reads your invoice and make them look forward to the next one (but be smart about it, no sexist, racist or political jokes-unless they are about Donald Trump).

By making your invoice a little more memorable you might even find that you get paid more quickly and I've never come across a business owner who complains about that.

BREE'S TAKE

Andrew's ideas are great; they remind me of one of his stories about a family with a gardening company that were struggling to get paid in a timely manner by their clients. Andrew felt that the problem was that there was no engagement between the business and its customers. They did a great job, they went above and beyond the call of duty in all that they did, but they still had to wait on average 90 days to get paid. Andrew suggested that they should start a storytelling photo series on their invoices, to create engagement.

So it started with a family photo stating, "We loving taking care of your garden, but we can't pay our bills on time if you don't pay ours on time. Please pay your bill promptly so we can continue to take care of your beautiful garden". Now I know that some of you will feel a cringe to do something as direct as this, but it worked and it worked wonderfully well. The payments started to flow in, along with notes of apology for being slow to pay. And people actually started to send photos of their family back with their payments, as a way of introduction.

But the problem wasn't entirely solved. So the next month the business owners sent their invoices with a photo of the family sitting in a wrecked old bomb truck, saying "To make sure we keep offering the best service we need to upgrade our truck, but to do that we need to get paid a little quicker. We would really appreciate it if you could pay your bills within 7 days.". Again the result was instant and there were even offers of prepayment from some customers to help the business owners raise the money for the new truck.

Of course this got Andrew thinking, so he suggested that they took it a step further and try to get all of their clients to pre-pay for their garden maintenance?

The invoice series evolved to include photos of the pet dog with an empty food bowl, the mother in-law chained to a tree, to mention a few. Each of which came with a nice message but also a request of some sort. What was the result? Within six months the business went from waiting an average of 90 days to get paid, to being fully pre-paid for all of their services.

The moral to the story is simple. Utilise your invoices as a marketing tool, and if you are up for it, make them personalised. You will be surprised at the results it creates for your business. But really the bigger message is about engagement. The better we can engage with our customers the stronger our business will be. We need to be looking for as many ways as possible to create meaningful engagement, and there are many.

64

Turn a Monday morning ritual into a quirky marketing campaign.

Something that drives me crazy is a voicemail message that you can hardly understand. The person sounds really bored, they mumble, it's the same message that they have had for the past ten years. They are doing everything to maintain being beige in a world that craves color.

My advice is to try doing this - every Monday morning, change your voice mail message on your mobile phone (or office phone or ideally both). Make it the first thing you do, and use it to set your mood for the week.

Put some thought into what you are going to say. Perhaps change your greeting (a new language for "hello" every week-there's a few hundred messages and it will be educational), read out an inspirational quote, tell a joke, give a business tip, say something about yourself that most people won't know. Get someone else to record your message and make it sound strange and quirky (like a lady recording a man's voice mail). Go to Fiverr and get a Darth Vader voice mail message and so on. Have way too much fun with it, but make it your ritual.

Sometimes it's easy to dismiss something like this as being silly, but in reality, it is a great way to stand out from the crowd, especially if you have a very busy phone.

People will start looking forward to this week's message, and in some ways, you can actually start to use your voice mail as a community-building tool and a marketing campaign.

A few years back I was working with a law firm and they felt beige. They were the same as everyone else, but they wanted to be different and somehow let their personalities shine through. So we came up with a campaign where we put lawyer jokes on their office "on hold" message.

The response was huge. Clients said they actually liked ringing their lawyer and they even rang back and asked to be put on hold so they could hear the end of a joke. The lawyers made fun of themselves and took it in turns to come up with new jokes every week (fortunately there has never been a shortage of lawyer jokes).

This simple idea created a lot of word of mouth. No one complained that they felt that the firm was less professional in any way, and it started a number of cheeky and fun campaigns.

We live in a world where you need to find some way to stand out, there are many, but quirky ideas like this are easy, cheap and fun.

BREE'S TAKE

Andrew hates boring voicemail, I hate voice to text (which he has by the way...) nothing is worse than trying to leave a message for someone in 10 seconds that is going to be transcribed. So if you ever call Mr. Andrew Griffiths, be sure to leave a message like I do, which is "I hate voice to text, call Bree" which usually gets translated and texted to him as "I have a cat called Britney".

Now that I've gotten that off my chest, I do love the idea of being more creative with your answering machine and hold music. Today's challenge is to look at the voicemail and hold music for all of your company phones to see what you could do that is a little bit fun and quirky.

65

When it comes to negotiating, are you a monster?

Some people simply have to win at everything. They treat every negotiation as a battle, never satisfied for both parties to come out with a fair deal. Instead they have to feel like they have gotten the best of their opponent. I think this comes from some misguided "Wolf of Wall Street" syndrome, that has "win at any cost" at its core.

We all know people like this and most of us dread doing business with them, because every interaction ends with a feeling of being "ripped off". They will negotiate on the purchase of a bus ticket. They are obsessed with the win, to the point where they spend their life burning people.

Negotiating is a part of life. In business we need to be good negotiators to make sure we can run our businesses as profitably as possible. But the key word here is fair. I always remember one of my earliest mentors sitting me down and explaining that if you are entering every negotiation with the intent of making sure that all parties can make some money, you will never have a shortage of people who want to work with you. And he was absolutely spot on.

I have to negotiate with suppliers, such as graphic designers, media outlets, printers and subcontractors. I want to have a good relationship with these companies and

I want them to do the best job possible for my clients. If I negotiate them down on price to the point where the project is only marginally profitable, they will lose interest, I will get a marginal quality job from them, and the real loser is my client.

I make it clear to my clients from the start, we want to do the best job at the fairest price. If they want a cheaper job done, they should find someone else to do it. This philosophy has enabled me to build an excellent network of suppliers who do a great job every time. They make good money out of each project, my company makes good money and the client gets the best end result possible.

Develop your own philosophy and approach to negotiating, and by all means, develop your skills as a negotiator. Take a mature approach to negotiating. Think of the big picture and the power of a strong relationship built on mutual respect, and the importance of everyone feeling that the relationship is fair and valued.

Saving a few bucks in the short term could have a serious impact on the long term.

BREE'S TAKE

Every sale I make, I do it with the intention of it being mutually beneficial, or, me giving more value to the other person.

I do this because I would never want anyone to feel like they haven't gotten what they paid for.

Look at your sales technique, are you too focused about what is in it for you? If you are, it's likely you aren't getting much repeat business.

Most customers are looking for more value these days, and they have the power of Google to check out whether they are getting a good deal or not. Remember there is more to a deal than price. Most of us focus on the price as the key motivator for a sale, but there are things like trust, knowledge, convenience and customer service that are valued commodities in a sale and people are generally prepared to pay more if these considerations come into play.

Think about it. You see an electronics product online from a website that you don't know where the business is located or even what country they are from. You check it out further and find that your local electronics store has the same product available, albeit a little bit higher priced, but you can at least go and check it out.

So you go and visit the store, talk to the sales person and they make you feel comfortable with their knowledge about the product. You realise that if you buy it from them and you have a problem, you now have someone you can take it to and talk to, which builds your trust further to purchase the product. The decision is made.

People make decisions differently, but we all want to feel like we have spent our money wisely, even if that means we pay more. Take some time today to think about what you can do to add value to your sale. It doesn't have to be extra products, it can be extra services and support. Just remember, that all people want to feel like they have spent their money wisely, and made a safe purchasing decision. It is most certainly not just about price anymore.

66

Three tips to increase your global online sales.

When it comes to selling online, just about anyone with a website has the potential to sell their product or service around the world. For the first time in history, the smallest of businesses can compete with the largest of companies in the international arena.

That said, simply getting a website and telling people that you can ship internationally is a good start, but there is so much more. If you want to attract more business from international markets, regardless of the type of business you have, you need to think globally as opposed to locally.

As we all become more comfortable with buying internationally, the opportunity to sell cross borders and time zones will continue to grow. Here are three tips that will help you get more business from around the world:

1. **Make your website "feel" global.** Many websites have very localised language, meaning they are written in a way that is relevant to their local market, but not to an international market. When someone is reading this information from afar, they may feel that the business doesn't want to sell internationally, or that it is too local to be relevant to them.

Wherever possible, write about how you can deliver your products or services internationally. Make it sound easy, give the potential customer confidence in your organisation. Talk about the relevance of your product or service on a global level, as opposed to a local level. This can literally mean saying "we deliver our products (or service) to many countries around the world." or "we look forward to continuing to offer the highest level of service, support and back up to all of our clients, wherever they may be in the world."

Another way to give your website an international flair is to have global testimonials once you start selling abroad. Ask your past customers to give some feedback in the form of a short punchy high-five. As you deal with more countries, list them on your website. It is all about reducing the perceived risk to a potential customer and testimonials are still one of the best ways to do this.

2. **Make sure you set up a 24 hour-7 day customer response.** Speed of response is one of the most important elements of success. Any business with an automated email that explains how someone will be in touch with you in 48-72 hours may as well not have a website. The problem with international orders is that time zones are generally different to yours, meaning there can already be a lag time of 12-18 hours before a response is received and this is too long to wait in our uber-connected world.

Try outsourcing after hours email responses. Or breaking your sales teams into split shifts to manage after hours' emails and enquiries. The faster your response, the more sales you will generate; this is universally applicable to any country in the world.

Recently I was visiting a travel site, enquiring about a holiday. I received a prompt email back from the site, with the relevant information. Then the consultant asked me a few questions about where I was from. She was interested to know a little more about Australia. We developed an instant rapport, swapped some emails and I booked the holiday. Why? Because it wasn't just an automated response, with no real interaction. It was two people having a conversation, trust was established, and purchasing was made easy.

3. **Integrate cultural training as part of your sales team training.** Anyone doing sales, either over the phone, or via email, should undergo some cultural

training. Learn a little about your markets, the countries where customers come from, the appropriate language to use, etc. It is easy to dismiss a poorly written email, but when English is someone's second language, their email might look a little amateurish-but you should never assume that they are not a serious potential customer. Undergoing some simple cultural awareness training, can result in increased conversion of sales enquiries.

Then you can do snappy things like create greetings for customers in their native language. Being an Australian, a typical greeting in this neck of the woods is "g'day." I always find it nice when I get emails from other countries and the greeting is a traditional Aussie "g'day." It shows that the sender has made an effort to connect and engage. Taking this one step further, and because I do work in a lot of countries, I made up a list of traditional greetings and sign offs, both formal and casual, for the twenty most common countries where I do business. I am amazed by how often people comment about the fact that I used the right greeting or sign off in my correspondence and how appreciative they are.

Once again, it is all about creating connection at an international level.

BREE'S TAKE

I love Andrew's thoughts on this. Many of us think too small when it comes to our dreams. We really are one very connected world now, and we need to think accordingly, especially in terms of doing business. It's a very cool feeling to start selling things to people on the other side of the world. And it makes you realise just how many more customers there are out there.

One of the things I have done for the past decade is run four parenting magazines, and we were once criticised for what the lady called "white washing". She felt our website and publication did not have enough variety of different cultures, nor did my team reflect a multicultural office.

I was a little shocked to read her email, but I took her comments on board and decided to do some self-reflection. I looked over the past 12 months worth of magazines that we had published. Thankfully I was able to pull together quite a few covers, stories and examples to demonstrate that we try very hard to be inclusive of families of different race, gender, special needs and different family compositions. I put her mind at ease that we were far from what she had stated. This exercise and the ladies comments made me realise that we do live in such a global market now. Even if you only do business in one geographic location, it doesn't mean your clients are. All of us have clients made up of many different people, all coming from different backgrounds, cultures, nationalities and so on. We need to consider this in our marketing and in particular, the images we use.

Today, take a look at your business. Could you sell anything globally? If not now, could you create something that could be in the future? A book, some resources, content or products? Really think about it and put some of Andrew's ideas above into practice.

Regardless of whether you have anything to sell or offer globally or not, fix up your website so that it speaks to a global and multicultural audience. All of us run a business in a multi-cultural town or city today, so at worst you are creating a website that will connect more meaningfully with your current clientele.

SECTION 8

THE BEST IDEAS FOR GROWING
YOUR BUSINESS WILL COME FROM
THE PLACES YOU LEAST EXPECT.

The concept of looking for ideas to grow your business from outside of your own industry warrants its own section. We are HUGE fans and advocates of a term called "cross industry innovation", which basically means studying other businesses in other industries, to look for ideas to do what we do better. This is a hot topic, one that is being explored by giant corporations and micro businesses alike. And of course, exploring this concept has never been easier thanks to the internet, do a search for "cross industry innovation" and you will see what we mean.

There is so much that we can learn from outside of our own industry, but most of us tend to look at the competitor up the road for ideas, which really doesn't make that much sense when you think about it. The ideas we get from the outside world can impact on everything from the products and services we offer, smart business practices, marketing ideas and much more. And of course, we can also get a few other ideas from a little closer to home like our existing customers, so we explore that in this section as well.

67

What can you learn from that one business that seems to get it so right, all of the time?

We all know that one particular business that just seems to get it right all of the time. They are consistent in all that they do, they are the leaders in competitive markets, they always seem to be one step ahead of other similar businesses and generally they do very well financially. To put it simply, everything they do, they do well and we need to learn from them.

Just as it's a good idea to visit your competitors' businesses (something I encourage all of my clients to do), it's also useful to take your team to visit a business that you really admire. Just as we have personal role models, having a business role model is a great way to develop an internal culture of continuous improvement.

Over the years I've done this with my teams and recommended it to many clients. The admired business doesn't need to be in your industry, in fact often it is better if it isn't. It simply needs to be a business that is very smart and one that you can learn from.

I often find that businesses become a little stifled by their peers and by their industry. Innovative ideas are confined to what the competitors do. Whilst I believe that it's important to compare your business with your opposition, there are many other excellent ideas out there that can be adapted and used in your business, by looking beyond the borders of your industry.

If you go to a beauty salon and they have a great promotional idea, with a little smart thinking, you can usually change a few details and use the same promotion in a lawyer's office or a restaurant or a mechanics workshop.

When taking your staff on a field trip to a business that you admire, talk to them prior to the visit about the types of things you would like them to observe. Have a good debrief after the visit and see what points they have picked up that you may have missed.

What about online businesses? I think you can do the same thing, it's just that the visit is virtual. Sit down as a team and go through the entire site, actually make a booking or buy a product. Perhaps make an enquiry and see how long it takes to get a response. Go deep, spend time and really take the site for a test drive. A lot can be learned from this exercise.

The bottom line, we can all learn a lot from smart businesses. Often they are right under our nose, we just need to think beyond trying to find ideas within our own industry. The gold lies with cross industry thinking and innovation.

BREE'S TAKE

I love this idea and I know that I've always had certain businesses that I've looked up to and admired. They have acted as role models for me and encouraged me to aspire to continually get better at what I do.

So do you have a business or two that you really admire? They can be a giant multinational corporation or a little corner store (we can learn a great deal from both I might add). Ask yourself a few simple questions:

1. What are the things you love about these businesses – and be very specific?

2. How do they make you feel? This can be tough to articulate but try.

3. Is there anything you don't like about these businesses?

4. What would you have to do to make your business more like theirs?

5. Where would you start?

Talk to your team, do they share your views?

A common theme that you will notice running through this book is the importance of being really good at observing other businesses and learning from them. We need to make these observations part of our day to day conversations with our team, with other business owners, and with our advisors.

68

What can we learn from the growing ranks of 'Petpreneurs'?

I spend a lot of time talking to entrepreneurs around the world, studying what they do, learning about their various industries and innovations and doing my utmost to work out their trials and tribulations. To me, the most impressive group of entrepreneurs, is without a doubt the Petpreneurs.

The pet industry is worth around $100 billion per year globally, a huge market and one that is growing rapidly. What is driving this incredible industry? Without a doubt it is the changing relationship between people and their pets. Pets are now considered a part of the family and as such, pet owners will do everything they can to care for them, entertain them and ensure they have a long and healthy life.

Petpreneurs are very smart. They know their target market extraordinarily well. They know what drives them; they know that they will spend what they need to do to ensure a good life for their pet and they are always looking for new products and services. And the Petpreneurs are keen to supply them.

We live in a world where there are two types of industries-those that have really learned to adapt and thrive in the new tech based world and those that are struggling to evolve and in many cases, probably won't survive. The one thing that the Petpreneurs of the world are crystal clear about, and a lesson for us all, is that they are totally focused on evolving with their market. This is the key to success for any industry or any entrepreneur.

Here are some of the interesting innovations that Petpreneurs have come up with in recent times. Some are still in the crowd funding stage but getting plenty of interest. Most of these illustrate the understanding that Petpreneurs have of the growing bond, between pets and their owners, and the role of the pet in the family line up:

- Sleeping bags for dogs to enable them to camp with their owners (because dogs can't sleep outside anymore).

- A new service that sends dead pets into outer space with prices ranging from $995 to $12,500.

- A smart device that can track tail wags and translate them into how the dog is feeling emotionally (they turn tail wags into chin wags).

- A headset that can translate a dog's thoughts so that humans can understand them.

- A British company has developed a washing machine that can be used by dogs. At this stage it is intended for support dogs but I'm sure it won't be long before we are expecting our dogs to do some of the household chores (my dog is not happy about this).

- "Wonderboo" is a small brown food truck in the Swedish capital which caters to health-conscious dog lovers and their pampered pets.

- JFK airport is going to build a luxury airport terminal for precious animals. The ARK-which will cost about $48M, and offer luxury pre-flight hospitality for about 70,000 animals a year.

- A gaming console for dogs keeps them busy when owners are out.

- A dedicated TV channel for dogs which entertains pets while owners are away. DOGTV is a 24/7 cable television channel which aims to keep pooches entertained. The channel features specialist programming developed using research from pet behavior experts.

- And last but not least, recently there was a concert held for dogs in Time Square.

So whilst in many ways the pet industry is cute, and people are coming up with clever ideas all the time, don't underestimate just how savvy this industry sector is.

BREE'S TAKE

As a pet owner whose fur babies took a little bit of a backseat once the real babies arrived, this industry makes me go WOW. Just wow. What this reminds us, is that there is serious money to be made in many industries these days, and we are in for truly exciting times in the years ahead.

We all need to learn from these innovative thinkers and understand these three points:

1. The key to capturing any market is to really know your market.

2. You have to evolve with your market or be left behind.

3. We need to keep developing products and services to meet their needs.

Now these might sound simple, but how many industries fail to follow them? And sadly, they go the way of the dodo. Take some time today to think about what you could do to innovate your business, or even bigger, your industry. Look at those industries that really are evolving and learn from how they do it. At the same time, look at those industries that have failed to evolve, and see how sad their demise is.

69

The best advice you could ever want or need is right under your nose.

Whilst the rock stars of the entrepreneurial world tend to be the ones who get most of the airplay (for very good reason-they are really impressive), I often wonder if we miss some of the best advice simply because we don't think to ask those less famous for their wisdom.

Last week I had the great pleasure of meeting a man who was the third generation owner of a sausage and ham making business. His name is Edwin, he is 75, at the tail end of his business career and ready to pass the reins to his son.

I asked Edwin for the best advice that he would offer to entrepreneurs starting out today. He thought about this long and hard, and then he quietly said, "This is not a big idea, or flash, or tech, but the thing I have learned the hard way, is the importance of learning to listen to your instinct. Most of the biggest mistakes I have made over the years, have all come back to me not listening to my intuition".

Sage advice that I agree with wholeheartedly. I love old entrepreneurs like Edwin. In fact, I love all business owners who have overcome the odds and proven that they can make a business work.

Is Edwin's advice any less valuable than advice from Richard Branson? Not to me, and that is my point. I think that in our hunger to look for words of wisdom from the big end of the entrepreneurial town, we often overlook the mountains of wisdom all around us. All we have to do is reach out and ask.

Every time I meet a business owner that has built a successful business, I ask them for their best piece of advice to help guide me. I have no doubt at all that I've been given the best advice imaginable through these encounters, that's why I keep doing it.

It might be the corner store owner, your accountant, the local restaurateur- it doesn't really matter. Reach out and ask them what advice would they give to the 18-year-old version of themselves? You might be very surprised by what they have to say and share.

Being successful in business takes an open and determined mind. Smart entrepreneurs are hungry for advice from those who have gone before them. Because they realise that by asking the right questions, they might avoid making the same mistakes.

Have you got an Edwin that you see every day who could share some wonderful pearls of wisdom if you simply ask? By all means, love and embrace the big names of the entrepreneurial world, but let's not forget the everyday business owners who are doing impressive things every day and have probably been doing them for many years.

My advice, find the Edwins close by, take the time to track them down, buy them a coffee and ask them to tell you their story. It will be time well spent for you, and a wonderful mark of respect for them. Everyone wins.

BREE'S TAKE

I have always had a strong rapport with those well advanced in life. It's often been a bit of a laugh for my friends that the oldest person in a room will always track me down and find me for a chat, but I've always loved my conversations and I always leave with a piece of gold.

I recall one man after a conference spoke about his regrets in his life. To see this man in his eighties so remorseful for not loving the people in his life more because he was too busy, and now facing a life alone, was really heartbreaking. I knew he was trying to kindly say to me "love the people in your life with all your heart".

Or the older lady that seemed fifty but was ninety that once told me "live your life, really live it and do all the things that you want to do, don't wait. Then when you are old, and your body stops working so well, you can live them again in your mind, and through your stories to your grandchildren".

If I can have as much life in my eyes and as sharp a brain and body as she in my nineties I will be super happy. Since that day, I have taken her advice and it's the best advice I've ever received. To the point now that if I have something bothering me, I ask myself, "Will 90-year-old Bree care about this when she is nearing the end of her life?"

If it's a no, then it's time to stop wasting time on it. Or, if I want to do something and I am nervous about it I ask, "Will 90-year-old Bree regret not doing this?" If I feel that I will regret not doing it on my death bed, then I just go for it.

Think about some older people in your world, or find an older stranger sitting on a park bench patiently waiting and watching the world pass by, and have a chat about life. I try and do it at least once a week. It will make you appreciate your life more, you may make their day, but I'm pretty sure they will make yours.

70

At a time when everyone has a camera on them, how can one photograph sell for $6.5m?

We live in a world where everyone carries a camera. Images are so plentiful, that if they cost anything at all, they can be purchased online for a few dollars. It seems that the law of supply and demand would keep images cheap.

So how on earth did Australian landscape photographer Peter Lik manage to sell one image for $6.5 million dollars?

Well you have to know Peter Lik to understand that. I have had the pleasure of being friends with him for more than 20 years. Starting right back when he was working from home, shooting pretty much anything that he could get paid for. And as always, there is much more to the man than the headlines suggest.

This is what sets him apart from others:

1. **He is the hardest working man I have ever met.** A lot of people say they work hard, but Peter takes that to a whole new level. When I first met him he was a 20 hour a day man. He was either on site taking shots, or sorting them, selling them or promoting them. He worked harder than anyone I have ever met, and he is always hustling to make a deal.

2. **He always backed himself absolutely.** Ten years ago Peter made his

boldest move. He packed up his camera gear and headed to Las Vegas. He opened a gallery in the revamped Caesars Palace, a bold, expensive and risky manoeuvre, that just so happened to pay off big time. But he was always bold, thinking big, making incredible galleries with incredible fit-outs. Investing every cent he made back into the business, he did this for many years. Underlying it all, was an absolute and utter sense of belief in himself, even in the tough times.

3. **He knows his market incredibly well.** People can argue about the aesthetic value of an image, is it art or isn't it? None of that ever bothered Peter. He had an incredible eye for what people were prepared to pay for, not just what they would admire or say nice things about. He could do this with coffee table books, prints, even furniture, he shot what sold. There is a great line "knowing your market is the key to capturing it" and Peter knows his market better than most.

4. **He values himself and his work and he isn't afraid to charge for it.** The fact that he sold one image for $6.5 million should prove this. But this is not an isolated transaction. Peter has sold other images for six and seven figures on a regular basis. This just happens to be the highest paid one to date. No doubt he will break this record at some stage soon. One of the biggest issues with entrepreneurs, is that they simply don't charge enough for what they do, because they lack confidence.

5. **He has stayed true to his course and he continues to strive to master his craft.** Peter has been a landscape photographer for decades. He has simply tried to take the shots that others haven't, or, redo the classics and make them better. Every year he takes his photography to a new level, as he goes to greater lengths to get the perfect image and he pushes himself harder and harder. Not many people would know that he almost died in a helicopter crash on a shoot in Northern Australia. That would have been enough to turn most people off. Not Peter-it pushed him forward, fired him up to push more boundaries. Like most 'one percenters', the elite in their space, he is absolutely and totally driven to keep getting better.

6. **He has avoided listening to the haters.** Anyone who is great at what they do, attracts those who snipe at the sidelines (those who are generally not very good at anything but experts in finding fault in others). In the creative world of photography and art, there have been and there continue to be, plenty of

people who say there are better photographers than Peter, or his work is not art. But none of them have sold an image for $6.5 million. To be successful for any period of time, you have to learn to block the negativity that sadly comes with having a high profile.

7. **He knows how to leverage his past success and past failures.** Not everything Peter has done has been a success. He's the first to admit his failings, but like most successful entrepreneurs, when he gets it wrong, he learns from his mistakes, adjusts his plan and pushes forward. At the same time, he knows that success begets success, so he is not afraid to promote himself and his success. The time for modesty is long gone in the cluttered, and distracted world that we live in. Sitting back and waiting to be found tends to result in a long wait, leading to disappointment.

Peter should inspire all of us who want to be extraordinary at what we do, no matter how 'tough' the market may be, or how competitive it is.

BREE'S TAKE

This entire section raises the concept of looking outside of your own industry for good ideas. With this story about Peter Lik, we get to see that what most people would think impossible, selling a single image for millions of dollars, is actually possible. Sure, it's not going to happen every day, and it isn't going to happen for every photographer, but if one photographer can do it, others can.

Often we are limited with our opportunities, not by any external circumstances but more by our own limitations, specifically our limiting beliefs. The key is to spend time looking beyond your own business and industry for ideas that challenge you. But at the same time these ideas need to inspire you to incorporate what you are currently doing and what you dream of doing in the future.

Talk about these ideas with your team. Get every team member to bring one idea in a week that they discover from the "outside" world. Do this and everyone will benefit in surprising ways.

71

Seven reasons to give thanks to Hipsters for changing how we do Business.

In the past ten years we've well and truly seen the rise of the Hipster entrepreneur. Personally, I love them. They bring some flair and attitude to the small business scene and in many ways, they've made it cool to be a business owner again.

In fact, I think that we have a lot to thank Hipsters for. They have changed a lot about the way we do business and the way we think about business. I think there are seven specific reasons why we should be grateful to small business Hipsters everywhere.

1. **It's very cool to do one thing and do it really well.** If you want to do nothing but sell great coffee, or make a particular type of food, or collect honey and nothing else, that is now absolutely OK. In fact, we love businesses that do one thing really well. Hipsters get this and they are very happy to find that one thing and do it better than anyone else.

2. **We don't all have to be building an empire.** For a while there it seemed that if you were in business, and you didn't want to sell it for a billion dollars in a year, you simply weren't trying hard enough. Now Hipsters have helped us come to terms with the fact that not everyone wants to build an empire, but if

you do, that's OK too. The bottom line, build the business you really want, not the kind of business that others expect you to.

3. **People love personality.** I think business was getting a little bland for a while. Everything was starting to look the same, like one big franchise. Hipsters have come along, covered in tattoos, beards and funky clothes, embracing their individuality and encouraging it with their staff. They have personality and they aren't afraid to use it. It just goes to show that customers want to do business with people who have personality, I know I do.

4. **It's nice to do things that take time to get right.** In a world that is obsessed with fast, a lot of Hipster businesses are fighting back and taking the slow approach. They do things well; they don't advertise that they are the fastest. Instead they actually say they do it right, not fast, so if you want fast go to a bland, faceless business.

5. **People will pay for quality.** I went into a barbershop in Sydney recently, a Hipster haven, and they charged $75 for a shave. Now there was a time when I would have laughed, saying there is no way anyone would ever pay that kind of money for a simple shave. Of course it is far from a simple shave and there is a line out the door, with people waiting up to an hour for a shave. People will pay for quality, Hipsters are proving that in every industry.

6. **It's nice to smile when you walk into a business.** Every time I walk into a Hipster run business I can't help but smile. They are having fun, they can have a conversation with you, they are proud of what they do and how they do it, they have a wonderful sense of team and they laugh a lot. Who doesn't want to buy from a business like this?

7. **Hipsters have taught us to be fearless.** With everything from food trucks, to mail order razor blades, Hipsters are all about giving it a go. If it doesn't work, you pick yourself up, dust yourself off, and try the next idea. They don't spend years beating themselves up. They try new things, they love new ideas, the more innovative and off beat the better. They teach us to not be afraid of giving a business idea a go, but do it well, charge what you are worth, and let your personality shine through.

BREE'S TAKE

My advice is really straightforward. Find a Hipster business and buy something from them. Check out their confidence, check out the playfulness, check out the energy of the team. Their marketing is simple, straightforward and kind of old school, and that is the point. In a world gone digital crazy, there is a craving for good old fashioned service, communication and marketing.

Now don't get me wrong. I'm not saying we all need to grow beards and get tattoos, and I'm pretty sure that being a Hipster doesn't guarantee you will run a great business, but there is certainly a lot we can learn from the rise of the Hipster business.

SECTION 9

STRESS IS GOING TO KILL YOU
IF YOU LET IT.

If you own your own business you know that feeling of waking up at 2am, heart pounding, your head full of all of the things you need to do tomorrow. No matter how hard you try, sleep eludes you, so you get up and start work. That's not a good feeling, and it certainly isn't sustainable.

We live in extremely stressful times, as proven by the fact that there are about a billion books showing us how to be mindful, present, calm, relaxed etc. In fact, we get stressed just thinking about all of the books we need to be reading to relax us.

The reality is we need to come to some kind of peace around stress. We're not suggesting you become a Zen Monk, but maybe a little less stressed, a little more functional and a little more able to get through the day, and arrive in better shape when it's over. This is a step in the right direction for most of us and is the core of this section. We're going to suggest a few ideas that might help you find some kind of calm in a world gone mad.

72

Do you start your day feeling overwhelmed?

Time, we all struggle to find enough and most of us feel under the pump from first thing in the morning until we finally mange to fall into bed at night. It feels like we do a lot, but achieve little. Often with a few simple changes in the way we do what we do, we can actually become much more productive and feel more in control of our working day.

Here are a few ideas that have worked wonderfully well for me:

1. **Get important tasks done before you check your emails first thing in the morning.** As soon as you check your emails in the morning, your day is shot. From that first moment on, we spend the rest of the day responding to other people and their requests, that just keep coming in. If you can spend the first few hours of your working day getting your top priorities done and then check your email, you will be amazed at how much you can get done. This is a very hard habit to change but the results are incredible.

2. **Batch your appointments.** Rather than space appointments over a day, I like to batch them. For example, I will have a morning of appointments, one after the other and I get them knocked over. This keeps the meetings on schedule, it keeps everyone on track, and avoids non-productive time breaks between appointments that are not really long enough to do anything significant except check emails, and once again, respond to everyone else's demands.

3. **Don't get pressured into committing on the spot.** Many people struggle to say "no" to a request for their time. Simply because they feel that they are put on the spot when the request is made. Whenever someone asks me to do something, I always say that I have to check my diary and other commitments before I can confirm. This buys me time to decide if I want to commit to this particular request. If I have the time, how I would like it to work and so on. I never feel pressured to commit to anything now and I make much better decisions as result of having some room to think.

4. **Have appointment free days.** Further to the previous point, the only way I get work done is to schedule days that are appointment free. These are the days when I don't see any clients, or have any appointments at all. These are the days when I am at my most productive. I schedule at least two of these per week and I just love them.

5. **Get better at finding out what the real deadline is.** There is nothing more frustrating than being given a deadline, working all hours to meet it, and then finding out it wasn't a real deadline. The client just manipulated you so that you would get the task done quickly. During your meeting you are told that "the task has to be done by Friday" and you pull out all stops to get it done. Then you find out that the person who requested it has gone on holidays for a month and they won't even look at your report until they get back. Very frustrating. I always make a point of finding out what the real deadline is, and why that deadline has been set.

6. **Tell a white lie about when you are leaving.** I figured this one out many years ago. The day before leaving for a business trip was always incredibly stressful and over committed on every front. I started to tell a white lie about when I was leaving. Specifically, I would say I was going a day earlier than I actually was. This gave me a full day in the office (or at home) to get everything done that I needed to do without the last minute panic of clients, suppliers and staff, needing my time. I still do this today, and I leave for every trip feeling relaxed and refreshed instead of stressed out and exhausted.

7. **Allocate time for the unexpected.** In my daily planner I schedule two one-hour blocks for the "unexpected" things that occur during the day. One hour in the morning, one in the afternoon. I do this daily, because the one thing that

really isn't unexpected is that you will need to do things that you didn't expect to have to do when your day started. If luck would have it and the unexpected hasn't materialised, you suddenly have a spare hour or if you are really lucky, two spare hours up your sleeve.

8. **Disconnect from the world.** When I write I turn off my email, my phone and all other connection to the outside world. At first this is very hard, but the more often you do it, the easier it gets. For me an hour spent working disconnected is equal to four hours connected. Manage people's expectations - let them know you are disconnecting and that you will get back to them, but it won't be until later. By responding to every email within a minute, we are training our clients to expect us to be connected. Managing other people's expectations takes time, but once they have worked out how you operate, if you are good enough at what you do, they will work around you.

I started to use all of these ideas because I was tired of feeling out of control. By breaking some of my own bad habits, I regained control of my world. Not only am I more productive, the quality of what I do is better, and so is my sense of satisfaction.

BREE'S TAKE

All great advice as always, so I'm going to tailor my thoughts and suggestions for those business owners with children. Here are a few tips that have helped me fit a working week into 25 hours (well I'm not sure I've ever worked a 25-hour week, but you know what I mean I'm sure)

1. **Get important tasks done while your family sleeps.** Before anyone wakes in the morning, or once everyone has gone to sleep at night, I dedicate 2-3 hours to do my best and most important work that needs to be done without interruption. Leave the dishes, leave the washing, and spend one hundred percent of this time doing the most important tasks whilst your family and

usually the rest of the world are sleeping. Let's face it, when they wake and your day starts, it gets hijacked with parenting duties and responsibilities.

2. **Batch your appointments.** Like Andrew suggested, I highly recommend batching as well. I have one dedicated day every week when my boys are in school from 9-5pm. This is the day where I plan to have back to back meetings. I power dress, get extremely organised, plan a pile of punchy fifteen minute meetings and then go for it. The work that comes out of these meetings can be fitted into the rest of the week, where I need to be more flexible. But I feel great knowing that the bulk of the meaningful meetings are done.

3. **Get super organised.** Look at your life and work out what can be insourced and done by your family. In my family, this means that the kids have to pack their own school bags, empty dishwashers and pitch in with other chores as well. Then look at what can be outsourced, get a cleaner, a gardener, or even better a Nanny to help if you need. Yes, we need to run a little like a military operation, but a lack of organisation will cause more problems than just about anything else. Organise what you can, and get help where you need it.

Maybe try to find ways to be more creative with being organised. Could you use a Virtual Assistant to help with planning your day to day life? Why not? Or find a Nanny who doubles as a Personal Assistant - a great option for business owners. This role means the hours they do for the business could be tax deductible, so they can be at home for a couple of hours supervising the kids whilst doing some office work.

RECOMMENDED READING - There is a great book called "Me Time" by Kate Christie, it's loaded with great ideas for Mums in particular to get more done. Check it out – it changed my life.

73

Overextended?
Here are five polite ways to say NO.

It is getting harder and harder to avoid living a life of over commitment. Every email requires a response, every phone call ends up with more things to do. Running a business is more complicated with responsibilities on a daily basis, we are required to attend more meetings, and our "to do" list just keeps getting longer.

One of the skills that most of us have to get better at, is learning to master our commitments, and I like to think of this as mastering the art of deflection. Now this isn't saying we will get out of our commitments. Rather we will get better at prioritising them, finding time to meet them, and developing new skills to put us back in the driving seat when it comes to deciding if we want to take a commitment or not.

Here are some strategies that I use on regular basis to overcome being over-committed:

When someone asks for your time, say you have to check your calendar.
Many people struggle to say no to a request for their time, simply because they feel that they are put on the spot when the request is made. Whenever someone asks me to do something, I always say that I have to check my diary and other commitments before I can confirm. This buys me time to decide if I want to

commit to this particular request, if I have the time, how I would like it to work and so on. I never feel pressured to commit to anything now and I make much better decisions as result of having some room to think.

Always ask for more information. Whenever someone is asking for advice or help in some way, I ask them to send through more information or more specific details and to explain exactly what they would like me to do and when they would like it done by? Once I receive this information I will make a decision. At least half the time I never hear from them again, which shows how un-committed they were. In other words, I won't commit time or energy, until they do the same.

Charge for your time. As an author and presenter, I have a lot of people contacting me for free advice. Sometimes it can be as many as three hundred emails a week. These are generally in the form of questions about specific aspects of doing business. In the past I tried to answer every one, but it soon became apparent that I would go broke if I spent all of my time answering people's questions for free. So I introduced a "One on One Package". This is a $500 product where people can send me their questions and I would offer a Skype consultation and some of my books. I explain very nicely that I run a business that offers advice commercially, and interestingly, about one in ten people buy the package. The rest I never hear from again.

Get creative at saying, "Sorry, no can do." Often the hardest part about being asked to commit to something, is how to say no without feeling rude. Several years ago, I found that my not for profit pro bono work was getting out of hand. I was spending up to two full days a week doing free work for a handful of charities, and it became apparent that if something didn't change, I would soon need the services provided by these organisations. I found saying no to any request for help very hard. So rather than saying no, I reframed how I could help the various charities. I decided to commit a maximum of 8 hours per week and once this was used, that was it. When I received a request for help, I would advise them of how I worked and they could book time in advance. But once I had reached 8 hours for any particular week, I was fully committed and that was that. In essence, this created a procedure that I could hide behind to help me say no without feeling guilty.

In the crazy fast paced world we live in, it is easy to commit every minute of every day. Then if one thing goes wrong, everything goes wrong. The compound effect is extremely stressful. In addition to saying "no" we need to find time in our day to play catch up. I suggest scheduling a one-hour time slot every morning and every afternoon to manage the unexpected. I also schedule at least one day a month to do nothing but work through my pile of incompletes and I have to say it is very therapeutic.

The better we become at managing commitment, the more effective we will be in every aspect of our life.

BREE'S TAKE

Again I am going to do this one for the "Parentpreneurs". If you are going to be a successful parent and a successful business owner that doesn't burn out, here are five things that I have realised along the way.

1. You can't do it alone. You will need to have a great support network behind you. A handful of family or friends that you can call on to watch the kids when an unexpected and annoying teachers strike happens, or during school holidays, or when one of the kids gets a vomiting bug and you have the pitch of a lifetime and today is the only day it can be done.

2. Daycare, vacation care, and afterschool care are services to be used when you need. Your kids are better off there having fun and playing, than being told to be quiet and watch an iPad while you work.

3. If you are working at home with sick kids and they are completely silent don't think that you can sneak in an important phone call. The little darlings have a well tuned radar that knows exactly when you are trying to make that important call and that is the exact moment that all hell will break loose. Tell the person you are calling that you are working at home and that the call may get interrupted, or reschedule the call. Trust me.

4. You are going to mess up and miss important things that the other parents get to go to. It sucks, other parents do judge you for not being as 'committed' to

volunteering at the school or doing other 'parenty' type tasks. But the sooner you come to peace with it, and work out ways to make up for it that work for your family, the better.

5. Raising a business and a family is very, very hard. There are more families doing it now than ever, so try and find a network of Parentpreneurs for support and understanding.

74

Eight ways to take the stress
out of meeting deadlines.

Let me start by saying I struggle with deadlines. I'm not Mr. Perfect. I take on way too much, I get overwhelmed, I say yes when I should say no and every once in a while I have a bit of a meltdown. However, I rarely miss important deadlines. Somewhere in there I manage to get a lot done, mostly to deadline, and I have tried really hard to get better at it.

Over the years I've learned a few tips. These are the ones that I think can really help if you struggle with deadlines and you would like to change.

1. **Start immediately by breaking the project into small chunks.** We've all heard this, personally I've found it really useful for getting things done. But there are two key points here - start immediately and break the project into chunks. By doing both of these you will get a solid head start on any project and it doesn't feel anywhere near as daunting.

2. **Block time to start working on the task or project right now.** If you don't allocate time, quality time, (and stick to it) you probably won't treat the project as a priority. So you will do it when you get the time, which of course is, you will leave it to the last minute and be stressed out and overwhelmed and do a sub standard job (even if the client doesn't see that - you know the truth).

3. **Set false deadlines.** As you saw earlier in this book, I do this when I travel. I tell a little white lie about which day I am actually leaving so I can have a day of peace to get stuff done. Basically the idea means reinventing the deadline, remove all evidence of the actual deadline, and put a new one into your calendar, notes, whiteboards etc. and make it one week earlier. If you get it done awesome, and you look super professional getting the project in early. If you need more time - perfect.

4. **Declare your deadlines publicly.** One of the best things I did with deadlines was to put a whiteboard in my office where all of my team's deadlines were clearly visible. There was nowhere to hide, everyone checked the deadline board daily- and the non performers were shamed into performing.

5. **Get an accountability coach.** Now for habitual deadline 'tragics'-those who simply can't meet a deadline to save themselves, perhaps it's time to get really serious and engage a tough accountability coach. A friend of mine has an accountability coach who holds $1,000 in a trust for failing to deliver on a deadline. If he misses any deadline, the $1,000 is given as a donation to a political party that he really hates. So far he has lost about $3,000, but it has changed his entire working world, and he feels it has been money well spent.

6. **Make a BIG public commitment.** Sometimes we need to issue a challenge and make a commitment, publicly. Perhaps declare this to be the year where you become the world's best deadline meeter! Sounds corny, sure, but if you are sick and tired of a bad habit, that impacts your life, sometimes we have to make a big declaration to really make a change. Come up with your BIG commitment and tell everyone - so you have nowhere to hide!

7. **Reward yourself.** OK, this might sound a little like giving yourself a dog biscuit for doing something you should be grown up enough to do, but hey, we are all human and sometimes we need the biscuit. What are some nice, easy, meaningful rewards that you could give yourself every time you meet a deadline? Reprogram your thinking about deadlines, make them something to look forward, to not something to dread.

8. **Establish routine.** I've been writing for a business website called Inc for about three years now. For 18 months, I had to have my article ready to go by 9.00am every Tuesday morning, rain, hail or shine. Did I ever miss a deadline?

No? In the last few months, I've gone to twice a week. Have I missed a deadline? Never. Why not? To me it is the routine. I know that I have a commitment that is scheduled, regular and important. And I'm in Australia, so my times mean 12.00am and 12.30am deadlines. Sometimes, I am writing at 11.30pm to get my article done, but I always get it done. Routine is powerful.

BREE'S TAKE

As a magazine publisher, my life is one big deadline. Here are a few things to keep in mind if you are working with someone who has given you a deadline:

1. **Negotiate your deadline upfront and don't make people chase you.** Often we are working with several if not tens or even hundreds of people at the same time, who also have deadlines. After you submit what you have agreed to submit, there are often many other hands the work has to go through. So you missing your deadline can be catastrophic and really cause a great deal of impact and stress on others, and that isn't fair. Become known as someone who always meets deadlines and you will get more work than you can poke a stick at.

2. **Keep the person who has given you the deadline in the loop.** If for some life or death reason you are going to miss your deadline, let the person expecting to get your work know as soon as possible. There is nothing worse than getting an email five minutes before something is due to say it won't be coming through. I would go one step further and a day or two before it is due, send a reassuring email to say it's on the way and it will arrive by the agree upon deadline (and then get it in early).

3. **Don't half commit.** If you aren't one hundred percent committed or keen on the project, do everyone a favour and don't agree to it in the first place. If you can't make the deadline with absolute certainty, don't accept the project. If you really aren't interested in the project, don't accept it, because you know you wont do your best work.

75

Could you go seven days without internet, phone and email, and survive?

I just arrived home after spending a week at a health retreat and what an interesting week it was. Part of the overall detox philosophy at the camp was the need to detox from the modern connected world we live in and I have to say, it was challenging.

Day one and I was like a junkie, pacing the room, looking for an internet connection or a single bar on my phone. Slowly a sense of dread started to settle in. How on earth was I going to cope with seven whole days with no contact with the outside world?

Interestingly I'm not sure what was concerning me more, the fear of missing an opportunity of some sort, the fear of letting a client down, or the fear of something happening and I wouldn't be aware of it. Rest assured, the only common theme here is fear.

What I really noticed was how much time I had on my hands when they weren't constantly connected to a device of some sort. All of this time let me do things that were far more constructive in many ways. I read seven books in seven days.

The fog started to lift at about day three. Part of this was due to the end of my caffeine cravings but I certainly felt like my brain was working much better.

Now that I wasn't spending the day doing a million things, multitasking like a madman, bouncing around all over the place. My thoughts were crystal clear, I could think something through at a high level from start to finish and make very clear decisions.

Another interesting observation was that I started sleeping really well, in fact more than 10 hours per night. Yes, some of this was due to the fact that they made us do exercise, but nothing excessive. I have no doubt that I was sleeping well because I was more relaxed as a result of not checking some device every five minutes, especially at night.

Towards the end of the week I had totally lost the need to have my phone attached to my hip. I had a sense of going with the flow and if anyone needed to get in touch with me, they would be happy to wait till I was back in the office (which as it turned out was true).

At the end of the week, I turned on my phone to about one thousand five hundred emails. Ninety-five percent were a waste of time, junk or just plain unnecessary. The rest I responded to and cleaned up in an about an hour and a half. Yet I seem to spend hours each day on email? So from now on I am definitely blocking email time, twice per day then switch it off.

Another interesting thing happened when I started to watch the evening news. The first three stories were particularly graphic, brutal, violent, cruel and sad, and I felt myself becoming physically sick, to the point where I had to turn the television off. These terrible stories had a physical effect on me. Wow; how desensitised had I become in the past, being bombarded with stories like this all day. From now on I am going to be very selective about what I watch and what I listen to.

Overall, was it a good exercise? Absolutely. Can I keep a hold of what I have learned and realised? I hope so. I'm also a realist, and whilst I can't ever see myself living off the grid, I do think I can better manage my world to live a more sane and serene life.

BREE'S TAKE

If you are like me and felt super excited about the prospect of a retreat like this, then it's time to do something about it.

Today's challenge is to note the amount of time you look at your phone, your computer, a television or any other device. If you are anything like me, I am guessing you look at your phone at least fifty times a day, for a few seconds here and there, sometimes longer, and spend upwards of eight hours a day looking at a screen. Once you know the amount of time in a day that you are looking at technology, you can make a decision as to whether you think it is too much or not.

So find out what you are averaging a day, and work out how much you think is healthy for your brain and peace of mind.

Then take some time to schedule a detox week, a detox day, or even some regular days or hours that are technology free so that you are in control of your usage. You will feel great for it.

76

Are you sick and tired of being a perfectionist?
It really is exhausting for you and those around you.

Most of my life I have battled with perfection. I don't mean that I am perfect in any shape or form, but I have tried to achieve perfection in my work. For some strange reason, no matter how hard I try, I keep getting clear messages that the world is far from perfect, and interestingly enough, that is okay.

Imperfection is a wonderful way to learn. It is the way we discover new things and new ways of doing tasks that being rigidly perfect would never allow.

As a writer, I encounter a lot of people who are seriously uptight about the use of the English language. I think they expect me to be equally concerned. They chastise me when I dare to start a sentence with the word 'and'. And this drives me crazy.

For me, language evolves. If it didn't, I imagine we would still be sitting around grunting at each other like Neanderthals. Please don't get me wrong, we should all aspire to do what we do with the best of our abilities, but there are times when near enough really is good enough.

Why? Simply because being too rigid and too inflexible, creates far more pain and anguish than perhaps the use of a wrong word, or placing an object in the wrong place, or someone turning up five minutes late.

The key is to learn to let go when it is appropriate. If you are an airline engineer working on a jet engine, it is important to get it right. But often the need for perfection is a need to control, which is caused by fear and self-esteem issues. I know that when I was a kid, my life had very little safety or control and my self-esteem was virtually non-existent. Because of this, I wanted everything to be perfect as an adult and I would control what I could to make sure this happened.

When your self-esteem is low you clutch to what other people compliment you on. For me, it was my work. I was praised for what I did and the results I got. So I started to take myself far too seriously, and again, my desired outcome was perfection.

Somewhere along the line I realised that I couldn't control everything, and more importantly, trying to control everything was exhausting. People don't like to be around other people who are that controlling or tightly wound.

Secondly, I realised that my work was a part of who I am, not all of who I am. So I learnt to appreciate positive feedback, but it doesn't rule my world any more.

With these two realisations, came a sense of freedom. I could finally relax and accept that sometimes near enough is okay. I still aspire to do the very best job I can, but I don't obsess over it and lie in bed at night beating myself up when I make a dumb mistake.

Instead I tend to laugh at myself, groan if it has cost me money and set about fixing the problem at hand. And then I move on. Some people seem to go through life always swimming against the current. Everything is a life or death struggle and there is a sense of the dramatic, surrounding every aspect of their life.

My biggest clarity with living this way is that the people around you, the ones you love and care for the most, really find it hard to just be themselves if you are busy trying to be the perfect mother, father, brother, sister, boss, employee and so on. Your struggle rubs off on them. In the long run, this means that they may not want to spend that much time around you.

We all spend a lot of time wondering what people think about us. Will they admire us, love us, like us or respect us if we are not 'perfect'? The reality is that they will probably admire, love and respect you even more if you are not perfect, and let's be honest, what other people think of us is none of our business.

Being great at what we do is a good thing. But feeling that we need to be perfect is not. Let your guard down, be human and be real and you will stop beating yourself up. Those around you will be more inclined to connect with you at a deeper level, which leads to all kinds of wonderful things.

BREE'S TAKE

I am a perfectionist's worst nightmare.

As much as I strive to be perfect and do my utmost, with so much on my plate, I am someone that also loves doing things under pressure, unplanned and what Andrew calls "winging it".

It often means that I don't feel like I have done my best work, but in my defense if I waited for the perfect time to do things, things would never get done. If I waited for the perfect time to start my business, and did a heap of research and planning, I probably wouldn't have started it.

I am someone that gets an idea and executes it, sometimes that very day, because I think "why wait for the perfect time? The perfect time is right now, whilst it's in my head".

I know I am not alone, and I think that is why Andrew and I work so well together; he is a planner and needs things to be perfect, whereas I am more about, just get it done the best you can, by the deadline.

He drives me nuts, I drive him nuts, but the combination of both of our skills is a perfect match because of these idiosyncrasies.

If you are someone that gets over-analysis paralysis, go and find the Tarzans of the business world, the people that will swing from the branches without even thinking about it. And all you crazy Tarzan's, go and find yourself a Jane, someone that thinks things through and plans things to perfection.

77

Are you struggling to make hard decisions?

Making decisions has gotten a whole lot harder in recent years, mainly due to living in a constant state of overwhelm that hits us from every direction. Now I am not talking about making a decision about what to have on our pizza, but more significant decisions like the direction we want our lives to take, decisions in our relationships, our business, big financial decisions and other important and real areas of our lives.

How many of us waste years in a dead-end job or relationship because we don't make a decision to do something about it? Part of the whole over-analysis paralysis issue is that feeling overwhelmed stops us from making decisions.

I meet so many business owners who should simply get out of their business. It doesn't make them any money, their lives stink, there is nothing on the horizon that is going to change and worst of all they know it. But they hang on for far longer than they should, and spend years struggling when they should have made a very hard decision to move on long ago.

When it comes to making decisions, especially the big ones, I adopt the following approach:

- I make sure I have the facts (not the emotions).

- I listen to my intuition, what is it saying?

- I think about the worst that can happen.

- I think about the best that can happen.

- I make a decision, accept responsibility for making that decision and move on.

- I know too many people who have spent a lifetime trying to make a decision. By the time they do, it is too late. Sometimes right or wrong doesn't matter as much as making a decision does.

There is also a sense of relief when you finally make a decision. It is very powerful when you stand up and say, 'I have made a decision - I am going to do this..........". The more you say it, the better it feels, and the easier it becomes to make the tough decisions.

The final part of this decision-making process is to learn that once you make your decision, move on. Just as it is a waste of life to be stuck in a state of procrastination, it is also a waste to spend a life stuck in regret over bad decisions. One thing I am very clear about is that I have learned so much from each and every mistake I have made in my life; I am now eternally grateful for making them.

So if you struggle to make decisions, about big or small things, today is the day to change. Start small if you need to and work up to the big stuff. Be realistic about the pros and cons and once you make up your mind, proclaim it out loud, and move on with your life happy with the decision you've made.

BREE'S TAKE

We all have decisions that we need to make that are weighing us down. I am someone that makes so many decisions on a daily basis that it's nice to let go of the reigns some times. Here are a few things I do to give myself some decision free time.

1. Allow someone else to order your meal off the menu at a restaurant, or ask the waiter to choose for you.

2. Book a mystery hotel on www.bookings.com instead of wasting time looking at all of the options.

3. Do a pot luck Friday lunch with your team once a week, have a roster and take turns to cook for the team. Create some rules, like it has to be done in the slow cooker, or it has to be international. That is one less lunch to think about.

4. Have a decision-free day. Tell everyone you aren't making any decisions today, and put someone else in charge. I've done it on a Sunday and put one of my kids in charge, they choose what I eat, what I wear and were we go. It can actually be really fun to put someone else in charge for the day. You have no idea what is going to happen and the kids love being boss for that day and it teaches them responsibility.

5. When someone comes to you with a problem, ask them what solution they think is best. My team know to come to me with a problem only if they have considered some solutions, so I can then help them choose the best option. I do it with the kids too, it works a treat.

78

Is this year going to be the year of the digital detox?

There is a lot of discussion around the concept of digital detoxing, but it feels like now it is finally getting traction. Most of us are struggling under the load of electronic connection and I get the feeling that soon humans will rise and start to regain some equilibrium.

So what is a digital detox? According to Wikipedia it refers to "a period of time during which a person refrains from using electronic connecting devices such as smartphones and computers. It is regarded as an opportunity to reduce stress or focus on social interaction in the physical world."

There is enough research to reinforce the importance of digital detoxing on both our productivity and our sanity. The problem is that we have all developed such bad habits when it comes to using our various devices, to the point where many of us are actually addicted to our phones, tablets, laptops and anything else that we can connect to the internet.

As I said earlier, I did a digital detox. Seven days without any internet or telephone signal. The first day was a nightmare. I literally felt like an addict searching desperately for one bar of bandwidth on my phone. It was hard, really hard, but after that first day it got much easier and then I started to enjoy the rewards.

I slept much better, my mind became incredibly sharp and clear, I could carry a thought all the way from concept to completion and I simply felt much better.

So how will this mass digital detox look? I believe a number of things will happen. Firstly, we will start to see experts and authorities who actually coach people through their digital detox. There may be support groups, internal facilitators, 24-hour helps lines, a pile of books, articles and much more, will all start to appear (in fact they already have).

Colouring in books took over bookshops, being touted as the new mechanism for adults to practice mindfulness and to help with the digital detox. And if you have tried some coloring in, it really is pretty darn relaxing.

Work practices will start to change. Meetings will become places where people talk, not spend time on their devices. There will be conversation rooms that are device free areas for people to actually talk to one another. We will be challenged on the emails we are sending, are they really necessary or are you simply wasting your time and other peoples?

It needs to be a gradual withdrawal. We still need to work and function and be available, but we will start to have periods where we leave the phone on the desk for a few hours. We might start to have digital-free weekends, where all devices are turned off. And the concept of the "signal free" holiday destination, is becoming increasingly popular.

Little by little we will introduce changes into our lives, that will make us feel more in control and less overwhelmed. The bottom line of course is that we really do need to do something about the over connected and over stimulated digital world that we live in, and the sooner the better.

BREE'S TAKE

Yep, we are all getting digitally overwhelmed. This stuff is supposed to be making our life easier, but in some ways I'm not sure it is. Anyway, here are a few simple ideas to try. They might just help you to think more clearly, sleep more deeply, and do what your do in a much more focused way.

1. No devices one hour before bed.

2. No television during the week.

3. No electronics, until after you have exercised in the morning. No exercise means no checking emails or social media until you get to the office.

4. No using electronics after hours unless you have read one chapter of a good book.

5. If you are in a social setting you can only look at your phone at set times, incase there is an important message from say the babysitter. Ideally, leave the phone at home and make sure the babysitter has someone else's phone number to call if there is a problem.

6. Log out of apps like Facebook so you aren't tempted to look at them all day, only login when you want to spend a set amount of time on the platform.

7. Have a tech free day or night, every week or month and play board games.

8. Pick up your phone and call someone you haven't spoken to for a while. Every week pick a new person instead of messaging them.

9. If it takes more than a few minutes in messaging, call the person.

10. Unsubscribe from everything that makes you feel a way you don't want to feel, email lists, Facebook pages, people and businesses.

I am sure you could come up with your own list? Implement just one idea a week.

79

Sometimes we all need a whining wingman.

A few years ago I was presenting at a conference where the MC introduced an interesting idea. He was a fantastic speaker, a true statesman with a light style and a strong message. At the beginning of the conference he made the following statement:

"At conferences things sometimes go wrong. The coffee can be cold, the speakers late, the fish over cooked, the toilets grubby and so on. It is easy to lose sight of why we are all here and to start complaining to anyone who will listen about all of the things that are wrong. But rather than do that, I want you to find someone in the room and they are going to be your moaning buddy. Every time you see them, get all of your moaning over and done with so you can actually focus on learning and growing. With everyone else you encounter, be positive, energetic and enthusiastic."

So we all found a moaning buddy and had a good moan about life, work, the excessively cold room, the cost of petrol and anything else that was bugging us at the time. Then we went about our day. Whenever we encountered our moaning buddy we had a good moan and a great belly laugh.

This was a very interesting exercise. For starters it really did get the negativity out of the way. It demonstrated that we can be positive and enthusiastic most of the time if we want to be, and that attitude is a state of mind.

I think the same should apply in everyday life. We should all have moaning buddies we can contact when we need to vent-get it over and done with, have a great laugh and then get on with the business of living and enjoying every moment of every day.

It seems that all too often more time is spent moaning and complaining, than actually getting on with things, and we all know those workplaces that are filled with nothing but negativity.

My advice, find yourself a good moaning buddy. Whenever you need to vent, give them a call, have a rant and move on. Let them do the same and cut your moaning time down to the bare necessity and life will be so much better.

Ideas like this can always sound kind of silly. Yet I have no doubt about the importance of attitude, language and thoughts when it comes to being successful, in all that we do. I hope you find yourself not just a good moaning buddy, but a great moaning buddy. I'm still in touch with mine, almost ten years after the conference.

BREE'S TAKE

I've never been someone to talk about my problems or what is irking me, I've preferred to keep them all inside and eventually explode. But as this chapter is all about how stress will kill you if you let it, and bottling things up inside is not good for your health. I think we all need a couple of whining wingmen, or wingwomen, to get some of our frustrations off our chest.

I have a couple of good friends and they gladly let me vent. I don't do it very often. One has even given me some personalised vouchers which allow me to "VENT FREELY ABOUT ANYTHING" which I can redeem at a moments notice.

Most of the time it isn't anything too major, it's lid of the toothpaste stuff that has just built up. I don't want someone to solve my problem, but I do want someone who can offer me honest feedback and advice. After I've vented, I'm good to go. The problem is back to being small and relatively inconsequential and I can get on with my life.

My only advice is to pick the people you vent to very wisely.

1. If you are going to vent about staff, pick someone who has staff who really does get it.

2. If you are going to vent about your relationship, pick someone who has a relationship you admire.

3. If you are going to vent about business, vent to another business owner.

Get the drift? We should never whine to someone who is just going to whine back with us. Unless you just want to get it off your chest and have someone that says "there, there you poor thing".

For me, if I whine to you, give me a verbal smack in the chops, tell me straight what it is you think I should do, that is productive whining, and I will respect you all the more for it.

SECTION 10

IF WE AREN'T GROWING
WE ARE DYING.

By now we're pretty certain that you will have noticed our not so subtle theme around the need to be growing as a human being to be successful in business. To be honest, for us it's essential. We invest a lot of time and money into both personal and professional growth and development and that's one of the reasons why we are successful.

Show us a business that is dying, or an industry that is dying for that matter and we're pretty certain you will find one where the people driving it are not growing themselves. Generally, it's a lack of will to grow, or perhaps uncertainty about the future, or just fatigue in a rapidly evolving world. Whatever the cause, it's a major warning sign.

We all know what it feels like to outgrow someone, perhaps in a relationship. The end is inevitable. The same applies in business. We have to be doing whatever we can to get better and we have to be doing it every day. This section might challenge you a little, we certainly hope so.

80

Want a better business?
Start by being a better person.

Over the years, I have coached numerous business owners, and the one thing that has always had the greatest impact, has been showing the relationship between how we live and act as a person, dramatically impacts the success of their business and the quality of their life.

I remember a client who was worth many millions of dollars. He had a wonderful family, a fabulous house, and travelled the world on a regular basis. He also was the most miserable sod I had ever met. To him, everything was terrible: the government, the economy, the city officials, and more. Finally I'd had enough of his moaning. We jumped into his luxury sports car and unbeknown to him, headed to the local shelter for battered and homeless women.

This may sound a little clichéd, but the visit had a profound effect on him. Talking to these women made him realise the ridiculousness of his negativity. An extraordinarily philanthropic man emerged from the miserable, self obsessed individual I knew before. But what changed the most, along with his attitude, was his business. He had been successful before, but with his newfound humanity, he became far more successful. Indeed, every aspect of his life improved dramatically.

The place to start is to develop your own personal code to live by. The following six strategies form the basis of my personal code that I work towards every day:

1. **Treat everyone you encounter with the utmost respect.** This is an attitude that great leaders share. They treat every single person that they encounter with enormous respect and they do it in a very genuine and humble way. From the cleaning person to the CEO, all are treated equally.

2. **Be ridiculously polite.** The old adage that "manners maketh the man", is more relevant than ever. Being polite really reinforces the concept of respect and humility towards others. It shows that you can focus on other people instead of yourself. People notice manners; more significantly, people notice the lack of manners.

3. **Small gestures make a big difference.** Taking a genuine interest in a photo on a desk, giving someone a sincere compliment, forwarding an email that you might think relevant to a customer... There are many small ways to show that you care and the more you incorporate these into your daily life, the more people realise you do actually care.

4. **Look for the win/win in every situation.** There is a perception that to be successful you need to be tough, one step ahead of the other guy, willing to do whatever is necessary to win. From my experience, the most successful people have figured out that if you aim for a true win/win situation, you end up being far more successful.

5. **Put yourself in the other guy's shoes.** Empathy is a powerful self-development tool. Learning to look at every situation from the other person's perspective, whether a customer, employee, supplier, or spouse, results in much better decisions.

6. **Be generous.** Nothing drives me crazier than a mean business owner-someone who spends nothing on the company, the staff, the customers, or the community. I believe that the more you give the more you get. I am not telling you to spend wildly; but I am saying that it is important to be generous in spirit, with everyone involved in your business, in any capacity.

BREE'S TAKE

I love the concept of having your own personal codes to live by. Take some time and create one, or a few. Here are some ideas for some one-page codes that I encourage you to create.

1. Your own personal code (like Andrew's above)

2. A business code

3. Your family code

4. Your relationship code

5. Your friendship code

6. Your money code

7. Your exercise code

The list is really endless, but it's amazing to have these codes for how you want to live your life. They become very real when you take the time to develop them and then print them out. Put your "Codes to Live By" somewhere where you can read them often during your day. If you have your own personal manifesto, with your own standards to live up to, you have a guide to live your best life. From my experience, this is the vital part of living a richer life.

81

A really simple way to stay motivated throughout the year.

One of the problems of doing business today is the sheer amount of data you have to manage and process. You tend to spend most of your business life responding to demands from others, which results in a frenzy of doing stuff but a sense of not actually getting ahead.

In this frenzy, it is really easy to forget what you accomplish throughout the year, which in turn can lead to a sense of just going through the motions on a day-to-day basis. It's hard to stay fired up and motivated when you feel like that.

A number of years back, I started a success board, which is nothing more than a whiteboard in the corner of my office on which I capture my achievements throughout the year. I wipe it clean on January 1, as I get ready to start the year, and as the months progress, I add my victories and special moments to the board. These might include anything from winning a project, getting a new client, hitting a milestone of some sort, taking a trip somewhere, or making a personal developmental breakthrough.

The year can start a little lean, but by June it looks pretty darn impressive, and by the end of the year, holy smoke. This isn't just a brag board; it is a powerful psychological tool that can have a big impact on how you do business.

So what exactly are the benefits of keeping a success board? I think there are many, but the most significant ones I have experienced are:

1. It helps remind you of the many successes you have had during the year. It feels really good to see all of your accomplishments in one spot, which is great for self-confidence and motivation.

2. It gives you a sense of progress. Research shows that most people feel a great sense of satisfaction when they are getting things done, and this is a tangible way of illustrating that.

3. On those days when you feel a little flat, one glance at your success board and you feel a whole lot better. And if you have had a bad experience of some sort, a grumpy person on the other end of the phone, or lost a client or a project for whatever reason, rather than going into despair. A quick look at your success board and the world is OK again.

Sometimes the simplest ideas are the most powerful. If you want a motivational tool that can inspire you when you need it most, start a success board today.

BREE'S TAKE

For me a board in my home is a bit of a space luxury I don't have, and I kinda feel weird having all my achievements out there for all my visitors to see. I once had a relative clean my home, who saw my goals on my wall and she never looked at me the same again. Since then I've been very apprehensive to have things like this out in the open. So if you are OK with having your dreams, goals and successes out in the open, like Andrew, awesome, but if you are like me and you prefer a little more privacy, try these ideas:

1. **Have an annual success diary.** Anytime you do something that belongs in your success book, write it out with the date, what happened and how the success made you feel.

2. **Have a success jar.** Get a jar, some pretty squares of paper and every time you have a successful moment, write it out and stick it in the jar. At the end of the year, read all of your comments.

3. **Go digital to keep track of your dreams, goals and successes.** Trello is a great platform to stick a list of your achievements, there are also many online platforms for note taking, or even get a good old spreadsheet happening.

4. **Do a series of video or audio grabs.** Nothing like actually capturing the excitement in your voice by recording yourself.

5. **Find a success buddy that you speak with once a week.** You speak about your successes for the week and document them for each other.

Bottom line is, there is nothing more satisfying than looking back at your successes, and having them in the one spot. It means that at anytime when you are feeling blue, disheartened, or in need of a pep up, they are there to remind you just how far you have come.

Most of us gloss over our successes, mainly because we simply aren't encouraged to celebrate them. Andrew is one of the few people who really genuinely celebrates and acknowledges the success of others. I know when I'm sharing my successes with him, I think he gets more excited than me, and that's a really nice feeling for me.

82

Seven ways to overcome feeling isolated and alone in your business.

Business isolation is a growing issue and it affects all kinds of people in all kinds of business environments. More people are choosing to work remotely, generally by themselves, losing that day to day connection of working around other people.

At the same time, competitive pressure is forcing people in the corporate world to work excessive hours, leading to extended periods of being alone with a growing sense of isolation.

So what are some of the symptoms of business isolation?

From my experience there are quite a few. We can suffer from a loss of direction, with some uncertainty and fear about the future. This can then lead to a loss of motivation, making it harder to get things done. We might struggle to make decisions and this makes us feel more frustrated, uncertain and isolated. It really can be a vicious cycle, made worse by the fact, that few people like to talk about it, as it can be seen as a weakness.

Regardless of the reason, for many people this is a new feeling and one that they don't really know how to handle. For anyone struggling with business isolation, here are my seven recommendations to overcome this feeling:

1. **Never lose track of where you are heading.** We need to have somewhere in the future that we are aiming for. Otherwise it is easy to flounder and move sideways instead of forward. This means continually revisiting our goals and our successes, to ensure we are heading in the right direction. Thinking about the future tends to get most of us excited. We get that feeling of 'what could be' and it spurs us in to action, to make our future vision a reality.

2. **Deal with the facts-don't let your imagination run away with you.** When feeling isolated our mind starts to run wild. Will the phone ever ring again? Am I going to lose a big client? Is my business going to survive? This type of internal chatter will drive us crazy. If you've been in business for ten years why on earth would the phone stop ringing? If you are delivering a quality product or service at a reasonable rate, why would you lose a client? When in doubt deal with the facts-not the chatter.

3. **Work on other parts of your life.** Spend time doing things outside of your business. The things you love that give you an interest outside of work. Don't get so busy building a business that you forget to build a life.

4. **Find a confidant-someone you can be really open and honest with.** This is ideally a friend who knows your business and knows you. It isn't a paid mentor, it is a friend who you can talk openly with about anything going on in your world, and discuss things like feeling isolated.

5. **Push ourselves to get out more.** It is important (really important) that you get out more. This might mean going to a networking event, visiting a client, making phone calls instead of just sending emails, doing errands, even spending time in a coffee shop to work on your laptop. This takes effort and the less we get out, the more effort it takes, but we need to interact with other human beings.

6. **Make the extra effort every day.** When working away from others, it is easy to stop doing the little things, like making the effort to dress and groom properly. We rationalise this by saying 'well I don't have any meetings today so I don't need to shave, or iron a shirt', which of course is all the more reason why we should. If you are feeling isolated, what are the small things you have stopped doing? Make them part of your daily routine and you will be surprised by how much more connected this makes you feel.

7. **Last but not least, accept that you are human.** Don't beat yourself up if you are feeling isolated. Don't look at it as a weakness, understand that you are only human and with this comes many needs, including interaction with others. We live in a world where it is surprisingly easy to become isolated, our mission is to work every day to avoid being isolated.

BREE'S TAKE

I've experienced this type of isolation many times before, but I am finding these days I have more people in my life than ever, but I feel a different type of isolation. It is isolation I feel from being at a different stage or journey in my business life than those in my current circle.

Here are some tips if you live in a location that means you are a little isolated from business people that will lift you higher.

1. **Get online**
   There are many groups on Facebook, LinkedIn, and websites that you can take part in that have entrepreneurs and business owners from all over the globe you can network with.

2. **Go to events**
   As we discussed earlier, invest in going to events where you are going to meet other likeminded people. This might mean getting on a plane to go to a specific conference or event. Ask other people in your network for recommendations.

3. **Get a mentor**
   There are many platforms that can help you find a mentor, or you can reach out to someone that you admire. It's great to have a mentor who pushes you harder than you ever thought possible (it has been extraordinary for me – Andrew has been my mentor for some time and I can't imagine my business or my life being where they are today without his guidance and at times, tough love).

4. Read more

We don't have to be face to face with people to learn. The first ten years of my business journey, I literally knew no one in the business industry in my town that I could speak to about business. I was eighteen years old when I first started. I took my work and business seriously but I never took myself seriously or called myself a business woman. It was only when I was nominated for a business award unexpectedly that I attended my first business event.

I'd been in business for ten years at this point, but I had never been to a networking event because I didn't feel like I was a serious business owner (I felt that I was too young to be a real business owner). I had no friends who were business people that I could speak with and I literally felt like I didn't belong. The only person I knew in small business was my brother who lived 3,000 kilometers away. His solution to help me was to shove business books and business cassette tapes in my face for which I'm eternally grateful for. It gave me a love of reading about business, and learning about business. I have no doubt that I wouldn't be writing this book if it wasn't for him. The books I read gave me the mentors I was looking for.

The thing is, we are a combination of the top five people we associate with. So if we want to become better people, we need to be associating with the types of people we aspire to be like. So whether that is in person, on paper, online, or on the phone. Always be on the look out for the people who can take you out of that stunted growth and isolation you may be feeling.

83

Why on earth would you read the same book every year for thirty years?

Every year over the Christmas break, I have a ritual that I have adhered to for over thirty years. I dig out a copy of Dale Carnegie's "How to Win Friends and Influence People" and read it. Yes, I've read it over thirty times now.

What more can I possibly learn from reading the same book after the second, third or fourth (or thirtieth) read? Well that's the interesting part. Every single time I have read this book, I've learned something new, I've interpreted some of the information in a completely different light. I'm reminded about the key messages in the book that sometimes I forget in amongst a busy life, and last but not least, I get just as much enjoyment reading it today as I did the first time I read it.

In fact, I re-read quite a few books. To me they are the classics of business, self-help and even fiction are those books that have been very influential on my life in so many ways. I find the same with each and every one of them. Whilst there is a familiarity about them, I always learn something that I didn't know before, that somehow, I seemed to have missed in past readings. The reading experience is somehow different, and the meaning I take from these books, is likewise a little different in an interesting way.

Of course the reality is that the book hasn't changed, I have. What is going on in my world at any specific time that I am reading the book is different. The trials and tribulations I am experiencing are not the same as they were last time. I've become older, hopefully a little wiser and it's fair to assume I've had more life experiences that make me a different person, open to interpreting information in a different way.

Whilst this might not be for everyone, re-reading those books that have had a profound influence on my life, over and over again, helps to keep me on track, inspires me to be a better entrepreneur and a better person. And I'm hoping I get to read "How to Win Friends and Influence People" at least another 30 times.

BREE'S TAKE

I love this book too! My dad gave it to me to read when I was sixteen years old, and I am really glad I read it. Today's challenge, grab a copy of "How to Win Friends and Influence People" and read it for the first time, or read it again (once you have finished our book of course). Perhaps buy a few copies and gift them to people you know who are just starting out in business. You never know just how impacting your gift may be.

84

The single best piece of travel advice
I've ever had, came from a trip to India.

A few years back I did a trip to India for a month. I was there for some work, but mostly pleasure. Before going I was surprised at the advice that everyone offered (most of it unsolicited I might add). Things like don't drink the water, don't eat the street food, watch out for the cows and the monkeys, etc.

Whilst they were all helpful tips, the street food is safe and delicious and I did get my foot trodden on by a cow, but I managed to avoid being bitten by a rabid monkey. However, the best piece of advice came from a friend who I think really understood India. He told me to take a book everywhere I go-and he emphasized "everywhere". For those who haven't been to India, there are queues and waiting required for pretty much everything, often with little to no reason for the wait.

When confronted with these queues, you have two choices, work out a way to deal with them or get grumpy and start being a pushy Westerner. The latter will have no impact at all, no matter how angry you might get, or frustrated you might feel. Following his advice, I never needed to get angry or frustrated; I simply pulled out my book and started reading. It was kind of nice and it grew on me over time.

The interesting part is that this habit stuck with me ever since going to India. I never leave home without a book or two. Whenever I am confronted with a wait of some sort, rather than get stressed out I pull out my book and start reading. As a result of this I have read hundreds of books in recent years, and I've learned a great deal.

Those snatches of five minutes here, ten minutes there, are the perfect place to read a few pages of a book, learn something, challenge preconceived thoughts, grow, feel inspired and pretty much everything else that can be achieved by reading a good book.

This has also made me much more patient and able to stop and appreciate a moment, rather than doing the standard grumpy thing. This is kind of nice when we live in a world that seems increasingly short on patience.

Of course now we have access to digital books, which can make it easier. Or so I thought. But what I noticed when I started to read something on my phone I tended to check email, see what was happening on social media and do nothing overly productive. So now I'm back to reading my book at any opportunity-and always a hard copy.

We live in a world where knowledge is vital; we need to commit time to learning more every day. Keeping a book handy is a great way of doing exactly that and perhaps learning to be patient at the same time.

BREE'S TAKE

I took this advice of Andrew's a long time ago, and it is one of the best pieces of advice from him that I've ever received. Carrying around some printed material to read and reflect on is a great use of time. Something else we both do is carry a notebook and pencils – you never know when some brainstorming inspiration is going to strike, so always be prepared.

My challenge to you is to grab that book that you need to read and start taking it everywhere with you. Get into the habit of having a book with you, and use those five minute windows of opportunity to do something far more productive than watch cat videos on Facebook. Read over breakfast if you are on your own, take a short reading break every few hours throughout the day, and ideally, put aside a certain amount of time every day just to read and learn.

85

Is it time for you to do a relationship audit in your business?

Often we don't take the time to really think about our relationships with the people outside of our immediate family and close friends. By these I mean the relationships we have with staff, customers, suppliers, professional advisers and pretty much anyone else who is a part of our business.

Sometimes we spend more time with these people than with our families, yet we don't really think about the health and status of these relationships. Every relationship will at some stage, run its course, and it is better for everyone to act on this as early as possible. In many instances it is simply a matter of one party out growing the other.

A while back I made up a list of the key people in my business world. It was a long list, but I narrowed it down to the 20 most influential people. The list included professional advisers, clients, staff, suppliers and so on. Next to each name I added three columns. In one column I wrote what I liked about the relationship, in the second column I noted problems in the relationship and in the last column I described how I would like the relationship to change.

This exercise had four very specific outcomes:

Firstly, it made me take time to stop and actually think about each relationship and the state it was in.

Secondly, it made me appreciate the aspects of the relationships that I liked.

Thirdly, it let me put into words what I didn't like.

And finally, it enabled me to clarify how I would like these relationships to evolve in the future. Or if in fact, any of them needed to come to an end.

Often this simple act of analysis will solve many frustrations that you may be experiencing in a relationship. All too often we let issues with people continue for far longer than we should. Simply because we don't actually focus any attention on it, other than day to day tasks.

At the same time, this exercise is a very good way to actually gain a deeper appreciation of the people in our lives. For me it was a very good reminder of the important people in my business life who I was taking for granted and I had the chance to do something about it. I had some very honest and open conversations about appreciation and gratitude.

After some practice you may find that you can do a relationship audit in your head, without the need to write it down. It is a quick and effective tool for clarifying why some relationships aren't working and what you need to do about it.

The people in our life have the greatest impact on our success. Sometimes we forget this. Maybe it's time for you to do a relationship audit and take the right action as a result.

BREE'S TAKE

I really like this idea, so let's do it together. Grab a piece of paper or start a spreadsheet. Please be careful what you write here and what you do with this document. We never want to hurt someone's feelings if they are to see this around your office…

Add five columns.

1. The first is for the person you are "auditing" your relationship with.

2. What do you like and value about this relationship?

3. What don't you like or find challenging about this relationship?

4. If the relationship was better, how would it look?

5. What improvements do you think the other person needs to make?

6. What improvements do I need to make?

7. How I am going to make this happen?

Of course, one big question that you have to ask in a bad relationship is, "is this relationship recoverable, or has it moved beyond that?"

86

Nine compelling reasons why writing a book is the best personal development program.

Over the past couple of years, I have helped over 300 people write and publish their first book. Without exception, every one of them found it challenging but hugely rewarding. A common statement is, "I learned so much about myself by writing my book." I'm the same. As an author, I know that with every book I write I learn more about myself, both my strengths and my weaknesses.

So why exactly is writing a book so good for personal growth?

1. **You have to stop talking and start doing.** Few days go by without at least one person saying to me, "I'm going to write a book one day." But it takes a lot to move from talking about writing a book to actually doing it - and this is the biggest leap of all. Growth comes from doing.

2. **You have to master the little voices in your head that try to talk you out of it.** If you are reading this, you're probably pondering writing your own book. From my experience as an author coach, another big hurdle to overcome is that little voice in our head that keeps asking "Who am I to write a book?" Self doubt, low self-esteem, and fear of peer review will stop most people from writing their own book. Stepping up and facing these gremlins head on, is wonderful for growth.

3. **You have to be courageous.** Another strange thing happens when you write a book - people read it (hopefully). To write something that others will read and judge requires conviction. Of course, not everyone will like what you write, and you need to be OK with that. It is courageous to share your thoughts, views, ideas, and opinions, and we all know that courage is a great sign of personal growth.

4. **You need discipline.** One of the integral parts of writing a book is the actual writing! No amount of good intention will replace long periods of time at a keyboard. On the days you plan to write, I guarantee the sun will be shining; there will be parades outside your house; free concerts in the park, and all kinds of distractions ready to take you away from your writing. You have to be disciplined enough to keep your eyes on your screen and the distractions at bay.

5. **You have to say "no" to people.** When you are writing your book, not everyone will be accepting of the fact that you are locking yourself away for months, using every spare moment to get your book out. They will try to distract you and demand you spend time with them. This is where you have to be strong enough to say "no." Those who truly love and support you will get it and do everything they can to help; others, not so much. Most people struggle to say "no" to others at the best of times. This changes when you write a book. You become stronger, and this skill stays with you long after.

6. **You can't half write a book.** When you know other people are going to read what you write, you are under pressure to produce a quality book. It has to be good stuff, it has to be researched, and it has to be correct. Sure, you put in your take on things, but you can't say things that are blatantly wrong or lacking in depth because others will see through it in a second. This means you have to bring your A-game to every page.

7. **You have to be ready for the spotlight.** It's easy to go through life blending in, being part of the crowd, and not sticking your head above the fence. As soon as you write a book, you have separated yourself from others. The spotlight will be on you, among your peers and within your industry. This takes a certain kind of inner strength, that is simply too much for many people. Being able to cope with this is certainly a way to grow as a person.

8. **You have to get comfortable talking about yourself.** Now, I'm not saying you become self-absorbed and narcissistic when you write a book, but people are going to ask you about it. If you are lucky, the media will ask about you too, your background and story. A lot of people find it very hard to talk about themselves, and in some cultures it is frowned upon. But if sharing your story can help others, that's a very good reason to share it. Being able to come to terms with who we are, where we have come from, our mistakes, and what we have learned by making them, and being able to talk about all of this openly, is very therapeutic.

9. **You will have done something extraordinary.** While it may feel like a lot of people are writing books, proportionally it's not true. Sure, there are quite a few people writing 10-page eBooks, but not many are publishing a real book a couple of hundred pages in length. There is a great sense of pride that comes from doing what very few people on the planet will do and that is very good for your self-esteem, confidence, and personal growth. Even more so if you have written a book with the burning desire to help people, to solve problems, and to make the world better in some way.

BREE'S TAKE

There are lots of stats floating around. The last one I came across said that 90% of people in America want to write a book. Seems kind of high, but I know in Australia, once you tell people you are writing a book it's amazing how many people say that they share the same dream. Of course lots of people talk about it, very few do.

If the thought of writing a book excites but scares you and Andrew's words have got you pumped up, here are some ideas to get started.

1. Decide you are going to write a book and commit to doing it.

2. Find a course or a person who can help you do this (obviously check out Andrew's website and drop him a line www.andrewgriffiths.com.au he does author retreats in Bali, throughout Australia and other places around the globe).

3. Find a writing buddy. Someone to hold you accountable.

4. Give yourself a deadline.

5. Make your book all about solving problems for other people.

6. Enjoy the journey, you might just find that you actually like to write.

7. Celebrate by holding a book launch when it's done with your nearest and dearest.

There is obviously a lot more to do, that if you follow point two they will teach you. These few things will help keep you a little sane during this massive task that will certainly change your life, as it has changed mine.

87

Can one person really make or break a business?

Over the past month I have been on the road a lot. Somewhere along the way I lost a small container filled with my favorite cuff links. When I got home I realised I had lost them and I started the task of contacting the 14 hotels that I had stayed at during my time away, to see if my beloved cuff links were sitting in a lost property box somewhere.

I rang them all, with pretty much the same response, "sorry, we haven't found them but leave us your name and number and we will call if we find them". Which of course means I will never hear from them, or so I thought.

Then a very strange thing happened. I received a package from one of the hotels and inside was a card and a set of cuff links. The message in the card said "Dear Mr. Griffiths, we are very sorry that your cuff links weren't here. We know how much we all treasure our special possessions like that. Please find a small gift enclosed to help you start building your cuff link collection again. We know this set won't replace the ones you've lost, but we hope it makes you feel a little better. Kindest regards-Franzi, Guest Services Manager".

I was completely floored. Imagine that. Now this is a hotel I have stayed at many times over the past 25 years. There have certainly been times in there where I stopped staying with them because the service was terrible, or the food was terrible or some other issue. In the past few years I have been staying there more regularly and I have noticed so many positive changes but the biggest reason I stay there is one lady, Franzi the Guest Services Manager. And this recent example is just one of the many extraordinary steps she has taken to make me feel like a valued customer.

A couple of months back I had booked into the hotel and prepaid for a room for five nights on a special offer. After three nights I had to leave, my plans had changed. I didn't bother asking for a refund because I knew that I purchased a cheap rate and we all know that you simply lose your money if you leave early.

Imagine my surprise when I got an email from Franzi saying that they have refunded me two nights' accommodation because I left early. They didn't have to; I didn't expect a refund but I was incredibly appreciative that they did.

So can one person really make or break a business? Absolutely. Now Franzi is part of a team, and I believe that exceptional service starts at the top of an organisation and it works its way down. I have certainly seen this happening at this particular hotel. That said, there are some people who thrive on providing amazing customer service, it's part of their DNA. They are one in a thousand and worth their weight in gold.

If I owned a hotel I would offer Franzi a huge paying job to do what she does so naturally. I think we all need to be on the lookout for that one person who really can make our business extraordinary and do whatever you can to get them to work for you.

BREE'S TAKE

One person can certainly make or break our business. I have been fortunate to have a few people that have made my business, but unfortunately I have also had the unpleasant experience of people that nearly broke my business.

The biggest lesson I have learnt is to hire for attitude not just for skill. A few times I've hired someone who seemed to have more credentials than me in an area my business was lacking, because that's what smart business owners do. I've been bitten a couple of times by these people who have often over promised on their capabilities and grossly under delivered. You have to learn from these experiences and move on.

But if you are like me, you give people the benefit of the doubt and live in hope that their never ending problems are the only reason they aren't doing their job and once their pets stop dying, their family members stop ending up in hospital, their car stops breaking down, their boyfriend stops breaking up with them, their bills start being paid, they get new clothes, they will get on with doing the job you employed them to.

The problem with allowing one person to act like this on your team, is it is like ebola. It can spread so fast to other team members that you better brace yourself, you are about to have an epidemic on your hands.

I put up with a lady not doing her job for a year. Nothing I asked from her ever really got done, and there was always an excuse that was external. It made my very hardworking team furious, they were forever moaning about her and it was a very tough time. After she finally left, I slowly lost nearly every person who was on my team. As much as they loved working for me, they were burnt out.

The situation had totally drained them and as hard as I tried I couldn't get their mojo back, there was too much resentment from picking up the pieces of someone else's work that went on for way too long and it became evident to me. Mental note, act much faster in future.

Moral to the story, a wrong person on your team can cause catastrophic damage to your business. You need to nip it in the bud straight away.

Since this situation I now have put in the following to ensure it never happens again, and my business and new team are better than ever because of it.

1. **Staff surveys.** I ask any new team members a series of questions that tells me how they like to be praised, how they like to be rewarded and how they like to be treated. What is their favourite food, colour, cake, and a whole heap of other stuff that I wanted to know. This helps me buy them gifts, celebrate their birthday and also ensures that I praise them in a way they like, some people don't like to be publicly praised, others love it.

2. **Staff performance check ins.** We do these monthly too. It's a quick one pager with ten questions, it's simple, but it enables us to see if they are having any problems. If there is anything we can improve on; if they have any ideas or concerns. It is mostly about us checking in with how they feel they are going. Sometimes we may talk to them about things they can improve on, but mostly it's how we can improve and support them to be the best they can be.

3. **Staff performance reviews.** These are a bit more detailed with some more questions and allows us to give them areas to improve on, or talk about extra training we feel they could use. We generally do these after their three-month probation and then once or twice a year.

4. **Weekly meetings.** Every Monday morning, we do a one-minute wrap with the team. Each person on the team has one minute to tell us what they are wanting to achieve for the week. This helps them to commit to the tasks and also get clarity about what they are going to do. Secondly it gives the entire team some insight into what their colleagues are up to, so they are more inclined to offer help, or give that person space, if they can hear that the person has a huge week on the cards. We also do an end of week wrap on Friday's to hear how everyone went for the week.

5. **Weekly reports.** My team leaders give me a weekly report detailing all of the wins we have had for the week. Measuring all of the numbers that we are watching from an engagement and sales point of view. They also address any issues that need to be brought my attention.

These few things have made my business much stronger. Moral to the story, always remember that the right staff member can make or break your business, so hire for attitude and skill, not just one or the other.

SECTION 11

GETTING MORE STUFF DONE.

If you think you are busy now and struggling to keep up, don't worry, it's going to get a whole lot worse. Well actually, maybe you should start worrying. We spend a lot of time talking to business owners around the world and without a doubt, we all share one common complaint; a lack of time to get things done. And it's getting harder and harder just to keep up.

Of course, we all have the same amount of time, so that really makes things mute. How we use our time is the issue, and most of us get caught up doing the wrong things on a day to day basis. Productivity is a giant topic, one that is easy to dismiss because there is so much information around about it, but seriously, if you don't start getting control of the "productivity tiger" pretty soon, things are going to go from bad to worse in a hurry.

In this section we share some of the ideas that have worked for us. They might not work for you, but we think they can. Challenge your team, challenge yourself, but most importantly, develop the right habits and rituals. Take control of your time and see the difference it can make to your life.

88

Stop beating yourself up for not getting everything done every day.

One of the biggest challenges that we all face is the steadily increasing number of things that we have to do on a daily basis. There is nothing new about this but many people struggle with a sense of daily frustration simply because they can't get everything done and in all likelihood they never will.

I get the feeling that this sense of frustration, is becoming a little more desperate every day. I'm suggesting a simple process that can dramatically change how you feel.

At the end of the day, when you look at your to do list, and start the afternoon "I'm not good enough" session, beating yourself up because you didn't get everything done, try making a new list.

On this list, jot down a few bullet points for each of the following five questions?

1. **What did I get done today that I'm feeling good about?** Now don't just give them a cursory glance, actually read through the list of things that you were able to cross off and give yourself a pat on the back for getting them done. This might sound kind of silly, but it is amazing how much better you feel at the end of the day when you acknowledge what you did instead of beating yourself up for what you didn't do.

2. **Who have I helped today and how did I help them?** Even on the busiest of days, I'm sure there are people who you helped and supported in some way. It might have been as simple as letting someone into a line ahead of you, being extra appreciative of someone who did something for you, or doing someone a favour.

3. **What did I learn today?** When we learn we grow and when we grow we feel better about ourselves. Think back on your interactions, meetings, conversations, emails, presentations-everything, and try to figure out what lessons you learned in the course of the day. They might be things about yourself, things about your customers, things about your team, it doesn't really matter as long as you are learning.

4. **What am I going to do differently tomorrow?** As you ponder the things you learned during the day, think also about how you will do things differently tomorrow. This might mean doing more of some things, less of others. It might mean deciding to smile more, or be more patient. Or, it might mean saying no, more often so that you can actually get more done.

5. **Which of my personal qualities that I used today am I most proud of?** Reflect on the day, all of the things you did, and try to identify which of your personal qualities you used the most. Acknowledge this quality. When you acknowledge your positive attributes you use them more, and this in turn makes you feel better about yourself and your life overall.

When you finish your "DONE" list-go home. End the day on a high note, celebrating and acknowledging what you've done, who you've helped, what you've learned, and what you will do with what you learned and hopefully appreciating yourself that little bit more.

BREE'S TAKE

To me this is incredibly important. How many of us beat ourselves up daily for not getting everything done on our ridiculously long "to do" list? So my challenge to you is simple – make this evaluation a daily habit. The only way that will happen is if you do it for the next 30 days.

So, the action you need to take will be:

1. Right here, right now, make a commitment to stop beating yourself up.

2. Copy these questions out and put them somewhere easily accessible when you need them for your daily check in.

3. Schedule your 'daily review' in your planner – and make it totally non negotiable.

4. Get your team to do the same, and discuss with each other what you are noticing.

5. If you miss a day, get back into it straight away, or your hopeful new ritual will become a dim memory and you will fall back into the routine of beating yourself up every day.

89

Master this and your daily to-do list could finally be brought under control.

Most of us spend our days totally overwhelmed, responding to countless demands directed our way. The one thing that we all complain about is the lack of time available to do all of the tasks that need to be done, a list that seems to get longer every day.

As much as modern technology has made communication easier, we are all spending a lot of time emailing, marketing through social media, reading material sent to us, and other such things that fit into the general category of "doing business." We feel under the pump from the start of the day, and it is a real battle to get everything on our to-do list achieved.

One simple thing that has helped me become much more productive has been learning to use five-minute increments of time really well. We all get these small windows of opportunity throughout the day, but we tend to dismiss them, with "It's only five minutes-what can I do?"

It might be time we spend waiting for someone to arrive; time before a scheduled phone call; time in between meetings; time spent sitting in the car; time between jobs; or any one of a number of short periods that separate our larger daily activities.

Generally, when these gaps occur, we simply kill time for a few minutes, not really doing anything of any significance. Check Facebook or Twitter, play a game, look out the window, or scroll through our inbox. I think this is a wasted opportunity. There are actually a lot of things you can get done in a five-minute block.

In the morning when I am planning my day and writing my to-do list, I have a column for the things I can do during my five-minute windows of opportunity. This way I actively look for these short breaks, because I have a list of small tasks that I can slot in straight away.

When you add these tasks up to do them all in one hit, they can take up quite a lot of time. But when done during the course of the day, a few here and a few there, you hardly notice.

I am amazed at how many of the smaller, easy-to-forget jobs I get done in a day simply by making better use of these small, five-minute increments. I feel much more satisfied because I am getting more done. I don't have as many irritating piles of "things to do," and my business is financially better off because most of the five-minute jobs that I do relate to following up with clients, thanking clients, and generating new work.

We all get the same amount of time, and how we use this time is important. As simple as this little idea might be, when it comes to productivity it is the little ideas that help us to get more done.

BREE'S TAKE

Love this idea, so let's take five minutes now and write yourself a list of five-minute job's that you can do. Print out the list and stick it on your wall, in your diary, on your computer desktop (you get my drift). Why not do it for your team as well to boost productivity?

Here are a few of my five minute jobs that I schedule into my day:

- Pick up the phone and make a thank-you call to a customer

- Write someone a quick thank-you note or send a thank-you email

- Pay a few bills

- Make up an invoice

- Do your online bookkeeping

- Proofread a document

- Order something you need online

- Review your business goals and plans

- Tidy up your desk/car/work station

- Read a small section from a book to learn a new skill

- Bullet point an article that you might need to write

- Book some travel

- Do something healthy- stretch, drink water, plan a healthy dinner

- Reconfirm a meeting

- Do a five-minute meditation

- Read through your daily goals, make sure you are on target

Once you master the art of using five-minute increments really well, you will be amazed at how much you actually get done on a daily basis. You will feel great and you might just tame that "to do" list after all.

90

One of the most important items you need to have on your daily "To Do List" and virtually nobody does.

A few years ago my typical work practice was to get to the office very early in the morning. I would set about making my 'to do' list for the day, which typically had about a million items on it in my attempt to do as much as I possibly could. Of course, it would be impossible to get everything done on the list in a month, let alone a week, but I didn't know any better.

One day I was having a coffee with a friend and I happened to jot down a few things in my notebook. She saw my 'to do' list (which ran over three pages), and with a look of shock, she asked, 'When do you find time to just sit and think?'

Now, that was a powerful question because I didn't allow any time to just sit and think. In fact, from the minute I arrived at my office to the minute I left I pretty well ran like a mad man all day, often not even bothering to stop and eat, fuelled on by coffee and sugar.

From that day on I made a point of putting aside some time each day to do nothing but think and reflect. Sometimes I might allocate 30 minutes; if I have a lot on my mind I might allocate several sessions in a day, equalling more than an hour a day.

I fly a lot these days, and I use this time as "thinking time". It is perfect; there are no phones, emails or meetings to interrupt you. I can completely lose myself to my thoughts. I put on a set of headphones, take out my notebook, close my eyes and just let my mind go to wherever it wants to go. If there are certain issues that need my attention I let these roll around in my brain until I get some clarity.

I am amazed at how empowering this feels and how it has reduced my stress and the feeling of being overwhelmed. Our brains need time to process information. The more information coming in the more time the brain needs to process it. If you don't give your brain time to work through things it keeps them in a holding pattern, with more items being added every day, which has to lead to a sense of exhaustion and being overwhelmed.

There are so many benefits in allocating time to do nothing but sit and think every day. The least of which will be a feeling of control and calmness instead of feeling thrown into the fray from the minute you turn your computer on.

The only way this will work, is if you look at this time as a significant investment in yourself and your business. Make sure your "thinking time" is in your diary. Change your work practice to suit and find a place that is conducive to letting you sit and think in an uninterrupted way.

BREE'S TAKE

Taking time every day to nurture your mind is one of the best things you can do for your productivity. Here are seven things that you can do in your "thinking time", or to increase your ability to have a great thinking time session.

1. **Meditate**

   This one is pretty obvious and has been around for thousands of years. A simple google will find a quick guided meditation. Some are as short as four minutes to give your brain a little rest and a reset. My team often find me laying on my office floor wondering what the hell I am doing. But that few minutes gives me a quick break and off I go again.

2. Walk

A quick walk around the block, even to get something off the printer is a start. It's a great reset for your eyes to look at greenery instead of a screen all day long and nothing like walking to get your mind to wander.

3. Exercise

Nothing strenuous, some squats, lunges, walk up some stairs, anything at all that will get your blood or muscles pumping and your brain juices flowing.

4. Dance

Sometimes I hear a really good song on the radio so I will turn up the music really loud in the office (if no one is on the phone) and dance as badly as I can. Often it gets the team to laugh, and they join in. It shifts the mood, raises the energy and then I go and sit quietly to ponder.

5. Play music

Whether you listen to some quiet music sitting with a cup of tea, or pick up that guitar or another instrument and have a bit of a strum and let your mind creatively wander, music is very good for the soul.

6. Have a nap

Twelve minutes is the ultimate time apparently, and it works for me. I set my phone on silent, and put on an alarm for twelve minutes' time. I turn off my brain as fast as I can and lay there. Sometimes I drift off, sometimes I don't, but regardless I wake up revitalised. It takes some training, but give it a go.

7. Pleasure yourself

Sorry if you just choked on your cereal, but yes, scientists say that releasing endorphins is a great way to get the brain stimulated. It can be as simple as sitting with your favourite cup of tea and some yummy chocolate, to laughing, or to you know what... I'll let your mind decide what you can do, that you find pleasing. But rest assured it doesn't have to be sexual.

91

This one tool will double your productivity overnight.

We all struggle to find ways to get more done on a daily basis. Doing business is complicated and demanding and we seem to be trying to pack more tasks into our every day. But rather than feeling like we are getting more done, we seem to be working longer days to fit it all in. It's hard to feel productive sometimes.

I was the same, feeling overextended, until I discovered a very powerful way to tilt things back in my favour.

Some time back I had a project where I had to give feedback to fifty people, taking part in an entrepreneurial program. The task was daunting and likely to take me an entire week to complete. So instead of writing the individual reports I decided to record them.

Productivity Tip: Record Your Messages

Using a cheap headphone plugged into my computer and a simple recording app, I recorded between five and ten minutes of personal feedback for each person. This enabled me to complete the feedback project in two days as opposed to five. Shortly after sending out the feedback, I started to receive emails from the entrepreneurs sharing just how much they loved getting the recorded reports.

They really liked that it was so personal, the depth of the feedback I shared. The ability to be able to have complex ideas explained in detail and the fact that they could listen to it, as they needed, whilst driving or exercising.

I was a little surprised by this. Initially I did it to save me time but I soon saw just how beneficial it was to the students. Then it dawned on me that I could use this technique in a few other areas of my business life that were causing me grief.

Like most people, I had a pile of special emails that I needed to respond to, but they were all a little complicated or requiring lengthy replies. I kept putting them off until I could find the time to respond accordingly, but it just wasn't happening. Taking my new approach, I started early the next morning and managed to record twenty complicated messages in about two hours.

Now this felt like the single most productive day I had ever had. It was barely 9am and I had achieved more in two hours than it felt like I had done in the previous week. And once I started to get responses to my emails, from my clients, staff members, suppliers and potential customers, all saying how refreshing it was to receive a message in this format, I was hooked.

Now I don't record every message, but I do record those messages that require longer responses than an average email. Those that need a more personal feel; or those conversations that are complicated or difficult for some reason.

This in turn means that I don't look through my email, mentally classifying them as "too hard to answer now", I simply group the tough ones, or the ones needing more explanation, and then I sit down and knock them all over in an hour. And best of all, now I get to go home with an empty inbox, which is one of the sweetest feelings.

When I am asked about the benefits of recording letters, emails and messages (and I am asked this often) my response is:

- You can say much more in a shorter amount of time; a 3-4 minute recorded message can be the equivalent of a couple of pages of written text.

- There are fewer miscommunications regarding the tone of the message.

- It is much more engaging and personal for the person receiving the communication.

- It is a great way to stand out from others and to be memorable.

- You can record responses from any device, from any location. This means sitting in a park, answering emails by recording messages can now be an enjoyable process as opposed to a dreaded chore.

- You get to clear your inbox of the "complicated" messages needing a response.

This could be one of the best productivity tools around. It certainly has saved me many hours each week and made difficult conversations much easier.

BREE'S TAKE

As someone that freezes when I receive an email that requires more than five minutes to reply to, these are great ideas. I have been caught out many times as I receive an email, glance at it and ascertain if it's going to take more time than I have right now to reply. Next thing I know, I have forgotten the email, and it's been a few weeks when I find it again. Then I fight with myself as to whether it's too late now to reply and the cycle continues.

I completely agree that picking up the phone or recording a message is a much faster approach.

I've even learnt the skill of sending emails that require only a few minutes for someone to respond to. I also ensure I lay them out in a very easy to read format so that it helps the people I am working with to respond quickly to my emails too.

Today I want you to think about any other regular correspondence you get.

Do your customers often ask you the same things?

Take some time now to write out a list of your most frequently asked questions. Then why not rip out your voice recorder or video recorder and answer all of them. Then, get them transcribed, load both versions to your website, and when someone asks a question you can send them a link to the answer, or do up a specific answer for that question.

It's done once, and you don't have to repeat yourself like a broken record.

92

Twenty-one 'in-case-of-emergency' ideas for writing articles and blog posts.

We are all being told that we need to write content, and of course we do, but there are those days when we've got nothing. The brain just can't come up with anything to write and we go into a panic and waste a lot of time looking at an empty page.

To overcome this issue, here is my list of "In Case of Emergency" blog post or article ideas. Of course if you write about all of these during the month you will have a pretty dynamic blog, filled with lots of great information that is certain to create a deep connection with your community.

1. Do a behind the scenes article on part of your business. Maybe something like "a day in the life of our delivery guy" or "come and meet the accounts department".

2. "How to" advice on whatever your area of expertise may be. This might be in the form of videos, articles, MP3 recordings, and interviews. Whatever is going to work best with your audience, and whatever is going to be easiest to produce.

3. Product reviews are always helpful. You can save people time, take the confusion out of their purchasing decisions and have some fun at the same time.

4. Business news-what's happening around your business? New people, milestones, new services, new products, things like that.

5. Meet the people-profile individuals within your business and again, have some fun with it. Show their personalities, what they like to do when they aren't working, what their great assets are and so on.

6. Have a soapbox rant once a month-what's driving you nuts? Now it's good to be passionate, but pick your topic wisely. Learn from those politicians that seem to lack the ability to sensor what they rant about.

7. Showcase one of your customers every week-who they are, what they do, find out their story and how it is they came to be doing business with you.

8. Unusual facts and figures about your business-how much stuff do you use, your most distant order, the funniest customer request?

9. Invite someone to write a guest blog post-maybe a supplier, a family member, a friend or a customer. Even get other people in the business to write an article from time to time.

10. How about a quote of the week? And explain why it is important or meaningful to you.

11. A monthly summary of what's been going on in the business for the past month. Highlights, challenges, bestselling products or services, anything new and so on.

12. Special offers (no one ever complains about special offers but make sure they are great offers).

13. Share some of the stories about the not-for-profit work that you do or the charities you support but go a little deeper, why are you involved, what's your back story for supporting the charity?

14. What are the most frequently asked questions that you get asked? Just answer one at a time, you don't need to answer them all at once.

15. Talk about new products and services being developed-don't wait for them to be finished, talk about them when they are in production.

16. Share your mistakes-show you are human when you get things wrong, and explain why it happened and what you did about it.

17. Do you have any free resources?

18. Can you recommend other businesses-maybe there is a business close by, like a restaurant, that you and your team love, why not post a positive review on your site?

19. Are there any events coming up that might be of interest to your community (even if they aren't your events)?

20. Your take on a news story that is relevant to your business, industry or community.

21. Write about your success stories. Now this isn't a brag post, but an overview of a project or product that you have developed for a customer that worked really well. The customer gets featured, you show your capability, and everyone wins.

BREE'S TAKE

After a decade of publishing over two and a half million magazines, it's safe to say I love content planning. All of Andrew's content ideas here are great. Now you are going to need a process to manage all of this content. Here are a few things to consider.

1. How many pieces of content are you going to need to write each day, week or month?

2. What platforms are you going to use to share this content? Your Blog, Facebook, LinkedIn, or a combination of a few platforms?

3. What is the process you are going to be using to manage this?

Once you know how much content you are going to produce, where you are going to share it and how you are going to manage, you can get cracking. To manage articles there are many platforms that you can use. My favourites are Trello, Google Docs and a good old fashioned Excel spreadsheet. Choose your platform and map it out by day, week or month and before you know it, you will be the king or queen of content planning.

93

Twenty-One seriously good ideas to help you win the war on productivity once and for all.

Clearly productivity is a hot topic these days. We're all complaining about having more to do and less time to do it. We have incredible technology, apps everywhere, productivity coaches and productivity workshops, but are we winning?

Personally some days I am, other days not so much. But I am always looking for more ideas, here are twenty-one of my favourites that I use. My advice is simple - introduce one idea a day, or even one idea a week and you will become the most productive person on the planet (well I hope so).

1. **Schedule time every day for the unexpected.** Every day we have unexpected things happen. These might be requests from customers, new opportunities, staff issues to handle or personal things that need our attention. At the start of the day we didn't know about them, but they appeared in the course of the day as "unexpected" gremlins. But, are "unexpected" things really unexpected? I allow two hours a day for "unexpected" things. One hour in the morning and one hour in the afternoon. I don't think I've ever had a day where I didn't use at least one of these hours. And of course if nothing unexpected comes up, I'm sure you've got plenty of other things to do in that hour.

2. **The best productivity tool ever**. For me it is the good old egg timer. I have a 15-minute hour glass that I use to monitor how much time I spend on social media, on calls, doing specific tasks that have a habit of taking far longer than I planned. Watching the grains of yellow sand flowing and realising just how quickly they flow has given me real perspective on what I can do in a 15-minute block of time, but it has also helped me to avoid wasting a lot of time.

3. **Invest in learning how to use your technology.** Most of us totally underuse technology. Whether it be our phone, computer, an app or a microwave oven. Who takes the time to read the manual? Very few people. I pay people to teach me how to use my technology. If I get a new app, or new computer, I pay my I.T advisor to spend a few hours and show me all of the features. I might get them in a few times to do this, just until I get the hang of it. Now I don't claim to be using all of my technology to it's full capacity, but I use a lot more than I did. And as most technology is designed to help us save time, in some shape or form, I'm far more productive as a result.

4. **Keep meetings to fifteen minutes.** There is nothing worse than a long winded meeting, that seems to drag on because people simply like to hear their own voice. Try and keep as many meetings as you can to 15 minutes (put the hour glass on the table to speed things along). Generally, you can have everything covered in a short amount of time, and you can do four meetings in an hour as opposed spending half a day. Clearly if you can master this, you will save a pile of time if you live in a world full of meetings.

5. **Take the time to do things once.** We all have those tasks that take longer and are more complicated than they need to be. But because we keep half doing them, instead of taking the time to do them properly, they take longer than they should and cause us no end of frustration. My philosophy is to take the time to do the job properly and do it once.

6. **Work out how much it costs you to use social media.** I recently worked out the actual cost of using social media on an hourly basis. What I mean by this is, how much does it cost me to run my business for an hour. Now once I had this figure in my head, idly wasting a few hours on Facebook had a real dollar value, and I certainly don't do it as much, which has in turn improved my productivity.

7. **Get really good at using five minute increments.** Throughout our day we have many little windows of opportunities, normally five minutes or less. What do we do with them? Check Facebook? Flick through email. Maybe waste time waiting for whatever we are waiting for. I stopped wasting that time by making a daily list of things I need to do that will take less than five minutes. Then throughout the day when I have this little window, I open up my list and get a few things done. Now collectively over a day, I get a lot done - if I sat down and did them all one after another they would take quite some time and bite into my day. Doing it this way I don't even notice, but I get the satisfaction of crossing a pile of 'to do's' off of my list.

8. **Plan your week, your day, your hour.** One of the big problems with productivity is losing control of our day. Hence I recommend doing a lot of planning, and revising your planning on a daily and even hourly basis. Many people say they don't really have time to plan, and I know we all know the value of planning, but do you do it enough? The best planning I do is "the next hour" plan. That's the one that makes me really productive.

9. **Learn to lie.** When I am travelling for work, I seem to have a crazy busy day before I leave. It's like everyone thinks I'm leaving the planet. Now I tend to tell a fib and say I'm leaving a day earlier than I actually am. The purpose of this is to give me a day without interruptions before I actually leave, because everyone thinks I'm out of the country. I get more done on that "bonus" day than in the week before. I think that sometimes it's OK to tell a white procrastination improving lie.

10. **Make decisions don't procrastinate.** I think many of us are so overwhelmed that simply making decisions has become a lot harder. Add to this the fact that we have so much more information to absorb and in many ways, we've all become procrastinators. I've learned to make decisions quickly. Get the information in front of me, commit time to "making decisions about important stuff" - and I do.

11. **Stop Multitasking.** This is simple, retrain your brain, do one task at a time and do it really well. We've all read that multitasking is a myth, it is. Get far more done by doing one thing at a time and your quality of work will increase, your brain will love you for it and you will finish your day feeling far less fried.

12. **Record responses and send MP3 files.** I've been doing this for years. Whenever I have a long email or document to send to someone, rather than sit down and spend hours writing it, I talk into my phone and send an MP3 audio file instead. Now of course this won't work with every document, but it will work with many. It saves a pile of time, my clients love it - and I do a better job because I don't dread sitting down for hours to write a long winded response to an email.

13. **Re-organise your workspace.** Periodically re-organise your workplace. Move things around, pull things out and clean behind them, bring in new furniture, put stuff where it will be efficient to help make you more productive. Often we don't move a thing for years and in fact our office is not really ideally laid out to suit our needs. So if it has been a while since you moved your office around, give it a go. Think about it before you do, use it to re-energise yourself and to implement more productive systems.

14. **Turn off all alerts.** This is a simple one that we could all do right now. Turn off as many alerts as you can. Especially the ones that really aren't that important. We are so attuned to beeps and pings and funny little sounds that drag us away from whatever we are doing and distract us. It is far better to get into the routine of checking what you need to check when it suits you, instead of becoming a slave to the sound of alerts.

15. **Start a "Drives Me Crazy" board.** Do you have things in your business that you've been meaning to address but you just never seem to get to it. They drive you crazy every time you use them or walk past them, but you never stop to address them. I suggest starting a "Drives Me Crazy" board. Carry some sticky notes in your pocket and when you come across an issue that drives you crazy, write it on your sticky note and put it on your "Drives Me Crazy" board. Then commit time each week to addressing the things that drive you or your team crazy. Give it a few weeks and you will be amazed at how many issues you resolve once and for all, and this will make you feel better and be more productive.

16. **Don't get guilted into committing on the spot.** I struggled with this a great deal. I would bump into someone on the street, they would ask me to come and do something, always for free, and I would feel too guilty saying no. So I would commit and walk away angry and frustrated with myself. Now, I never commit on the spot. I always say something along the lines of

"that sound interesting, let me check my diary and my commitments and get back to you". This gives me time to think about whatever it is that I'm being asked to do and decide if I want to do it. It's much easier to decline via an email if I don't want to do it.

17. **Take the time to delegate cleanly.** In the past I've been terrible at delegating. I always found it irritating and I would rush through what I expected of the person I was delegating to. I have learned that if I slow the process down, and actually do a thorough delegation process, it will ultimately save me a lot of time with questions, mistakes, crossed wires and other results of poor communication.

18. **Don't confuse distractions with opportunities.** When I had an office with staff I used to get really frustrated with the constant interruptions. I let my team know and accordingly, they stopped interrupting me which initially I thought was great. Of course the problems started to arise as I realised that I wasn't giving them the direction they needed. It was my business and I was sabotaging it. So I reframed my thinking and decided to look at interruptions with my stuff as an opportunity, to do what we do better. I just retrained them to be better at interrupting me. Choose a better time, make sure I'm not in the middle of stuff, email and check for a good time and so on.

19. **Ask a busy person how they do what they do.** We all know that one person who seems to do ten times more than you, and they do it in such a relaxed and easy way. Sure, they are probably paddling like a duck below the surface, but to all outward appearances they are a sea of calm and a "getting stuff done" machine. Ask them for their advice, their tricks, their systems, and whatever words of wisdom that they can share to help you. I've found that people will gladly share their secrets if you just bother to ask.

20. **Retrain those around you to help you be more productive.** Most of our bad productivity habits have occurred over time. They sneak in. When it comes to people, we need to retrain them. For example, all of my friends and family know that when I'm writing a book - leave me alone. They are wonderfully supportive, they get the challenge of writing a book and they support me. How do you retrain those around you to help you get more done?

21. **Hold out for as long as you can before checking your email.** Most of us check our email soon after rolling out of bed. I've found that the longer I can hold off on checking my email, and spend that "email free time" doing more meaningful work, the more productive I become. Let's be honest, the minute you start checking your email, you've lost control of the day and you will spend all of your time responding to others. Unless of course, you are brave enough to only log into your email a few times a day. But that's a whole other article.

BREE'S TAKE

All of these are great ideas, Andrew and I have been using a lot of these for a number of years, and they have helped us enormously to be more productive. Sure, we all have days where we are not as productive as we would like to be. But try implementing one of these today to see if it helps your productivity, and then try out a few more to see how you go. Imagine if we could use all twenty-one of these each day? We'd be the most productive human on the planet.

SECTION 12

WHEN THE GOING GETS TOUGH.

Business is hard, there is no way around it. We're not living in Disneyland where there are unicorns and butterflies and crazy people in costumes wandering around (well not in our businesses anyway). We get it. We can certainly show our share of business battle scars, but we choose not to focus on them, instead we prefer to talk about the outcomes of these wars and how we got better as a result of the tough times.

We would be lying to say there weren't times that we wanted to give up. The times that weren't just tough, they were impossible and on every level; personal, financial, relationship, health - everything. But we survived. We got through them and we're guessing you've got through a few of your own.

This section is all about coping with the tough times. Learning from them, growing from them and making sure we do everything we can, to avoid having more of them.

94

Five ways to cope with a major business setback.

One gloomy Thursday morning, I received the call that could have announced the end of my marketing business. My biggest client had gone broke, the court had taken over the company, and it was highly unlikely I would get any of the money that was owed to me. At the time, their account was around $200,000.

I remember feeling like I had been kicked in the belly. I had no idea how I was going to survive this? I had a few employees on my team and we sat around for most of the day, simply shaking our heads in disbelief.

Thus began our period of wallowing.

For the next few weeks, we really struggled to come to terms with what had happened, and more importantly, what would happen. We were all kind of frozen. It felt like someone had died and there were no answers to be had.

So we wallowed.

But I soon realised that the biggest threat to my business wasn't my client's demise. It was our self-indulgent wallowing. I had to leap into action. The following steps saved my business, and they just might rescue yours following a big setback.

1. **I set up meetings with each of my clients.** I needed to make sure that what had happened, was a one-off anomaly and not the beginning of a series of events that were guaranteed to end my business. My clients all reassured me that there were no problems; in fact, some offered me more work, knowing that I had extra capacity.

2. **I got into serious business-development mode.** This was tough, especially as business had been good for a while and I hadn't chased new clients for quite some time. But I had to make generating new business my number one priority.

3. **I rounded up some cash.** The cash may have stopped coming in, but it still had to go out. I had to figure out exactly how much cold hard cash I had and I needed access to more right away. I knew that the longer I waited, the harder it would be to get. I may have been shocked, but I was OK-the real crunch was going to come in a couple of months. I got some extra credit cards, sold a few toys, and put together a small war chest of money to hopefully get me through.

4. **I made some hard decisions.** I had to lay off some staff, which was really hard. But if I didn't, the whole business was going to go and everyone would lose their jobs. I downsized my office, moving to a new cheaper premises. These were hard decisions, but now was the time to make hard decisions.

5. **I tapped my network for support.** People want to help. That's what I learned when I reached out to my network. People responded, offering support in many ways. Now I don't mean financial support-they offered advice, introduced me to new potential clients, spread the word that I was looking for more work, offered a shoulder to lean on. And some tough loving whenever I fell back into wallow mode.

Luckily for me, the moves I took saved my business and in fact created a much better business for me today. My advice is simple: Go ahead and wallow for a little while. Lick your wounds, be grumpy, experience the mixture of emotions associated with any setback. And then give yourself a good talking to, and take some serious action.

BREE'S TAKE

If you are in business, you are guaranteed to have a major setback at some point. It goes with the territory. If you are lucky you will only have one major set back.

Take some time today to work out the five biggest issues that could impact your business at any point, and put a plan into play as to how you would fix it. Think of it like a fire escape plan.

Some issues you could map out on your fire plan, for could be;

1. A key member of staff suddenly leaving.

2. A key member of staff becoming ill or injured and unable to work.

3. A key piece of machinery breaking down.

4. Threat of a natural disaster.

5. You becoming ill.

6. Your family becoming ill.

7. Loosing a major client.

8. A disgruntled staff member.

9. A staff member that steals.

10. Your office loosing power and internet for a week.

There are literally hundreds of things that can happen, but I suggest mapping out five of the biggest issues that scare you, so that you can put a simple plan into play, should that situation arise.

If a fire was coming for your business, would you and your team know what to do? Would they know what to grab if they had time, so that your business may be able to salvage some important items?

When you think through a bad situation, and work out a plan of attack if it were to arise, and document it, we tend to be much more prepared for that worse case scenario.

It's not nice to think about these issues, but putting strategies into play will give you some peace of mind when things get messy. Times like that, in the heat of the moment, thinking clearly isn't easy, use the Girl Guides motto, "be prepared".

95

How can we stay sane when it feels like
the world is going crazy?

We are living in a world where there is way too much bad news bombarding us twenty four hours a day. At times, it really does get hard to stay positive and focused when it feels like the world is going crazy.

Of course apart from retaining our sanity, we also need to maintain our productivity. We can't slide into depression, throw our hands up in the air and run away. I'm not saying we should live in denial, or ignore what is going on in the world, but like all information coming in, we need to manage it, learn from it and move on.

These are seven strategies I use to cope in a crazy world:

1. **Proactively protect your mind-don't just sit back and absorb the negativity.** Interestingly enough, according to Seth Godin, the world has grown less violent every decade for the past thousand years. It sure doesn't feel that way. What has changed though is the sheer volume of news that we are being bombarded with every minute of every day. When something bad happens, we certainly know about it. It makes really good sense to protect your mind by being extremely discerning with what you watch, what you read and what you listen to. Sure, find out what is going on, but then that is enough. Do we really need to read or listen to a hundred articles about the same murder?

2. **Look for the good–not for the bad.** When the world seems to be going crazy, it can be hard to see the good. But rest assured it is there and in fact there is far more good going on than crazy. It's just that you have to know where to find it. This means we need to consciously hunt down the things that make us feel good, the websites, the articles, the radio, the television shows, the people, and the places we love. A lot of people complain about cute pet videos on social media, but really, I would much rather watch them than videos of violent crime that have been aired on every medium a thousand times.

3. **Do as many kind deeds as you can.** In the darkest of times the smallest acts of kindness have the greatest impact. Whenever the world seems dark and gloomy, I find that the more kind deeds I can do for others, the better I feel. Little things like giving someone a parking space, donating to a charity, carrying a bag or reaching out to help someone who needs some support. Do what nurtures you, do it selflessly, and do it as often as you can.

4. **Avoid the situations where negativity rules.** It's interesting to see how quickly conversations turn to negative topics, and of course it is quite natural when the topic is current. But we all play a role in keeping these conversations alive. I find that I have to make a conscious decision not to participate in the conversations that are all about doom and gloom. Whenever they take that direction, I leave or disconnect. I also make a point of avoiding those people who seem to revel in talking about the latest bad news story, they can't wait to dive straight in and get to the nitty gritty of the latest calamity.

5. **Do more of the things that make you smile inside and out.** We all have those things that make us feel good, and I mean good right to our core. I know that if I am feeling down, spending a few minutes playing with my little dog really helps. Being bombarded by her cheeky demands to play fetch, and her demands to be cuddled–all melt my heart and make me feel such love and adoration for her. The world is a very nice place when she is snuggled up on my lap. I get the same feeling going for a long walk in the rainforest or on a beach or even reading a great book. We all have those special things that evoke a wonderful sense of inner peace, contentment and gratitude. The key is to remember what they are and do them often, especially when it feels like the world is going crazy.

6. **Get excited about your future.** It is easy to lose hope when there doesn't appear to be a lot of good news around. But these are the times that we have to focus inwards, appreciate our businesses, the difference we make to others, the opportunities ahead, and the way we can make the world a better place and focus on all of this. Visualise where you are heading and what you are going to achieve, and that excitement is contagious in a good way.

7. **Treat this as a daily practice.** We know that if we want to be fit, we need to exercise daily. If we want to grow our business, we need to work on it daily. The same principle applies with building a strong and positive outlook on life, we need to work on it daily. Many of us have developed bad habits around what we watch, what we listen to, what we read and what we say. I work at this every day, to be as positive a person as I can be, then help others be more positive. It doesn't sound like much, but it is me doing my part to make the world a better place. My advice is, make this approach to life a conscious decision, and even more importantly a philosophy to live by.

BREE'S TAKE

Throughout this book Andrew and I have written a lot about attitude, the people in your life, growth and development, and all of those less specific and more emotive business tools. We both agree that these are in fact the most important business tools. Business success or failure is largely due to our state of mind.

Today I want you to write out a list of the most negative things in your life – people, situations, thoughts and those things that make you feel unhappy. Write it all out.

Now look at the list. Are there any items on there that you can resolve? Are there any items on there that you need to forgive? Are there any items on there that you need to cut from your life? Are there any items on there that you need to give yourself an uppercut about and change your thought process about? Because they are actually good things and you are just thinking about them in a negative way.

Write it out and take some time to think about it, then action what you are going to do about it. It could be getting rid of negative media, right through to disengaging from a negative friend.

It's a tough process, but one I guarantee, you will be grateful for and one that will allow more space for the positive things in your life and in your business.

96

Ten ways to pull yourself out of any business rut.

From time to time we all fall into a bit of a business rut. For some reason nothing seems to be working. If there can be a problem there will be a problem; we have issues with staff, customers, suppliers, politicians, global warming-everything and everyone. It all gets to be too much.

The key of course is to work out how to pull ourselves out of a rut as quickly as possible. Here are ten strategies that I've used in the past:

1. **Try to figure out exactly why you are in a rut?** When we are clear about the "why" it becomes much easier to get back on track. We need to put words around it, something like "I don't feel like I have any challenges in my business" or "it always seems like a financial struggle and I don't feel like I am getting any closer". Often this moment of clarity is enough to get things back on track.

2. **What's your big reason "why" for working so hard?** This is important. We need to have a big enough reason to justify why we are doing what we are doing. This applies to motivation overall. If there is not a big enough reason to do something, generally we won't. It might be time to re-evaluate exactly what your big reason is and why.

3. **Remember where you came from.** I think that one of the biggest reasons people fall into a rut is that they don't feel like they are making any progress. I always try to tell my clients that they need to take lots of photos, keep old brochures, keep printouts of old advertisements, logos, websites, uniforms etc., as a way to measure just how far they have come. When we do this we have a sense of progress.

4. **Move things or change things simply for the sake of it.** This might be as simple as moving the furniture around in your office, to moving an entire workshop around. One thing I tend to do if I feel like I'm in a business rut is to change my logo and corporate branding. Luckily I don't get into a rut every month, that would be expensive for me and confusing for my clients. But a new look for your business does go a long way to reigniting your enthusiasm and passion. I recommend this a lot to tired and worn out businesses.

5. **Introduce 'NEW.'** From my experience most business owners love the concept of new ideas, new projects, new products, new clients and new money, more than they love the idea of actually doing the work. What "NEW" things can you introduce into your business to get that energy flowing and the enthusiasm back?

6. **Have a holiday.** Let's be honest, there is never a good time to have a holiday, especially when you own your own business. We are always too busy, there is never enough money, and it is the wrong time and so on. I suggest to people that the longer the list of reasons, why now, is not a good time to have a break. The more important it is, that they have one. Even a mini break, a day off, a weekend away, anything to help get the mind and the body feeling good. And most importantly of all, do it without GUILT.

7. **Goof off.** Being in a rut means that everything is just a little bit harder. You tend to spend a lot more time sitting and staring at a computer screen. Getting started on projects is hard (normally fear of a looming deadline does it in the end) and your overall productivity is about half of what it normally is. Now these are the times that I think it is OK to goof off for a while. Do something you really love to do, maybe go to a movie, go for a walk or catch up with a friend for a coffee and a chat.

8. **Find a confidante (not a misery buddy).** At times like this it is great to have a good confidante who you can share your feelings and frustrations with. Now this is not a misery buddy, we don't want someone who is going to reinforce the fact that you are in a rut, and enthusiastically keep you there. This is someone who will listen to you, let you get whatever your issues are off your chest, but they will also be wise enough to help you pinpoint what the real issues may be.

9. **Get rid of what drives you nuts.** Every business has certain things that drives the business owner nuts. This might be a certain customer, a certain piece of equipment, a dumb system that doesn't work anymore or a cupboard full of junk. Now is the time to get rid of at least one thing that drives you nuts. It might be that one customer who you can never please, who despite everything you do, is never happy and takes up so much of your time, that other better customers get neglected. Whatever your one thing is, address it today.

10. **Complete your 'incompletes.'** Whenever I am in funky zone (AKA a business rut), I find my pile of big, irritating, complicated stuff that I call my "incompletes" and I shut the door, turn off the phone, close my email and methodically work my way through all of those things that for whatever reason, I have been putting off. There is nothing better than seeing an empty "in" tray with no "incompletes" in it. It feels like the slate has been wiped clean and you can think clearly again.

Now, interestingly enough, all of the above will certainly help and lift you out of a rut, even if there doesn't seem to be a logical reason behind it. How on earth can moving your furniture around help you to get your mojo back? I don't really know, but it does. So if you are in a rut, please try these ten ideas, they have worked for me many times.

BREE'S TAKE

Andrew has some great ideas here (he's a clever fella isn't he?) so I suggest answering these questions and putting them somewhere safe so that you can pull them out to look at, when the going gets tough.

MY EMERGENCY BUSINESS RUT BUSTER.

1. What's my big WHY?

2. How does what I do make the world a better place?

3. What does this business give my loved ones?

4. Where could I go today to make me feel more positive?

5. Where could I go on a holiday to completely regroup?

6. What makes me smile?

7. Who can I talk to to make me feel better?

8. Who should I avoid talking to because they make me feel worse?

9. Who can I talk to, who will give me some tough loving?

10. What is my reason for not giving up?

Feeling like you are on a hamster wheel and that the world is on your shoulders is not a nice place to be. So the sooner you can get out of it, and get on with it, the better.

97

Don't sell your soul when times get tough.

Whenever we face a few challenges on the financial front and we find that it has become harder to get sales, we have to be careful to avoid the temptation of "getting the sale at any cost." Rest assured, there is always a cost to pay when you try to get the sale at any cost.

There is no point in discounting to the point where you literally make no money, or even worse, the sale is going to cost you money. As much as it is tempting to get the cash in, even when you know you are losing on the deal, it is an act of desperation that tends to end in tears. Eventually it will catch up with you and it is surprising how many businesses send themselves broke by doing this.

Several years ago I did a job for a publishing company. They produced specialist magazines and books that they sold on subscription right around the world. They asked me to help them as business was tough, but their new subscriptions were good, yet they still seemed to be going backwards. I spent an hour looking at the cost of their products etc. and found that for every subscription they sold they were losing almost $100 over the year.

Now this business had sold in the vicinity of 20,000 subscriptions - so when you do the sums, clearly there were big problems. The subscriptions were priced way too low, because that was the price the company thought they could sell them for, not what they should have charged. This compounding error almost sent them broke. We had to do some fancy footwork to get them out of the crisis, but luckily we did.

Another temptation in tough times is to lower your standards and expectations regarding your standard sales protocol. This may mean that you extend credit when you wouldn't normally, or that you give away more than is realistic, or that you over promise on time frames that you can't possibly deliver on. Simply so you can get the sale. In other words, the sale is corrupted in some way that is bound to come back and haunt you.

My advice here is simple. Avoid the temptation associated with "getting the sale at any cost." From my experience and observations of many businesses, it leads to both short and long term issues that can destroy a business. Keep the sale clean, be certain that you are making a profit and don't compromise your standards. Instead focus on adding value, servicing your customers better and being innovative and professional in all that you do.

BREE'S TAKE

I've certainly been in tough situations and my first thought was to discount what I was selling. I'm so glad I never did. I've always looked for more creative ways to make what I'm selling more appealing.

As Andrew says, once you start discounting, you train people to expect it, and that's a hard expectation to break. Look to value add, look to partner with others, sell on your merits, not on your price, and you will thank yourself for many years to come.

Most people will discount, so hold your nerve. Be wary of those customers that try to manipulate you and play on your fears. It can be challenging, but it has always worked out for me and I've never had to sell my soul.

98

Your business has been damaged or destroyed by a natural disaster, what now?

Every year, around the world, tens of thousands of small businesses are badly disrupted by natural disasters (and sometimes manmade disasters). I know that in Australia alone, we face fire, floods and cyclones constantly. The cost both financially and emotionally is huge. Businesses can be disrupted for anything from a few days to a few months. So what should you do when disaster hits your business?

1. **Start by setting up communication to the outside world.** The first step in the rebuilding process is to make sure you are connected to the outside world, and this normally means a working telephone and an email connection. It might mean hiring some computer equipment or getting your mobile phone set up for internet connection (if you haven't already. Even setting up a TV in your building helps to make you feel connected to the rest of the world).

2. **Break the rebuilding process into smaller, more manageable chunks.** When standing in a devastated office, shop or factory, the amount of things that need to be done can be totally overwhelming. The best way to deal with this is to break the big and overwhelming "to do's" into small more manageable chunks. Start on the smaller jobs, one by one, and before you know it you will be back on track.

3. **Let your suppliers know what is going on - they will want to help.** Remember that if your business is not making money neither are your suppliers, so it is in their best interest to help you get up and running as quickly as possible. Even though it might be a few weeks before you are ready for stock or replacement equipment, place the order now so that you are in the system. Talk about payments - it is better to be upfront and clarify what you need, especially if there is an insurance claim pending. You might be surprised at how flexible your suppliers will be.

4. **Talk to your bank and credit card providers.** Cash flow is going to be a big issue, particularly in the short term. Make the call to your bank and to any institution where you have credit and let them know what has happened. Most of the time they will be supportive by deferring repayments. Regardless of whether you need this right now or not, think about longer term cash flow. On another note, if you take credit cards in your business, you might want to get a hold of a manual machine, to at least be able to process credit card payments with the old "click clack machine". It is very likely that there will be many power interruptions once the rebuilding process starts. Down time due to power cuts or telephone line upgrades can mean lost sales - clearly the last thing you need now.

5. **Keep your staff informed.** This is a tough time for employees in small businesses in particular. They know that the business owner generally doesn't have a lot of money, and with none coming in, plus the cost of the rebuild, their job is in jeopardy. Tell your staff what is happening, be honest and lay it on the line. As hard as it is, the pressure of doing what you need to do as well as trying to protect your staff from hard news is simply too much. You might just be surprised by the response from your staff - most will roll up their sleeves and do what they can to help, regardless of whether they are getting paid or not.

6. **Keep new records, take photos, keep samples of damaged stock and equipment.** When confronted with a pile of rubble or a foot of mud, our initial desire is to get rid of it all so that we can start with a clean slate. But it is important to take photos along the way that show the extent of the damage to stock, to buildings and to equipment. This is important for insurance claims, many of which won't be paid unless there is some record or proof of damage.

7. **Manage your physical and emotional well-being.** It is very easy to get sick at a time like this. The emotional toll is enormous, something we can easily overlook. Add to this working long hours in less than ideal conditions and the potential to get really ill is extremely high. You simply have to take care of yourself as this is a marathon event.

8. **Let your customers know what is going on.** As soon as you are operating again, even if it is in reduced capacity, hang that shingle out, turn on the lights and yell it from the street corner. It is vital that you get customers coming back to your business and spending money as quickly as possible and believe me, they will want to support you and your business.

9. **There is always an upside.** I know that it is hard to see the upside or the bright side of things at a time like this, but life somehow always seems to give us an unexpected positive when faced by adversity.

I feel that in this instance it is a chance to think about your business, the changes you have been meaning to make but never quite seem to get around to. It is the opportune time to think about your future, what you want out of your business and where you are heading. It is a time to rebuild not just your business but also your dreams and your goals.

Most importantly it is a time to think about what you have, not what you have lost, and to be grateful.

BREE'S TAKE

Disasters happen and often with little notice. You need to plan for this situation to occur, even if it is unlikely. Fires, floods, cyclones, and even cyber attacks happen and the best plan is to be prepared.

Take some time now to think about two things.

1. What you would do if you had one day to prepare for a disaster that could wipe out or impact your entire business?

2. If your business was wiped out or impacted by a disaster, what would you have wished you had done, to prevent some of the impact ahead of time?

The first question will help you build a strategy as to what to do if you had notice, ie. grab servers and hard drives, put auto responders on your emails so that the world knows you could be out of contact for some time should the impact happen and how you can be contacted. Divert phones, back up files to a cloud system, unplug your computers from the internet straight away, should your business be under cyber attack and the list goes on. Once you have this strategy, share it with your team, should you require them to implement it. Then everyone knows exactly what to do and when to do it.

The second question will ensure you have long-term measures in place such as insurance, important items backed up on the cloud and also backed up on various other off site locations. And I'm sure there will be a long list of other items.

These are not nice things to think about, but trust me, if you have a plan now, when you are thinking clearly, you will not have an "I wish I had done that" conversation in the aftermath of a disaster of some sort. The key is to do everything you can to protect your business and that means really thinking about what could go wrong and what you would do about it if it did.

99

Eleven ways to get through any tough time in business.

There are two types of business, those that have had tough times and those that are going to have tough times. Generally tough times relate to money dramas, either a lack of business, or a client that goes broke or a combination of the two. Of course there are other issues that can create tough times but more importantly, what do we need to do to survive them?

I have experienced a lot of tough times in business and I've certainly helped a lot of businesses to get through tough times as well. From these experiences, there are eleven absolutely non-negotiable things that have continually proven to be the most helpful to get through and actually come out the other side in better shape.

1. **Don't make things worse by doing nothing.** Whenever you see a disaster looming, the single most important thing to do is take action. Sometimes we can be a little like a deer in the headlights, not quite believing what is going on, frozen on the spot. The problem is that if we don't leap into action, things will always get worse and they will get worse quickly.

2. **Deal with facts not fiction.** In the middle of a tough time it is really easy to start freaking out based on "what could be" as opposed to what actually is. It is imperative to get all of the information about what is going on and to only

deal with facts, regardless of what is going on in your head. Most of the things we worry about never actually happen, so don't let your imagination get ahead of the reality of the situation.

3. **Always cement your relationship with your existing customers.** In a weirdly ironic way, when times are tough, many businesses actually stop servicing their existing and loyal customer. A depressed mood descends on the business and this in turn affects customer service. That's why businesses in this negative space lose far more customers than they should, which of course only makes matters worse. Now is the time to build bulletproof relationships with each and every customer you are fortunate enough to have. You need to be communicating with your customers, engaging them, finding out what is going on in their world and most importantly of all, becoming very clear on what your customers need from you.

4. **Use this situation to rethink your business.** Tough times are crossroads in our business and they provide an opportunity to make hard decisions about what is working and what is not. This is the perfect time to stop and really reflect on your business and make the changes that deep down you know you need to make.

5. **It is time to get out and chase business.** Just as we can stop servicing our clients during tough times, business development can also grind to a halt and we all know that this spells disaster. As hard as it may be, when times are tough, you have to ramp up your business development and push through the hard times. Winning a few new projects, or finding some new clients might just prove easier than you think and it will go a long way to making you feel better.

6. **Be careful whom you spend your time with.** One of my favorite sayings is that "if you lay down with dogs you get up with fleas." It is more important than ever to avoid the harbingers of doom, those people who are negative all the time, they only ever focus on what they haven't got as opposed to what they have and so on. Don't let yourself get caught up in the negativity vortex. Keep away from people who are like this and find the positive, proactive and energetic business owners who are too busy getting on with it to get caught up with the misery brigade.

7. **Be prepared to try "NEW".** When what you are doing isn't working it makes sense to try something different. Now this sounds logical, yet I have watched so many businesses slowly go bust simply because they kept doing the same thing, right to the end. We have to be prepared to do new things, try ideas outside of our comfort zone and look to others for advice.

8. **Invest in your business.** This is the very best time to invest in your business. It is time to give the outside a coat of paint, upgrade the website, come up with a new corporate image, train your staff, invest in new technology and really anything else that will make your business look more impressive and run more impressively.

9. **Invest in yourself.** Just as I believe that it is an important time to invest in your business it is also an important time to invest in yourself. This means learning new skills through books, seminars, online training, mentoring, and coaching, really whatever it takes. To do this you need to invest time and money.

10. **Find someone to mentor you through the challenging times.** If you have someone who you admire and respect and who you know has been through a similar challenge, why not reach out and ask for help? Be totally honest with them, tell them the problem, exactly how bad it is and what help you need. They can't be expected to take on your problem, but having them to talk to, and to offer advice on how they got through their own challenges could just prove invaluable.

11. **Learn from the experience.** This can be such a cliché but it is true. Most business owners are really good at beating themselves up for things that go wrong but there really isn't much to be achieved from this. Far better to take a step back and learn from the experience. What would you do differently next time? What were the clues that you should have picked up on? What are you going to do to make absolutely certain that this never happens again?

BREE'S TAKE

OK, if you haven't had a tough time in business, read every word that Andrew has said and read it carefully. His advice is incredibly valuable and it will help you survive when you do have a tough time.

If you have had a tough time, which I suspect will be anyone reading this who has been in business for more than a few months, take a moment to reflect back on the situation and the advice offered here. What would you have done differently? What can you learn from that situation? And is your business in better shape now than it was? Put measures in place to make sure that any vulnerabilities are addressed.

Business can be tough, we need to be incredibly resilient to survive and thrive.

100

If you treat your suppliers badly, it might just come back to haunt you.

Do you get frustrated when you are contacted by a company asking you to submit a quote for a project, which you do, only to never hear from them again? Not so much as an acknowledgement of receiving your email or a "we'll be in touch soon" message. And even worse, as you follow up, they don't even have the courtesy to return your call.

This is irritating and to be honest rude, but what does this do to the reputation of the company that asked you to submit the quote in the first place? Clearly not much. Often we think that our reputation is only built by what our customers say about us, but it's not that simple.

We all talk about businesses, those that we recommend and those that we don't. If you have a bad experience with a company that wasted your time and was rude, it's unlikely you will have anything good to say about them.

Over the years I've found that if I've had a bad experience with a company in this way, I'm not the only one. Talking with other suppliers in the same competitive space, it soon becomes obvious that this company has a reputation for being unprofessional. Once this reputation is developed it is hard to shake - and I have no doubt that it will have a direct impact on their business.

The best businesses that I have worked with have always treated their suppliers really well. This showed a really strong, positive and professional internal culture that was all about treating everyone well, staff, customers and suppliers. And no surprise, these businesses are very successful.

Of course they also had suppliers who were raving fans and suppliers who would go way above and beyond the call of duty to do anything to help their customers. Relationships like this can make or break a business, particularly in the tough times.

When it comes to treating suppliers professionally, I suggest the following:

1. **If you ask for a quote have the courtesy to acknowledge receiving it.** Remember it takes time, energy and money to do quotes, show respect by taking a few seconds to acknowledge receiving it. Ideally explain to the tendering business roughly how long the decision making process will be and advise them that you will be in touch one way or another.

2. **Let the unsuccessful businesses know they missed out.** When you decide on a company to award a particular project or order, make sure you have the courtesy to let the unsuccessful applications know. Let them know why they were unsuccessful and you will find that most business owners will be disappointed but really grateful for the feedback.

3. **Try to resolve issues as opposed to just cutting a supplier off with no notice.** If you've got a problem with a supplier, try and work it out, don't just stop using them with no explanation. At least give them a chance to rectify any issue and be open to the fact that even though they are the supplier, the problem could still be from your end.

4. **Give your suppliers realistic time frames.** We are all suppliers to someone else, and nothing is more frustrating than those clients who continually issue unrealistic time frames. Most of the time the reason for the unrealistic time frame is their disorganisation, which now you have to pay for. Remember how this makes you feel when you are working with your own suppliers.

5. **Build a reputation for being good at paying your bills.** Always pay your bills on time. It's amazing how you can grow a fantastic reputation as a company by becoming known as a great player. Who wouldn't say nice things about your company with a reputation like that?

6. **It's all about respect.** Always treat your suppliers with respect. Even if they don't act as professionally as they should, don't use this as an excuse for you to act badly. Respect their time, respect their money and respect their advice.

7. **Give feedback and build your supplier relationships.** Don't be afraid of giving feedback to a supplier at any stage in your working relationship. Smart suppliers will always take this on board. Most importantly look to build long term, win/win relationships that are good for all involved.

BREE'S TAKE

Take a long hard look at all of your suppliers and rate your relationship with them out of ten. Then identify ways that you could make the relationship stronger. But be really honest with yourself, what impact are you having on the relationship, is it in fact your fault that the relationship isn't as good as it could be? Remember, your suppliers are part of the success of your business, so your relationship with them is certainly one that is worth nurturing.

101

Ten strategies to survive working with family, friends and lovers.

If you own your own business it is only a matter of time until you find yourself working with a family member, a friend or even a lover (or two). Whilst there are many upsides, there can also be some very deep and dark pitfalls.

Family members were enlisted to work in the family business, simply because they were available. They could be trusted (generally) and they would work for very long hours for very little money. If the business made money they shared the rewards and if times were tough, they tightened their belts and did what they could to help it survive.

So how do you survive working with family, friends and lovers? Here are ten of my strategies:

1. **Set the ground rules and make them clear.** Even if you already have your family business up and running, it is never too late to make the time to set the ground rules so everyone knows what is expected of them. A lack of ground rules or clarity around expectations leads to all kinds of problems and confusion. Spell them out and put them in writing to leave no room for confusion.

2. **Good pillow talk versus bad pillow talk.** OK, hopefully we all know what good pillow talk is, but bad pillow talk is any discussion in the bedroom that is about business. We need to have very clear boundaries between the business and the bedroom and under no circumstances should the bedroom conversations move into topics like "did you send out that invoice?" or "did you ring that client?" or "did you pay that bill?". Couples who work together can easily slip into the routine of talking about business all the time and that is ultimately bad for the relationship which is bad for the business.

3. **We need clear roles and responsibilities within the business.** This might sound obvious but a lack of clarity around who does what and who is responsible for what are two of the biggest causes of friction in family run businesses. Blurred lines around responsibilities can be very confusing and frustrating for all involved. Spend time working this out early in the piece and then let people do their job.

4. **We need to have time apart and outside interests.** From my observations (and experience) when you live and work together you can easily stop having your own life and interests outside of the business and the relationship. Making time just for you and your own interests is vital. It isn't being selfish it is being smart. You will be better as a person, which will be better for the relationship and that will be better for the business.

5. **Have a way to solve disagreements (ideally before they happen).** Having a mechanism to solve conflict is vital in any partnership but often family run businesses haven't figured out how to do this, especially if there are only two people in the business who are equal partners. In the past I have used a third person, who we both agreed upon as an adjudicator. Whenever there was a problem that we couldn't resolve, we went to our adjudicator to cast the deciding vote.

6. **Have a clear vision on where the business is heading and make sure everyone knows about it.** Time needs to be spent ensuring that everyone in the business is clear about where the business is heading. Clarity is not a sign on the wall with some corny mission statement, clarity is sharing dreams, aspirations, goals and expectations. Sometimes it is surprising to see just how aligned your dreams are and sometimes it is scary to see just how misaligned they are. Clearly the latter can lead to big issues, so it is better to find out early on.

7. **Accept that we all work, think and act differently and that is OK.** We have to accept that other members of the team will want to do things their own way. We need to be able to share our experience, but also give them the room, the space, and the respect, to do things their own way.

8. **Know your strengths, know your weaknesses and be big enough to admit to both.** This is a golden rule for success in any business, but particularly so in family businesses. We can't be good at everything and any business that works to an individual's strengths is always going to be more successful than one where the wrong people are doing the wrong jobs.

9. **Never stop having fun, playing and most importantly, celebrating your victories.** One of the upsides of working with family, friends and lovers, is that you are working with people you really like (hopefully). It is important that we keep a fun and playful environment happening. Too many businesses become very serious and this seriousness then gets taken into the home environment as well. Celebrate loud and celebrate often.

10. **If you leave the business, leave the business.** Selling the business to younger family members is a common form of succession planning. But a lot of people struggle to let go once they have taken the leap. By all means you have a lot of experience to offer, but you have to come up with a way to share that experience in a positive way that helps the business to grow but also lets the newer members of the business, put their own ideas into practice. After all, one day you won't be around, and they will be left on their own.

BREE'S TAKE

Working with family, in particular ones that you live with, is hard. Spending that much time together, but not really spending any time together can mean that it's all work and no play. Lots of resentment can build as the perception can be that the business gets most of the passionate energy, and that the business is more important than the relationship.

Being aware of what sort of problems you will encounter will help. If you haven't yet journeyed down the path of employing a friend or family member, here are three things that you need to consider.

1. Are you bringing them into the business to help them or the business?

2. If they applied for a job with you, would they get it on their own merits?

3. If it doesn't work out work wise, will your relationship survive?

It always has to be what is best for the business and what is best for your relationship and which is a really fine line that is hard to manage. But, if it works, it can be the most amazing thing to be able to work on something you love, with someone you love. I wish you luck.

WHERE TO FROM HERE?

Well you've made it this far, that's of course assuming you haven't just jumped to the last page to see what words of wisdom we would be offering to close Volume One. The "where to from here?" is all about using the ideas in our book to challenge your thinking, to reinforce your thinking and to provide new thoughts for old thinking that is no longer really working. Keep this book close. Pull it out regularly. We guarantee that something that maybe didn't seem that important on the first read, will in fact be life changing when you're flicking through the pages a year or two later.

We believe that building a successful business, one that doesn't just survive for a few years, but one that grows and in fact thrives, year after year, takes a very determined and holistic approach. We have to work on ourselves as business owners, just as much as the mechanics of the actual business.

We have to be brave, we have to be open minded, we have to be so seriously driven and committed that some people will call us obsessed, which of course we absolutely are. We know it's not about the money, even though others will think that is all it's about. We know it's the thrill and excitement of building something, backing yourself and believing in yourself, often when those around us don't.

We practise what we preach in "Business Over Breakfast" every day. We push ourselves hard, we push each other just as hard, we make mistakes and we learn from them. We have good days and we have tough days. We have a ridiculous amount of fun with each other and those around us. We are obsessed, but we like to think we are obsessed about good things, the things we can do to change the world for the better as a result of being successful in our businesses.

Most importantly of all - we challenge the way we do everything, every day. We thrive on thinking differently, on coming up with new ways to do what we do. We are passionate about our businesses and our life and we are curious beyond measure. And it starts the minute we get out of bed every morning.

We encourage you to be the same. Never apologise about your obsession. Build a business with meaning. Change the world however you can. Have way too much fun every day. Surround yourself with likeminded people. We do.

Bree James and Andrew Griffiths
Authors - Business Over Breakfast, the series.

Would you like Bree James to inspire and energise your audience at your next event?

Bree James started her entrepreneurial journey at the age of 10 and she really hasn't stopped since. When it comes to inspiring and educating an audience, Bree can share her own experiences, realisations and observations that will ultimately encourage everyone in the room to step up and take action.

She can also help people to have belief and faith in themselves, particularly during those times in business where the going gets tough. Honest, direct and a lot of fun, Bree James will be a major asset for an event targeting business owners and entrepreneurs.

BREE JAMES

breejames.com.au

ANDREW GRIFFITHS HAS DELIVERED OVER 500 PRESENTATIONS IN 15 COUNTRIES OVER 30 YEARS.

Clearly Andrew knows a thing or two about doing business. Add to this the fact that he is Australia's #1 Small Business author, with 13 bestselling books sold around the world and he is a wise choice as a speaker for your next conference.

Andrew's style is fun, engaging, visionary and passionate. Audiences leave energised, invigorated and keen to get back to their businesses to start implementing his advice. Andrew can cover a huge range of topics, all are inspirational and relevant and customised to suit his audience.

To find out more about getting Andrew to talk at your next event please visit www.andrewgriffiths.com.au

ANDREW ★ GRIFFITHS
Enterprises

EMPOWERING ENTREPRENEURS GLOBALLY

Need a little morning inspiration to get your business day off to a healthy start?

THE BUSINESS over BREAKFAST SHOW

Check out Bree and Andrew's podcast show "Business Over Breakfast". Each episode is fast paced, designed to explore one main business idea every episode, and of course, it's a lot of cheeky fun. As well as diving deep on a specific business issue or opportunity.

Bree and Andrew always have a special guest, they share specific tips and advice to take away and start using right away, and they get to tell the listeners about some weird and wonderful business ideas from around the world.

CHECK OUT THE BUSINESS OVER BREAKFAST SHOW ON ITUNES, OR YOUR FAVOURITE PODCAST PLATFORM TODAY.

SMALLVILLE

WHERE GOOD BUSINESSES GO TO BECOME GREAT.

With over 100 contributors and more than 1000 articles so far, Smallville is rapidly becoming Australia's #1 Small Business platform.

Check it out and you will see what all the fuss is about and why you need to be stopping by for a visit every day.

www.smallville.com.au

SMALL★VILLE

FOR SMALL BUSINESS OWNERS WHO THINK BIG

COMING SOON
MOB MAGAZINE

As business owners we need every resource possible to give us the competitive edge when it comes to doing business. The world is spinning faster, information and advice is what makes the difference. MOB Magazine is the combined efforts of 40 of the best business minds in the country, providing the most relevant and important information, delivered as one practical resource.

There is no magazine like MOB - and it's coming soon.

MOB
MAGAZINE

Join the mob movement...

mobmagazine.com.au

The Family Market is HUGE and growing every year

Are you capitalising on families?

The family market is worth billions of dollars per year in Australia alone. PakMag is a parenting magazine that we have produced over a 10 year period with a hugely successful history in specialising in the family market. We have helped many businesses of all sizes, across all industry sectors, to grow their share of this lucrative and very significant market. Marketing To Families provides Research, Training and Consulting with a range of products and services that can be customised to suit your specific needs but with the same very definitive outcome; a greater share of the family market.

To find out more, please contact one of our specialist advisors admin@marketingtofamilies.com.au

pakmag
RESEARCH - TRAINING - ADVICE

MARKETING TO *families*

WE ALL NEED A LITTLE HELP IN OUR BUSINESS EVERY ONCE IN A WHILE...

Between them Bree James and Andrew Griffiths have well over 50 years business experience. That always sounds kind of cool, but even more significant than that is the fact that they have built many of their own successful businesses and helped many other people to build successful businesses. As business coaches and mentors, they are realistic, honest and street smart. This means that if you want to work with one or both of them, you're business can't help but grow dramatically.

To find out more about being coached by Bree or Andrew or both of them, shoot an email to info@andrewgriffiths.com.au.

COME ON A 4 DAY RETREAT WITH BREE AND ANDREW

Have you always wanted to write a book but didn't know where to start?

Or perhaps you've written a book but you want to learn how to leverage it and make a business out of it?

And maybe you want to be a professional speaker but need to develop your skills and learn more about the business?

Well Bree and Andrew run 4 day retreats on these three topics in Bali and throughout Australia. Visit **www.andrewgriffiths.com.au** and check out the workshop section and you will find a pile of information about how you can immerse yourself in a 4 day retreat, with a small, enthusiastic group of people wanting to achieve the same goals as you.

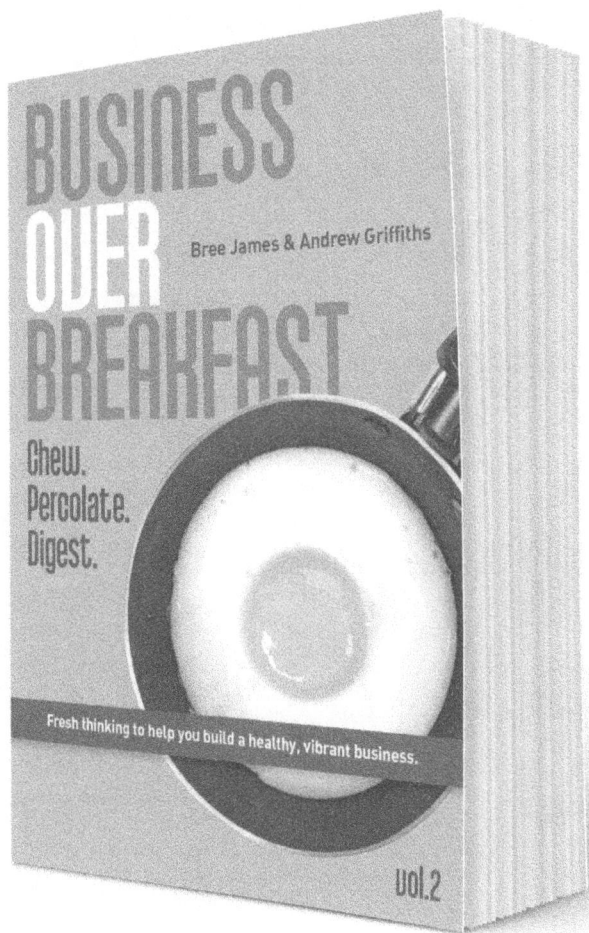

BUSINESS OVER BREAKFAST

Bree James & Andrew Griffiths

Chew.
Percolate.
Digest.

Fresh thinking to help you build a healthy, vibrant business.

Vol.2

COMING SOON